ADVANCE PRAISE FOR *NORTH OF NOWHERE*

"This book is a must-read for everyone! Dr. Wilson captures stories about lived experiences through her personal heartfelt reflections. From shattered families comes the power of hope, to forgive, to respect. Dr. Wilson challenges all of us to make a commitment to positive action, to advance reconciliation. It is about working together: Upintowin, lifting each other up. The thousands of stories culminate in this most powerful story from the North: 'Love is the direction.' Hai Hai, merci beaucoup, thank you."
—Chief Dr. Wilton Littlechild, Ermineskin Indian Residential School

"My parents met in residential school and I feel the fusion of their angst and strength—and the arc of their lives—in these pages. Marie Wilson's incisive journalistic rigour, her gentle humanity, and her privileged view into the accounts of Survivors lead us on a captivating yet harrowing—and ultimately beautiful—journey that no one can turn away from. Residential schools deeply wounded our people—and our entire country. As a doctor, I can say with certainly that this book contributes to healing. And we all need healing—of our hearts and minds and our collective psyches—after all that has come to pass."
—Dr. Evan Adams, actor and chief medical officer of the First Nations Health Authority

"Marie Wilson is the truth keeper entrusted with the accounts of the First Nations, Métis, and Inuit children who went to residential schools, the memories of those who did not make it home and the fate of us all if we do not learn from the past. The savagery of 'civilization' comes into stark relief as children emerge from the pages to awaken the national consciousness and render the TRC Calls to Action imperative."
—Cindy Blackstock, executive director, First Nations Child & Family Caring Society

"Beautifully written, Marie Wilson's *North of Nowhere* is a stunning work of truth, power, and wisdom. An imperative read for all Canadians to understand the layers of shrapnel left by the residential school system that will leave you with emotion and hope. Wilson is an incredibly brilliant and gifted writer." —Angela Sterritt, author of *Unbroken: My Fight for Survival, Hope, and Justice for Indigenous Women and Girls*

"We ask and demand so much of our leaders and healers. And we expect that while they work, they also hold space for us. In that space is our healing. The Commissioners heard it all—an emotional snapshot, a glimpse of our collective history—and held it throughout and carried on, every day. Words like Marie Wilson's, from her beautiful soul, are the salve." —Susan Aglukark, Juno Award–winning Inuk musician, author, and philanthropist

"Commissioner Dr. Marie Wilson recounts and celebrates the courage of everyone involved in one of Canada's most important chapters of coming to terms with residential school Survivors and their families and their communities forever changed by policies that amounted to cultural genocide. What a profound and riveting read." —Richard Van Camp, author of *The Lesser Blessed* and *Godless but Loyal to Heaven*

"During Canada's Truth and Reconciliation Commission, I watched Marie Wilson listen so deeply to so many Survivors who shared their terrible truths, and I wondered: How could she bear to witness it all? We find out in this heartfelt book, crafted from the careful observations of a seasoned journalist, mother, and grandmother. An insider's look at the TRC, a meditation on love, and a timely reminder that we as a country cannot ignore our painful past if we hope to move forward together." —Duncan McCue, professor of Indigenous journalism and (story)telling at Carleton University, author of *Decolonizing Journalism: A Guide to Reporting in Indigenous Communities*

"*North of Nowhere* is both a necessary call and a collaborative invitation for all Canadians. A beautiful blend of both a heartbreaking account and an inspiring call to rise, told with the care and empathy of a mother. Even in the midst of residential school despair, there are glimpses of hope in seeing how sport could briefly lift the spirits of struggling children, serving as a powerful reminder of the importance of sport in reconciliation." —Lizanne Murphy, Canadian women's basketball Olympian

"As a Truth and Reconciliation Commissioner, Marie Wilson walks with us, guides us, and helps us see, hear, and accept the difficult truth of our country. With beautiful writing, superb insights, and sensitivity, she leaves readers not guilty or damaged, but optimistic for a shared future as we travel a national road to reconciliation." —Whit Fraser, Viceregal Consort of Canada, author of *True North Rising* and *Cold Edge of Heaven*

"Marie Wilson's *North of Nowhere* is a necessary book. Within its pages, a reader will find the story of a remarkable woman with tremendous humility and strength who has chosen to serve the country and all those affected by residential schools. The Truth and Reconciliation Commission journey and the pathways to its 94 Calls to Action come into focus in very personal ways, not only through Wilson's reflections but also and most powerfully through Survivors' testimony and truths, which punctuate like sledgehammers. Marie Wilson places her own life and story in the service of reconciliation, as an agent for truth and as a reporter for the TRC story, whose legacy has profoundly changed this country for the better. But most of all, this book is about love. Love of her family, love of Inuit, First Nations, and Métis, and in turn, a collection of moments exemplifying the love she has received in return." —Natan Obed, president of Inuit Tapiriit Kanatami

"*North of Nowhere* is a book that is bound to ignite dialogue. Marie Wilson elicits emotional and insightful responses that move us along our own journeys of understanding the truth of Canada." —Former CBC broadcaster Shelagh Rogers, and author and speaker Monique Gray Smith

"In *North of Nowhere*, Marie Wilson honours her vow to residential school Survivors to 'do no harm' and to bear witness to and honour their experiences. Marie has achieved her purpose to educate readers and inspire reconciliation and, most importantly, hope." —Perry Bellegarde, former National Chief of the Assembly of First Nations

"Marie Wilson's remarkable memoir is a schooling in painful facts and brave reckonings. The stories she tells of heartbreak and soul-break lift off the page, and what evolves is a kind of spiritual strength that has a touch of the miraculous." —Elizabeth Hay, author of *All Things Consoled*

"This book made me laugh, get emotional and helped reset my journey on the role I need to play. As a child of residential school Survivors, I was motivated to continue to learn my language and strengthen my pride as an Indigenous person. If every Canadian reads this book, the Truth and Reconciliation Calls to Action can be achieved." —Cadmus Delorme, former chief of Cowessess First Nation

"Marie Wilson's *North of Nowhere* is profoundly moving and surprisingly optimistic. With humility and wisdom, she takes us behind the scenes of the Truth and Reconciliation Commission. *North of Nowhere* is a powerful book that shifted my perspective, and, thanks to Wilson's lucid prose, helps the rest of us glimpse what is needed." —Charlotte Gray (CM), author of *Passionate Mothers, Powerful Sons: The Lives of Jennie Jerome Churchill and Sara Delano Roosevelt*

"This is a book for all Canadians. It presents an account of the Truth and Reconciliation Commission's work that is both painful and inspiring to read. The stories and experiences that Marie Wilson shares are deeply personal, and they call us each to look within ourselves to find the ways we can be part of the important work of reconciliation." —Nora Sanders, former General Secretary, United Church of Canada

"Truth and Reconciliation Commissioner Marie Wilson has given Canadians a powerful, readable, personal, and uniquely informed review of the historic damage done to Indigenous people in Canada and a compelling reminder of how and why we can change that legacy." —The Right Honourable Joe Clark, former Prime Minister of Canada

"Marie Wilson's masterful work speaks for children whose voices have been silenced and whose stories have remained untold, allowing Survivors to continue their healing through the inspirational examples and words of many others. She opens a doorway, allowing her readers to both witness and reconcile with this dark chapter in Canada's history." —Jane Middelton-Moz, therapist, author, and founder of the MSW Indigenous Trauma and Resiliency (ITR) Program at the Factor-Inwentash Faculty of Social Work, University of Toronto

"*North of Nowhere* is a brilliant mix of intelligence, wisdom, and a sharp eye describing a painful truth that we all need to face. Marie Wilson had the courage to bring some diamonds out of the dark mines of despicable crimes. This book should be in every Canadian classroom and living room. We can only change what we understand." —Eric Le Reste, CBC journalist and producer

"Marie Wilson has the power to inspire people. This power emanates from deep inside her being. In *North of Nowhere*, she combines her rare insight with her ability to be a beacon of inspiration. She has turned the story of the Canadian TRC into a healing narrative for the whole world." —Sylvia Vollenhoven, South African journalist, managing director of Vision in Africa

"Through vivid personal stories, Marie Wilson transmits both the tremendous technical challenges of the TRC journey, and even more importantly, the passion, courage, and heart that are needed to move toward reconciliation, one story at a time. *North of Nowhere* fills a crucial void in the literature on truth commissions and transitional justice: the heart element of this work." —Virginie Ladisch, International Center for Transitional Justice

"*North of Nowhere* is a must-read for public and private funders and philanthropists who share a sense of outrage at the intergenerational harms of residential schools." —Nancy MacPherson, former managing director, the Rockefeller Foundation; former acting chief impact officer, the Mastercard Foundation

"TRC Commissioner Marie Wilson beautifully centres the Survivors at the heart of her book. *North of Nowhere* includes stories of heartbreak and of loss but also celebrates stories of resurgence and redemption." —Tammara Soma, assistant professor at the School of Resource and Environmental Management, Simon Fraser University

"Journalist Marie Wilson brings us into the emotion-charged rooms, the sacred spaces of Canada's Truth and Reconciliation hearings. This is a triumphant restorative narrative—a testament to the healing that happens when we share our deepest, darkest truths." —Judy Rodgers, founding director of Images & Voice of Hope, board member of The Peace Studio

"The long-matured work of a true elder, this magnificent book is a sober masterpiece of sacred activism. Its level decency of tone, its lucidity, its determined hope in terrible circumstances, both transmit and model those qualities we all now need to build a new world out of the smouldering ashes of the old." —Andrew Harvey, author of *The Hope: A Guide to Sacred Activism*

"This amazing, compelling, and moving book from former journalist, Commissioner, and Warrior Marie Wilson is not only a testimony of the stories, the tears, the smell, the ache, and the hopes heard during the TRC and the behind-the-scenes camaraderie between the three Commissioners. It is a real gift to humanity to immortalize the spirit of the TRC hearings, a call for a new beginning, and a special blessing bringing the circles of truth and light to healing." —Denise Amyot, former president of Colleges Institutes Canada and former ADM and CEO of a federal Crown corporation in the Government of Canada

NORTH OF NOWHERE

SONG OF A TRUTH AND RECONCILIATION COMMISSIONER

MARIE WILSON

ANANSI

Published in Canada and the USA in 2024 by House of Anansi Press Inc.
houseofanansi.com

House of Anansi Press is committed to protecting our natural environment. This book is made of material from well-managed FSC®-certified forests, recycled materials, and other controlled sources.

House of Anansi Press is a Global Certified Accessible™ (GCA by Benetech) publisher. The ebook version of this book meets stringent accessibility standards and is available to readers with print disabilities.

28 27 26 25 24   1 2 3 4 5

Library and Archives Canada Cataloguing in Publication

Title: North of nowhere : song of a Truth and Reconciliation commissioner / Marie Wilson.
Names: Wilson, Marie (Journalist), author.
Description: Includes bibliographical references and index.
Identifiers: Canadiana (print) 20230623670 | Canadiana (ebook) 20230623689 | ISBN 9781487011482 (hardcover) | ISBN 9781487011499 (EPUB)
Subjects: LCSH: Wilson, Marie (Journalist) | LCSH: Truth and Reconciliation Commission of Canada. | LCSH: Truth commissions—Canada. | LCSH: Indigenous peoples—Canada—History. | LCSH: Indigenous peoples—Canada—Social conditions. | LCSH: Indigenous peoples—Canada—Government relations. | CSH: Indigenous peoples—Canada—Residential schools. | LCGFT: Autobiographies.
Classification: LCC E96.5 .W55 2024 | DDC 971.004/97—dc23

Book design: Lucia Kim
Cover photography: Tessa Macintosh
Song lyrics on page xi excerpted from "In the Walls of His Mind" by Stephen Kakfwi used with permission from Stephen Kakfwi.
All epigraphs from *A Story of the Seven Sacred Laws* by Elder Dr. David Courchene are used with permission of the keeper of his estate at Turtle Lodge in Manitoba.

House of Anansi Press is grateful for the privilege to work on and create from the Traditional Territory of many Nations, including the Anishinabeg, the Wendat, and the Haudenosaunee, as well as the Treaty Lands of the Mississaugas of the Credit.

Canada Council for the Arts | Conseil des Arts du Canada
ONTARIO ARTS COUNCIL
CONSEIL DES ARTS DE L'ONTARIO
an Ontario government agency
un organisme du gouvernement de l'Ontario

With the participation of the Government of Canada
Avec la participation du gouvernement du Canada | Canada

We acknowledge for their financial support of our publishing program the Canada Council for the Arts, the Ontario Arts Council, and the Government of Canada.

Printed and bound in Canada

FSC www.fsc.org MIX Paper | Supporting responsible forestry FSC® C016245

To the Survivors of Canada's "Indian Residential Schools," I offer this book as a written monument to honour and remember you—lest we forget.

To the Dene, Inuit, and Metis peoples of the Northwest Territories, and especially the K'ahsho Got'ine of Radeyilikoe (Fort Good Hope), Northwest Territories. You have welcomed me into your North as friend and family.

To Stephen, wherever we are, you are my North Star. You promised to make me interesting. Rather, your love made me rich. You, our children, and our grandchildren are the invaluable treasures of my life.

To Kyla, Daylyn, Keenan, Maslyn, Tydzeh, Sadeya, and Ry'den, I love you forever and always.

To all the children and generations to come, may you know love, family, and belonging.

In the Walls of His Mind

I remember the years they took all the children,
And they locked them away where they taught them to pray.
There were children each night who were silently crying.
They are in the walls and the halls of my mind.

Do you remember the years when you were the children?
When they locked you away and taught you to pray?
Are your voices each night still quietly crying?
Be free from the walls and the halls of your mind.

—Stephen Kakfwi, residential school Survivor and former premier of the Northwest Territories

Contents

Author's Note

AS A FORMER JOURNALIST, I have often said that the Truth and Reconciliation Commission (TRC) was the biggest, toughest, most fulfilling story assignment ever handed to me: Get to the bottom of the story; dig up as many facts as possible; cite more than one source; include as many witnesses as possible; and cross-reference for consistency of information. Finally, provide meaningful context to tell the story clearly and accurately. So, of course, this reporter-turned-Commissioner took notes.

Years later, I have used my notebooks as source material to report the TRC story from my personal and particular angle as a Commissioner. My notes are from public TRC sessions only. All participants and specifically all Survivors were informed when they registered to speak that all proceedings during the session would be open to the media and the public, live-streamed via the internet, and recorded for future use. The Commissioners included reminders of the public nature of the session in all our opening remarks and in pamphlets.

In cross-referencing the accounts of witnesses who spoke during these public events, as captured within the pages of my notebooks, the consistency of information was glaring. My notebooks reflect both distinct experiences and recurring themes—the individual and the collective. For this book, I have chosen to do the same. Except for a few cases, the words of residential school Survivors are anonymous. This allows the voice of one to speak for many in a shared experience. In some cases, I have presented composite quotes from several voices to strengthen a common point.

My own story, embedded within this book, is my contribution to ongoing reconciliation. It is offered in hopes of advancing our understanding of the residential school experience in Canada as a story of great national significance to *all* Canadians, including all non-Indigenous people.

My notes helped me focus and listen to Survivor statements, and they were a tool to help me accurately summarize each hearing day in my closing remarks. But I discovered later that my note-taking was also a practice of self-care. A respected therapist told me that it had been a healthy way for me to let the details of what I was hearing flow through my body and back out again, rather than getting stuck as vicarious trauma inside me. So, the stories I heard travelled from head to heart to hand to pen to paper.

Still, I know that words can evoke traumatic memories for some. I sincerely wish to hold true to my Truth and Reconciliation Commission Mandate promise to Do No Harm. *To anyone triggered by the contents of this book, please seek support and care in the way that is best for you. The Indian Residential School Survivors Society crisis line provides twenty-four-hour support at 1-800-721-0066.*

A portion of the proceeds from this book will go to a fund established for the creation and perpetual care of a national monument for residential schools in Ottawa, Canada.

PROLOGUE

North of Nowhere

MY MOTHER-IN-LAW, GEORGINA, was captivated by TV, the same as everybody else. It was late in the 1980s, in Fort Good Hope, Northwest Territories (NWT)—the early years of television in remote northern Canadian communities. We got TV reception decades after most other places, and one channel only. With no outside road connections, the national public broadcaster, the CBC, suddenly brought in a much bigger country and a much wider world. From morning to night, blue screens shone through tiny windows of humble houses. No one wanted to miss anything. The national anthem, followed by the official time signal, followed by a black-and-white graphic of a caricatured Indian with a headdress, and then that buzzing hum—this was what now marked the end of the day.

Georgina was a woman of few words. She watched. She listened. Sometimes she laughed. But she didn't say much. In the early years, I took her silence personally—I thought she didn't approve of me. I learned to keep my distance, not to ask too many questions. With time, I eventually understood that her manner had nothing to do with me. She was almost eighty before she told her kids that, like most of them, she had gone far away to residential school. Worse, most of her family died while she was gone, the rest shortly after she got back. Deep losses shaped the woman I knew. Not affectionate. Not warm. Not close.

So, this particular day was a big exception. For starters, the two of us were alone in her house. And then, out of the blue, she spoke up. To me. Loud and clear. Something on the TV had caught her attention. Provoked her. Something about the Northwest Territories—

"Northwest Territories! I don't live northwest of anywhere. I live right here!"

~

Years later, I look back on that day with my mother-in-law through a new lens. I have since lived at the heart of a national truth-telling probe into those very residential schools that so altered her life and kinship bonds, and those of tens of thousands of others like her. Today, I see deeper meaning in her television outburst, a hidden clue to the big work of reconciliation that has barely begun in Canada.

Her words said so much about the identity of the Northwest Territories and Canada itself—about how it has historically been seen, named, carved up, and subdivided. The Northwest Territories used to be a lot bigger. In 1870, the NWT included all three northern territories and several provinces: Alberta, Saskatchewan, and parts of Manitoba, Ontario, and Quebec. But over the years, it was reconfigured with new names and provincial or territorial birthdays. The latest subdivision in 1999 was for the creation of Nunavut. By its very name, the Northwest Territories is a colonial construct—northwest of somewhere else, a place presumably more important to those who named it. Northwest of Ottawa.

But to my mother-in-law, Georgina, who spent her life on the land and among the plants and animals of this region, *this* was her universe. All of its parts already had Indigenous names. This was her home. The centre of everything.

She lived her life right here—north of nowhere.

INTRODUCTION

Walk with Me

"WE WERE JUS' little kids. They were supposed to take care of us and look after us really good, but no, they were jus' ever mean to us and didn't treat us ever good, or nice, or anything."

I heard these words in a hot, steamy room as snow evaporated from oversized boots, mukluks, and moccasins, the air thick with the intermingling smoky smells of tanned moosehide, wood stove, and tobacco. People and parkas were jammed into a modest hall in a northern Dene community on a cold, subarctic winter day, standing, sitting, and crouching along its walls. There were hundreds of them, all reverently hushed to hear the stories of their family and community members. All day and into the early darkness of a northern night, many of them shared their stories for the very first time, stories of heartbroken childhoods like the one I have just remembered as if it were still unfolding...

Back then, I was in the midst of Canada's first and only Truth and Reconciliation Commission (TRC). It was a non-stop journey for six and a half years, criss-crossing our vast country and beyond. After thirty years of journalism and teaching, international work and executive leadership, I was selected in 2009 as one of three Commissioners.

We set out to research and document the complete history of more than a century of so-called Indian residential schools, to educate the general public about the true history of this country, and to inspire ongoing reconciliation between and among Indigenous Peoples and all Canadians. In other words, our job was to dig up almost 150 years of scattered, hidden history, to find ways to drill it into the heads and hearts of people who generally knew nothing about it, and to convince everyone along the way that things could and should be different from now on—more honest, more respectful, more inclusive, more loving ... more *Canadian*.

By the time we were done, we had recorded almost seven thousand voices from every region of the country—Survivors of Canada's imposed residential schools for Indigenous children. It was an onslaught of information, emotion, and enlightenment. And I was in the thick of it, as a Commissioner, giving all that I had to offer and receiving all that I had to learn. I stood out in our trio: as the solo woman, as a mother and grandmother, and as a non-Indigenous person. That difference prompted the most obvious of the many questions I got asked along the way. Where did you come from and how did you get to be a Commissioner?

In many ways, my journey to that moment began in Mrs. Hibbard's sunny grade-two classroom at Queen Elizabeth II Public School in small-town Canada. I can still see the multicoloured Rand McNally map on the wall, with the largest section in my favourite little-girl colour: pink! It was the Dominion of Canada. As a seven-year-old, I did not know all that was hidden within those two words: *Dominion* and *Canada*. We learned about ten provinces. The national motto we had to memorize back then still stands: *A Mari usque ad Mare* ... From Sea to Sea, meaning from the Atlantic to the Pacific. The third and longest Canadian coastline—the Arctic—was not even on that map from my childhood. Neither was the part of the country where I have now spent the majority of my life—the Northwest Territories.

I grew up with the same knowledge gaps as most other children of my generation, in educated ignorance about both our vast geography and rich, pre-dominion history, when lands now known as Canada were already inhabited by some of the oldest Indigenous civilizations on the planet. Instead, we learned rhymes about Christopher Columbus, 1492 and the ocean blue, and the "discovery" of the Americas, as if they began to exist only when people from various parts of Europe showed up and started naming places after their own heroes, relatives, and hometowns, and pejoratively labelling the people who were already here. Even the good old *Complete Mother Goose of Nursery Rhymes* for the children of my day had nasty, scary things to say under the racist banner of "Ten Little Injuns." The words of the poem still haunt me to this day; the last line sums up the prevailing attitude and endgame that has historically shaped Canada's laws and policies toward Indigenous Peoples: "And then there was none." But mostly, in my schooling anything to do with First Peoples was simply missing altogether, except when we played Cowboys and Indians, made Thanksgiving crafts, or dressed up for Halloween.

Other rooms that marked my childhood were in St. Paul's Church on Main Street of our little town. My limited understanding of church was as a Sunday morning event at a place where we went to hear stories about a nice man who did kind and sometimes magical things so that we would want to be kind, too. I remember singing a song about how much Jesus loved "the little Indian boy" and "the little papoose." I remember every week putting one or two pennies my parents could barely afford onto the flat wooden plate for the children's collection, and hearing about how we were "helping the little Indian children up north."

I never once imagined those children living anywhere other than in their own homes, with anyone other than their own parents. I did not know that while I was singing about them, so many were being raised, taught, redefined, and abused in institutions run by churches, including the one I attended. Years later, I married someone who had been one of those children. Without knowing it, I now had an entire extended family of multigenerational residential school Survivors, all raised by others, far away from home. Slowly, painfully, and in parallel, such secrets began to emerge within my marriage and within our country.

The purpose of the TRC was to reveal and document what had been happening for more than a century to my husband and 150,000 other children, while the rest of us were learning half-truths about Canada in our classrooms. Our Commission shed light on one of this country's earliest, longest-lasting, and most damaging policies: Indian residential schools. That policy characterized the very nature of the Dominion of Canada, with its built-in European imperative to dominate the colony. It is a policy that has defined and damaged relations between Indigenous and non-Indigenous Peoples for most of our 150-plus years as a country.

~

The deepest and often loneliest part of any TRC hearing day was afterwards, back in some unfamiliar hotel room. Phone calls home filled a partial void. But I could only say so much without transferring a traumatic load to my family, especially my Survivor husband. He did not need to hear residential school stories that could trigger his own memories. For his sake, I held in the toughest details of my Commissioner days, alone with my thoughts.

One night, I got to thinking about my time as a young teacher in Africa in my early twenties. For two long years, I'd had no phone or other reliable means of communication with home. To my surprise, once I got back to Canada, I was still lonely. The extremes of African poverty had left me in a state of bewilderment as I returned to the comparative opulence of middle-class Canadian life. Something as routine as grocery shopping had become an overwhelming dilemma—too much choice. Who in the world needs an entire row devoted to heavily packaged breakfast cereal, while others in the world still lack the basics? I returned homesick for all that I had missed during my two years away, but I soon felt distance anew from everyone around me, even those I most cared about. They didn't know what to ask about my time away, and I didn't know where to begin or end in the telling of it.

Heavily influenced by my African experience of seeing military men overthrow a democratically elected government, I decided to switch my career path from teaching to journalism. I returned to university in London, Ontario, where speakers from northern Canada were headlining an awareness campaign. Most of us knew little to nothing about these compelling leaders or their distant homes within this huge country. Although they were from distinct nations, they were all facing a common dilemma: major industrial developments pushing onto their traditional lands—from massive gas pipelines in the Northwest Territories and Yukon to hydroelectric dams in Quebec and British Columbia to uranium mines in what is now Nunavut. These pressures were mounting on the doorsteps of their communities faster than their rights and lands were being recognized and protected.

London was where I first met Yukoner Daniel Johnson, who has uplifted his Southern Tutchone language as a musician and educator and reclaimed his name Daniel Tlen. It was where I first experienced the late Jose Kusugak—for to be in a room with Jose was never just an encounter. It was a fully engaging experience. It was also where I was first exposed to Jose's passion for Inuit languages, linguistics, and incomparable circumpolar identity. And it was where I first met the young Dene rights advocate Stephen Kakfwi. He carried forward the name of his grandfather and the vision of his people, later becoming the head of the Dene Nation and, later still, the premier of the Northwest Territories. Of greatest importance to me, he became the heart of my own story, my life partner, father and grandfather to the children of our family.

I had a lot to learn about the struggles of these young northern leaders, but I already recognized the alarms they were sounding, lessons I had first learned from the complexities of the Africa I had only recently left. Competing waves of colonization by the British, French, Portuguese, Belgians, and Dutch, among others, had wreaked societal havoc throughout the African continent: the displacement of historic kingdoms, traditional leaders, governments, and languages, and the subdivisions of lands and tribes along lines determined by marketable resources rather than geography, kinship ties, and animal and human migration patterns. Outsiders, whether corporations or countries, were determined to reap the benefits of all that wealth.

Now, these Indigenous voices from northern Canada were expressing the same concerns for *their* homelands: destruction of natural environments, division and relocation of communities, annihilation of traditional economies and decision-making, loss of self-sufficiency, disintegration of distinct identities, and depletion of regional wealth by non-Indigenous beneficiaries. Eventually, some of the major industrial projects proposed for the North did get delayed or were stopped altogether. But there has been no stopping the multigenerational impact of residential schools that carried on for more than a hundred years in the background and continues to resonate and devastate today.

Not only have residential schools contributed to the physical and cultural upheaval of Indigenous peoples, they were specifically intended and designed for that purpose. The schools were a central part of a wider Canadian landscape of legislated attacks on Indigenous family structures, languages, cultures, and spiritual practices; restrictions on movement; displacement and dispossession of Indigenous lands; and denial of democratic and human rights. Rather than ensuring education and opportunity, residential schools in Canada contributed significantly to the social impoverishment of Indigenous peoples causing a parallel trail of economic poverty.

As an unintended social by-product—you might call it a backfire—residential schools also nurtured a combustible, silent anger that eventually fuelled a determined resurgence of Indigenous leadership. In the early 1970s, throughout the North, it brought major industrial projects to a halt. In the 1980s, throughout the country, it rose up in a collective voice, compelling the recognition and entrenchment of Indigenous rights within the Constitution of Canada. In the 1990s and early 2000s, in provincial and territorial courts and right up to the Supreme Court of Canada, that anger finally exploded when residential schools were legally denounced for the multigenerational centres of harm and criminality they had been. Ever since, in this country and well beyond, multifaceted forces and multicultural voices repeat the call for truth and reconciliation.

The TRC had a huge job with many distinct parts. It was physically exhausting work. We pushed ourselves hard, trying to take the Commission as deeply into this vast country as we could, always knowing we did not have enough time or money to do all that we might have wanted. Our original five-year Mandate eventually became six and a half. The work was also emotionally and spiritually exhausting, at times soul-crushing. We recorded statements from close to seven thousand residential school Survivors, all voluntary participants from among the estimated eighty thousand who were still alive at the time the TRC was established. Our Commission's 2015 final report and Calls to Action are based on the many recurring themes that emerged from those voices, from coast to coast to coast.

Over those years I also noted recurring themes of a different sort—the common themes in the many questions I was asked, over and over again:

How did you get to be a Commissioner?

How did your Commission hold it together, while many others struggle or collapse?

How could you bear, day after day, to hear such terrible things that happened to children?

How did you take care of yourself, and what kept you going?

What is the worst thing you heard?

What moved you the most?

What do you hope will come out of the Commission's work?

How has the TRC changed you?

What will you do after the Commission?

Where is your hope?

While the TRC was still in motion, the demands of my days left little time to answer such big questions. I needed to give my full attention in order to keep moving forward, to avoid sinking down into the horrors of what I was so often hearing. I needed to protect myself so that I *could* keep going, so as to honour my part in seeing the TRC through to completion.

Now, with the hard work of reconciliation just beginning in this country, I believe these questions asked of me are still valid, warranting deeper reflection. I want to share the wealth of what I have experienced. I recognize what a privileged vantage point I had as a TRC Commissioner. No one else sat where I sat. No one else saw through my eyes or felt the vibrations of this experience at closer range. It was a life-altering experience that permeated into me, and that continues, beyond the Commission, to reframe the way I see myself and the world around me.

I also have tens of thousands of other reasons to speak up. For that is the promise I made to the Survivors of Canada's residential schools—the thousands of adult children who became national teachers by unveiling their childhood experiences—and to the still unknown thousands of little ones who did not survive. I promised, as a sacred trust, that I would never stop telling their stories to Canada and the world, as long as there was breath in me. Today, I breathe into each new day with gratitude, accepting the mystery that I cannot know how many breaths will be given to me. And so, I write as a trustee. To keep my voice alive. To keep the spirit of my promise living.

As a Commissioner, I hope to offer insights into aspects of our TRC that I believe made a positive difference. As a citizen, I aim to provoke further thinking about the potency and imperative of reconciliation in Canada. And as a loving mother and grandmother—one who has now borne witness to the devastation of so many generations of children's lives—I seek to heal my own aching heart ...

I see things more clearly now. And differently, in the new light of the many gifts shared with me along my TRC journey, including invaluable teachings. One of them has to do with the multi-year cycle of ceremonies for sickness, loss, grief, letting go, and the honouring of who or what has passed before. I have begun to see myself within that cycle, recognizing that each stage of my life helped equip me for my cherished role as a TRC Commissioner, and that all those stages are still contributing to the new role I one day hope to earn, as an Elder.

So, walk with me, for this story is also about you, about all of us.

Find out what it was like to sit for hours and days and months and years in the face of so many haunting memories and pent-up devastations, so much unflinching hope, and grace beyond measure. To witness it. To bear it, even as it took up all the air. The tears and sweat and blood and spew of it. The nearly unbearable pain. The fear. The holding back. The release. The relief. The terrible beauty of it all.

How did I, of all people, find myself in such rooms? And what in my own life prepared me to hold the sacred trust of all that unfolded?

As a woman, wife, mother, and grandmother; as a teacher and a journalist; from the narrow confines of a small town in southern Canada to the main stages of redefining our country, this is the song of a Truth and Reconciliation Commissioner.

Three truth and reconciliation Commissioners standing strong together: Marie Wilson, Murray Sinclair, Wilton Littlechild. Photo: Mindy Willett

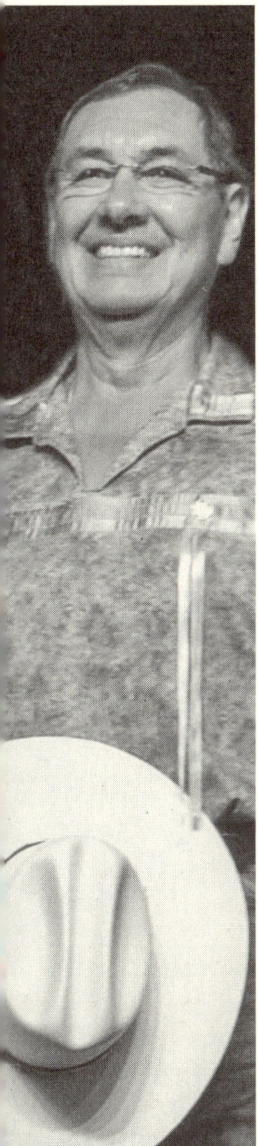

PART I

THE COMMISSION

Differences are not intended to separate, to alienate. We are different precisely in order to realize our need of one another.

—Archbishop Desmond Tutu,
chair of the Truth and Reconciliation Commission of South Africa

CHAPTER 1

The First Circle

PICTURE A MID-STAR HOTEL in the cluster across the highway from the Edmonton airport, Indigenous-owned and with a reputation for great food. On June 18, 2009, we met there, two weeks before we were officially on the job. Willie drove north from his home in Maskwacis. Murray flew west from Winnipeg. I flew south from Yellowknife. I felt new excitement on that old flight I had done hundreds of times before. I was heading toward my first real encounter with two men I had admired from afar for years—my new colleagues.

The Willie I'm talking about is Chief Wilton Littlechild, Cree lawyer from Alberta. The Murray is Murray Sinclair, Anishinaabe judge from Manitoba. And me? Marie Wilson, journalist, TV host, teacher, and executive manager from the Northwest Territories. Marie Wilson, southern Canadian turned northerner. Marie Wilson, world traveller, Canadian born but one-time resident of France and Burkina Faso. I am perhaps that most undefinable thing of all—a non-Indigenous Canadian. At least not indigenous to this place. I was raised to be proud of being Scottish-Canadian. And I am a woman. I am a daughter, sister, wife, and mother. I am a grandmother.

The three of us were interviewed individually, then tied together by a large committee representing Survivors of "Indian residential schools" (a government-imposed term), their lawyers, the Assembly of First Nations (AFN), Inuit Tapiriit Kanatami (ITK), around fifty Catholic Church orders, four Protestant church denominations, and the Government of Canada. It was the largest, most diverse selection committee I had ever experienced, a two-day process overseen by a former Justice of the Supreme Court of Canada. Our first encounter as three Commissioners of the historic Truth and Reconciliation Commission of Canada had all the nervousness, energy, anticipation, and excitement of an arranged marriage.

Our arrivals were staggered, so Murray, as Commission Chair, had told us to meet at his hotel room when we got there. When I arrived, he filled the door frame with his warm smile and commanding presence. I remembered that rich baritone voice from many years before, when he was speaking to a crowd at the Yellowknife Inn about his work leading the Aboriginal Justice Inquiry of Manitoba. I remembered his impact and inspiration as the first Indigenous judge in Manitoba, the second in all of Canada. The room was in awe.

Willie arrived soon after, in what I came to recognize as one of his signature summer golf shirts. I had also met him decades before, in a chance encounter on the other side of the ocean, when a mutual friend from Alaska introduced us on a Geneva sidewalk. It was outside the building where an international group was having diplomatic arguments about what would eventually grow into the United Nations Declaration on the Rights of Indigenous Peoples (UNDRIP). They were taking a break after a day of fighting over the importance of including the letter *s* in "Peoples." Willie was wearing a golf shirt that day, too—always the lawyer but also always the athlete. Professional sports had been his first career. His induction into multiple athletic

Halls of Fame and his founding role in the North American Indigenous Games would later mean as much to him as being an architect of that UN Declaration.

It turns out, Willie was also a virgin. Who knew? Certainly not Murray, nor me. We had sent Willie on a coffee run to Tim Hortons, that Canadian icon, when he confessed: he'd never had a cup of coffee in his life! Within seconds we dubbed him the "Tim Hortons virgin." And so our time together began. That gift of easy laughter would prove to be invaluable medicine over the years ahead.

Unlike my fellow Commissioners, I was not a lawyer. But as a teacher-turned-journalist, I had spent a lot of my professional life reporting from rooms defined by laws and observing political decision-making, strategizing, and occasional grandstanding at all levels of public and Indigenous governments. I was in Ottawa in the 1980s during multi-year negotiations to get section 35 Aboriginal Rights entrenched into the highest law in the land. I was part of the national broadcast team for those constitutional talks, listening and reporting to Canadians. I was a featured reporter when Pope John Paul II came north to Fort Simpson in 1987. He apologized to the Aboriginal Peoples of Canada for the Catholic Church's part in displacing them from their homelands, and I remember the impact of his words: to "affirm the right to a just and equitable measure of self-government, along with a land base and adequate resources necessary for developing a viable economy for present and future generations ... so that Canada may be a model for the world in upholding the dignity of the Aboriginal peoples." In the 1990s, I travelled back and forth to South Africa, training print and radio reporters in television skills to cover their first democratic election after the end of the racial segregationist policy of apartheid. As the authoritarian state broadcaster transformed itself into a public broadcaster, it was a time of journalistic reckoning: a recommitment to seek and tell the public the truth, no matter what.

And now here we were—the judge, the jock, and the journalist—each devoted to justice and the law, human rights, fair play, fact-finding, truth-telling, and accountability. A new common purpose would bind us together. For the next several years we would be researching, recording, and documenting more than a century of forced residential schooling for Indigenous children, educating an ignorant Canada about the history and ongoing legacy of those schools, and inspiring nationwide efforts toward lasting reconciliation. The background, perspective, and expertise that each of us brought to such a huge, wide-ranging job turned out to be an essential, near-perfect mix. But on that day in Edmonton in June 2009, we were still just getting to know each other.

As we settled into that first Commissioners' circle and started to build a shared understanding of the work ahead, each of us offered our personal connections to the residential school story. Willie had first-hand experience—he is a Survivor. He was the Elder in our Commissioner trio, a fluent Cree speaker raised by grandparents, steeped from birth in cultural knowledge and traditions, and also a practising Catholic. From that first meeting, we turned to Willie to lead us in prayers and guide us in protocols.

Murray was the child of residential school Survivors. He was the youngest of our team, also raised by grandparents. He told us about his decision not to enter the priesthood as his devoutly Catholic grandmother had wished. Instead, he decided as a new young father to reclaim his Anishinaabe culture and practices, staying committed to that effort ever since.

And me? I'd been living with a residential school Survivor for more than forty years. I had lived in his remote hometown and learned the basics of Dene language, culture, and spiritual practices, including ancient drum prayers sometimes overlaid with Catholic rituals. My mother-in-law, several brothers- and sisters-in-law, and many neighbours, friends, and co-workers were also Survivors. The majority of the population in the North is Indigenous, with more Survivors per capita than anywhere else in Canada. For half my adult life, I had been living with the still recent, raw, and inescapable impacts of the schools in my own home, facing them on the streets, and confronting them in my workplaces.

But I didn't grow up knowing these things. And I didn't grow up in the North or in an Indigenous family. Far from it. I grew up in one of the most southerly parts of Canada: small-town southwestern Ontario. Unlike my TRC Commissioner brothers, I was raised Protestant. Glaringly, I was also the only one among us raised by my own parents.

Yet we soon identified much in common. We shared easily about our spiritual practices and their importance to our well-being. We were all married and, coincidentally, we all had three kids: two daughters and a son. Each of us had one or more adopted children, a common addition in Indigenous homes. And we all had treasured grandchildren, who would become the inspiration for many of the stories and laughter we shared over the years ahead. Our children and grandchildren were the deepest reason each of us felt compelled to take on this job—for the well-being of them and all future children, after the profound damage done to several generations before them.

We immediately agreed to keep Survivors as the focus of everything we were about to do. They were at the heart of this story. Some had been fighting for their voices to be heard since the 1980s and '90s, some for entire lifetimes before that, well before the start of our TRC. They brought legal actions against the churches and the federal government to seek redress for the abuses of residential schools. Some went as far as the Supreme Court of Canada. Eventually, individual and regional cases grew into one national class action lawsuit. Survivors agreed to settle out of court to save precious time, as former students were rapidly aging and passing. In 2006, the Indian Residential Schools Settlement Agreement (IRSSA) was approved. The agreement is a long document with many parts, but a key obligation was to establish a Truth and Reconciliation Commission, a TRC.

The first paragraph of the TRC Mandate reads more like poetry than a legal obligation, written in italics to stand out:

> *There is an emerging and compelling desire to put the events of the past behind us so that we can work towards a stronger and healthier future. The truth telling and reconciliation process as part of an overall holistic and comprehensive response to the Indian Residential School legacy is a sincere indication and acknowledgement of the injustices and harms experienced by Aboriginal people and the need for continued healing. This is a profound commitment to establishing new relationships embedded in mutual recognition and respect that will forge a brighter future. The truth of our common experiences will help set our spirits free and pave the way to reconciliation.*

The entire Mandate is twelve pages long. The rest describes our Commission structure, lengthy to-do list for a five-year term, and guiding principles, including Do No Harm.

The central obligation of the TRC was documenting residential school history, realities, and consequences. We would collect and archive millions of documents from hundreds of government and church archives spread all over Canada. We would commission and oversee fresh research to help fill in the gaps in written records. Most compellingly, we would gather Survivor statements. The core of our work was recording and documenting the lived experiences of as many residential school Survivors as possible. To create opportunities for all that statement gathering, the Mandate also called for an unspecified number of community events, as well as what were called National Events, with opening and closing ceremonies. We needed to support commemoration, too, by recommending how to distribute monies earmarked for that within the agreement. We had to produce interim and final reports, with recommendations, in English and French. And we had to establish a national research centre. It would archive and preserve all this newly compiled information; keep it accessible for research, analysis, and education about residential schools; and keep the spirit and purpose of our Commission going into the future.

Long before the statements started flowing at the first community hearing, we knew that our loved ones were about to pay a huge price for our roles as Commissioners. Residential schools had been in every region of the country; Survivors were just as spread out. To get to as many of them as we could, our time away from home would be extensive. This would be especially hard for me, with often an extra travel day getting to and from Yellowknife. On top of being gone a lot, what emotional loads would we be carrying home with us? It was a fine balance: to be home enough and to be honest enough about our work to get the support we would need without damaging family members or relationships in the process.

I had just lived through what I've sometimes called my own personal TRC. I had fresh memories of our family implosion, marriage disintegration, two-year separation, and eventual reconciliation. The crisis was largely fuelled by my Survivor husband's residential school experiences. His first sickening efforts to face the long-buried facts of what had happened to him eventually blew up our family. It was a long, painful crawl back to a shared life. I already knew I would have to filter what I could tell him from the road. Any details about the experiences of other Survivors could trigger traumatic memories for him, too. It was unfair and unreasonable for me to expect support from him in that way. The Commissioners needed to make sure our home partners had the protection, support, and sense of community we would be putting in place for ourselves, even though we would often be far apart. We decided our spouses would travel with us for major events and opening and closing ceremonies. It would help them stay aware of our work, keep them safe, and bring them, and us, loving support.

We knew we would need all the help we could get during this difficult process. We would make time and space for whatever tools we needed to keep ourselves and Survivors strong. Many Indigenous communities embrace Indigenous spirituality; many others are Christian; and some embrace both traditions. That same range of belief was reflected within our Commissioner team. We agreed to respect and accommodate sacred practices of all kinds, in many languages. And in our meetings as a trio, we would take turns offering prayers.

I am forever grateful to Murray for recognizing that each of us would also need the support of a spiritual advisor for self-care. I knew immediately who to ask—someone who had been there for me several times before. Peter Short was my local minister before moving away to eventually become the national moderator of the United Church of Canada and a chaplain for the Canadian Armed Forces. His church is a community of compassion and care: he carries the gift of knowing how to make sense of ancient scriptures for modern times, how to take the church from the pulpit to the people, how to say just what you need to hear. I would leave his sermons thinking he had spoken directly to me, providing a nugget of spiritual guidance for the days ahead. And he always ended with this message: "Church is over. Let the service begin."

Peter walked that talk in his own life. I have a clear memory of him in the old downtown Yellowknife hospital, at my bedside. The day after my daughter's birth we had left the hospital; a couple of days later we were back. She looked so perfect, but something was wrong. An anxious, bereft mother. Her naked newborn babe, now blindfolded, with a little hat, on display under the spotlight in an aquarium-like incubator, countless pinpricks on her heels. A mother wants to hold her new baby. To smell her. To memorize the face, the gurgles, the cries. To inspect the tiny fingers and toes. To cradle the head and caress the soft, velvety earlobes. A mother cracks open when that bond is severed, even temporarily.

This was my second child but the first time anything like this had happened to me. As a United Church minister for many years and a father of three older children, Peter brought reassurance that all would be well with my child. He asked me about the meaning of her name: Daylyn—the rushing waters of rapids. "She will live fully in the flow of life," he said. With wisdom and quiet presence, he calmed my churning. Together, unhurried, we listened for the rhythmic little breaths coming from across the room. A week later, baby Daylyn was wide-eyed and snuggled back in my arms—home.

A few years later, Peter guided me through a professional challenge. I had accepted the job of CBC regional director for northern Canada on two conditions: that I would launch northern Canada's first-ever daily television news programming (in multiple languages across four time zones); second, that the region would no longer be run from faraway Ottawa, as it had been since its colonial beginnings as the CBC Northern and Military Services. I got the position relocated to Yellowknife, renaming the region CBC North. As the first woman in the role, I had inherited a man's world, complete with girlie calendar decor. Culture change is not easy. One day, Peter Short came to see me at the CBC and walked straight into my wall of discouragement and frustration. He had wise encouragement for that situation, too: "Sometimes you just have to act as if things are the way you know they need to be, until they become so." It was a vital lesson for me in vision, determination, practice, and hope.

More years later, by miraculous coincidence, he reappeared when I most needed him during some of the darkest days for our family. I told him that I had cried every day for the past six months, that I couldn't seem to stop. He listened quietly, then said, "Jesus wept." No judgment. No shaming. Instead, Peter Short placed me in the company of the ageless, reminding me that at some point in our lives we have all been there, in the depths of grief and despair. Sometimes you just have to cry it out, tears being their own contribution to healing, cleansing, and whatever is to come next …

When I asked Peter to be my TRC spiritual advisor, he responded as if I had offered him an honour. When I told him I was a little nervous, he talked about the age-old practice of tempering. For metal, it involves heating to a very high temperature and then cooling down. For other trades, it can be the gradual callusing of hands, to protect from deeper injury or extreme conditions. Whatever the field, it is a process of strengthening for a tough job to reduce brittleness, strain, and internal stress. Peter said, "You already know how to do this, Marie. You've been preparing for this all your life."

He knew. As the years of the TRC unfolded, and as I steadied myself to hear story after story of the broken childhoods of our country, images of my own life and childhood would emerge. Over and over, I would think, *So that's why that happened to me. That's why I met that person. Now I know why that was an important chapter of my life. Now I see how that helped prepare me for this moment.* My TRC experience was a convergence of all my past experiences: professional and personal, good and bad, happy and sad, deflated and hopeful. It was a profound convergence of care, with the support of Peter and countless other friends and helpers I would come to know along the journey, starting with my fellow Commissioners.

Our Mandate's long list of what to do didn't say anything about how to do it. That was up to us. That was where our own vision, skills, and creativity would kick in, playing to each of our strengths and experiences. We needed to know each other better, to develop trust among ourselves and with Survivors. So, we decided that for the first six months we would stick together, do everything and go everywhere as a single unit of three. We would observe and learn from each other while giving residential school Survivors the reassuring signal of our solidarity and commitment.

~

That Edmonton meeting in June took place before the official start of our term as Commissioners. I'll never forget the date we did become official—July 1, 2009. Canada Day. The irony was not lost on me. Rather than celebrating this nation in all its greatness, the Truth and Reconciliation Commission was setting out to expose the longest-running human rights abuses in Canada's history: imposed residential schooling for Indigenous children, sanctioned by government, enforced by churches.

First, we needed to get grounded in key relationships, especially with those who had negotiated what we were now responsible for, and figure out how to stay true to the Mandate they had entrusted to us. So we went to Ottawa. The capital city is home to the Government of Canada. It is also the headquarters of national Indigenous organizations that signed the Indian Residential Schools Settlement Agreement: the Assembly of First Nations and Inuit Tapiriit Kanatami. The church parties to the agreement were more scattered and complex, with Protestant churches based in Toronto (Anglican, United, and Presbyterian) and fifty-three Catholic Church entities located across the country in distinct orders and dioceses, including the majority Oblates and Grey Nuns. We experienced very different beginnings with the federal government, the Indigenous organizations, and the churches. The government prepared for our arrival through briefing notes and bureaucracy. Indigenous organizations reached out to us through relationships and ceremony. The four national churches that ran most of the residential schools had distinct internal stances, even within their own denominations, ranging from historical remorse to historical amnesia, from willing partnership to legal protectionism.

But first we needed to meet the TRC team. With few exceptions, our staff were based in Ottawa. The federal government had set up a TRC secretariat for a previous Commission—one that had floundered and dissolved in a matter of months the year before ours. We had inherited the workspace, staff, and structure of that original secretariat. A federally hired executive director reported to the deputy minister of Aboriginal and Northern Affairs (the federal department now called Crown-Indigenous Relations and Northern Affairs, or CIRNA). All the TRC staff reported to or through that executive director, who also controlled and managed all the Commission's money and other operational resources. The three Commissioners were off to the side, with no direct authority over any of it.

We spent several hot, sweaty days in July 2009 in various boardrooms of the nation, where we made a number of organizational intentions clear. The Commissioners, through our Chair, would assume leadership and direct authority for the executive director and the secretariat. We would restructure to reflect our mandated areas of activities. We would establish an Inuit sub-commission to ensure

Inuit-language fluency and cultural expertise within the TRC. And we would relocate the TRC office to new headquarters in Winnipeg. Our court-ordered and court-supervised status had a lot to do with this decision. It was critical for us both to *be* independent and to be *seen* as independent. Getting out from under the shadow of Ottawa would help with that.

In those first weeks in Ottawa we also met with individuals beyond the parties to the Settlement Agreement. Several had been involved in various inquiries and commissions before ours. They offered important advice, both organizational and worldly. Of all the guidance, the most memorable—and the most personal—came from the late Sheila-Marie Cook. At the time, she was the Secretary to the Governor General of Canada, but she'd gained a lot of commission expertise before that as a leading expert in strategic planning and management. "Be prepared to face all the major life events that come along within every Commission," she said. "Births and deaths, marriages and divorces. Life won't stop for your Commission, and you'll have to be able to deal with it." Her kind but stark message provoked a moment of quiet reflection among the Commissioners. Over the years ahead, the wisdom of Sheila-Marie's words proved to be prophetic and, in some cases, hit extremely close to home. Within the next two years—with barely time to pause, much less grieve—I would face the loss of my mother.

The government's outreach to us as new Commissioners was through a senior bureaucrat. The residential schools file had been assigned to the department known back then as Aboriginal Affairs and Northern Development. Michael Wernick was the deputy minister in charge. He invited us to a reception of senior staff in his office, where he gave each of us a small, greenish maple leaf pin. Murray and Willie got smaller lapel versions; mine was a little bigger, more like a brooch. They came with a card explaining they were made of oxidized copper from the roof of the Parliament Buildings. Something recycled from the very structures that had landed us in our present-day morass. The weathered copper was pretty, but I couldn't help thinking that it would take much more than the re-adornment of existing structures to get us anywhere close to our agreed purpose of meaningful reconciliation.

The official welcome by the Indigenous organizations was something else altogether. Phil Fontaine was in the last weeks of his final term as national chief of the Assembly of First Nations, the organization once known as the National Indian Brotherhood. It represents the largest association of Indigenous Nations within Canada. As a residential school Survivor, Chief Fontaine had signed onto the court case against the government and the churches both on behalf of the AFN and as an individual plaintiff. Although others in various parts of the country had started multiple local court cases, he was the first to bring the issue to national prominence, with a high-profile interview on CBC Television's flagship program of the day, *The Journal*, with its iconic media host, Barbara Frum. This TRC welcome was a kind of finale for Chief Fontaine, a signature moment in his long, public role seeking justice for residential school Survivors. He brought us together for an unforgettable lifting-up ceremony to equip the three Commissioners for our TRC calling.

A photo I treasure shows the three of us sitting on the floor of a stage in the Canadian Museum of History in Gatineau, Quebec, just across the river from Ottawa. TRC Commissioner-Chair Murray Sinclair, TRC Commissioner Wilton Littlechild, and TRC Commissioner Marie Wilson—each of us wrapped in a colourful star-blanket quilt. Mine is shades of dark and pale blue. National Chief Phil Fontaine is sitting just above and behind us. He has our backs. The picture captures one precious, solemn moment in a ceremony full of prayer and symbolism.

First, we were offered the smoke of burning sage for cleansing. Then the still-burning smudge pot was placed nearby on the floor, where a pipe ceremony was about to take place. I was in the direct line of its smoke. I could feel my lungs constricting, my eyes watering, my shallow breath turning to gulps of panic. I was having an asthma attack! I felt as though I was about to fail my first public test as the one non-Indigenous Commissioner. I felt the dreaded weight and shame as my face and eyes set out to betray me at a time when we were all still getting to know each other.

As discreetly as the stage allowed, I leaned over to Murray and gasped, "I'm so sorry, but I can't breathe."

He saved me. He didn't make it a big deal; he just asked the Elders leading the ceremony to move the pot farther away because it was creating a problem for Commissioner Wilson. Then Murray kindly whispered to me that we would have to watch out for this in the future, to make sure I was always okay. I was so grateful and could feel myself calming down.

But then he whispered something else: "You can't sit cross-legged. Women can't do that."

I had copied the way he and Commissioner Littlechild were sitting, thinking that would be the safest way to get it right. I was very self-conscious and didn't want to embarrass my fellow Commissioners in our first public outing, this special event that was completely new to me. I had been in countless sacred fire ceremonies back home in Dene country, but they had always been outdoors and standing up; none of them involved sitting on the floor in a circle inside a building, especially not on a stage in an auditorium, all eyes fixed on us.

I had bought a special dress for the occasion. It was the best that Yellowknife could offer on such short notice: turquoise and black, fitted on top with a flowing skirt. As I repositioned myself, I was glad the skirt was full enough to cover my legs. It turned out it hadn't been enough, though, to cover up my ignorance. I would have a lot to learn over the coming months—we all would—about the differing protocols for women and men in various Indigenous traditions throughout the land, their practices as diverse and distinct as the Nations themselves.

After the pipe ceremony, the lifting-up began with a teaching about humility. Seated on the floor, we were reminded that we could not do our work alone. To stand strong, we would need support from others. Four helpers approached the corners of three blankets where we had been called to sit down. Working from all sides, my helpers supported and raised me up from the floor of the stage to a standing position. Four women—one First Nations, one Inuk, one Métis, and one non-Indigenous Canadian—lifted me up and blanketed me. They wrapped me in the warmth and beauty and security of that star-blanket quilt—my comfort, my reassurance, my gift to mark this sacred moment.

I later learned that Elder Maggie Hodgson and Paulette Regan had been part of the circle of women who lifted me up—and they never did stop lifting up my spirits over the months and years to come. Maggie, an Order of Canada recipient, had already been working on reconciliation for years as one of the founders of the international forum Healing Our Spirit Worldwide (HOSW) and a national founder of the original Reconciliation Day movement in Canada. Dr. Paulette Regan, a scholar on residential schooling and author of *Unsettling the Settler Within*, was part of the TRC research team and did important analysis and writing for the Commission.

Once lifted up, we were each then called upon to speak. That day, I publicly committed to my role as a Truth and Reconciliation Commissioner as "a sacred trust."

Next, we received a large, polished, deep-green carving from the Inuit homeland. Today we know Mary Simon as Her Excellency, the first Indigenous Governor General of Canada, but back then she was head of the national Inuit organization Inuit Tapiriit Kanatami. Also a former

Canadian ambassador to Denmark and the Arctic, ITK president Simon had chosen the meaningful gift of an experienced diplomat. Noting its weight, she reminded us of the tremendous weight of our responsibility to remember that her Inuit people also number heavily among residential school Survivors. The carving's form, size, and colour reflected the great potential for beauty in the work that lay before us.

Months later I heard Aboriginal Affairs Minister Chuck Strahl lament how Indigenous people and the government so often "talk past each other." He said that the one talks about relationships, history, and ceremony, while the other talks about legislation, limits of authorities, and the rule of law. Those back-to-back welcomes during our first TRC days in Ottawa reflected that same dichotomy, showing how even symbolic gestures could talk past each other. The government had pinned us with a beautiful yet recycled adornment from an aging structure. The Indigenous organizations had handed us a rock transformed by careful, creative vision, wrapped us in unique new blankets, and lifted us with ceremony, prayers, and promises. Our TRC challenge would compel us to look both ways: old and new, realities and possibilities.

We needed to choose our own TRC symbols carefully to build an image, look, and feel that captured the spirit and intention of this Commission. There had never been a Truth and Reconciliation Commission like ours. We looked at previous examples, such as South Africa's, Peru's, and others, but no other had the same legal context, mandate, or authorities. No other dealt with harms specifically targeting children. There was no established rulebook or tool kit. We would be learning as we went.

First, the slogan. I was surprised to learn that the historical meaning of the word *slogan* comes from my Celtic roots. It meant a Scottish Highland war cry. In a way, that meaning was relevant to our modern-day TRC context, as many Survivors would eventually tell us that residential school was like a war zone. They had been taken, hardened, disciplined, sometimes locked up, and put on rations, their heads shaved. They had learned to fight, to defend themselves, to protect others, to steal food, to communicate with secret codes, and to carry lifelong bonds with their mates, which some called "inmates."

For the Commission, the slogan became a banner of words that would constantly remind us that Survivors had been children when the first harms of school hit them and rocked their families. They would always need to remain first and foremost in our TRC efforts. Our carefully chosen words spoke out from a large panel by the Commissioners' table at the front of every single event we held. For Survivors and others who made public statements, these words became a focal point for their sharing. For many, it helped them remember. The slogan also helped them think beyond themselves: *For the child taken, for the parent left behind.*

Then, the logo. Start with a circle, fill it with flames, surround it with story. No words on the logo, leading people to ask questions. What does it mean? That helped with our Mandate to educate the country. The circle represented a place for everyone, binding us all to the call for truth and reconciliation—Inuit, First Nations, Métis, and all Canadian society. The flames were individual yet interconnected—a circle of fire with its power to purge, cleanse, heal, warm, nourish, draw people together, and light the way. We were shining light on a shadowy part of Canadian history; all parts of the TRC circle would help illuminate the whole.

The TRC colours followed naturally from the flames of the logo—shades of orange. Posters, pamphlets, and early TRC T-shirts were all bright orange. Eventually, orange shirts gained wider recognition and new symbolism. On her first day of residential school, Survivor Phyllis Webstad had a new orange shirt taken away. The Commission would hear many such stories of confiscated treasures. Whether traditional moccasins, mukluks, mitts, hats, parkas, or something store-bought, all were childhood losses made worse when beloved mothers and grannies had made or bought the items. To residential school children, having such things seized was more than the loss of a material mark of love from home. It also marked the lost transfer of expert skills needed to make them. One Survivor broke down and cried about kamiks, those timeless, waterproof sealskin boots essential to keeping Inuit feet dry and warm in the coldest homelands on the planet. As a former student, now a fifty-something woman, she confessed her shame at never having made her own pair of kamiks—never learning how. Where does one learn to make such a beautiful, durable, and essential piece of footwear, capable of saving lives? Where, but at the side of a mother or grandmother who has spent a lifetime perfecting the pleat of the sole, the stitch of the toe, the depth of the foot, the turn of the heel, the width of the cuff, the signature design of the maker? What about the complexity of expertise needed to harvest your own animals for food, clothing, and fuel: cleaning the gun, planning the route, loading the sleigh, reading the water and skies, the wind, snow, daylight, the stars, stalking and tracking, aiming patiently for a responsible kill, offerings and prayers of thanksgiving? Then the straining, sweating hours of work to gut and clean with the precision of a surgeon, to haul and pack with the strength and endurance of an Olympian, and still, to find inner reserves and the way back home by the only navigational tools available ... the land itself, the land and waters and skies that have become part of you. Where was the opportunity to learn, to practise, and to perfect such timeless survival skills in residential school? It was nowhere ...

The orange shirts first seen at the TRC now focus much wider public awareness, thanks to Phyllis's powerful campaign to share her personal orange shirt story, especially among students still learning about truth and reconciliation. Orange is the perfect colour to do that, a primary mix of red for heart and yellow for light. When I imagine reconciliation, I see orange—where heart and light come together.

The TRC logo, by design, had seven flames to represent the seven sacred teachings common to many Indigenous nations within and beyond Canada. They are sometimes called the seven sacred laws, or grandfather teachings: respect, courage, love, truth, humility, honesty, and wisdom. When one of the spiritual advisors explained the teachings, I felt peaceful familiarity. I was raised with these same values. The seven teachings are common to many of the world's wisdom traditions, with variations in wording. We decided the teachings of the logo's flames would also serve as themes for our TRC National Events.

The TRC Mandate called for us to work with an Indian Residential School Survivor Committee (IRSSC). We renamed it the TRC Survivors Committee. Like the Commissioners, the ten members of the Survivors Committee (SC) came from various parts of the country; they, too, were expected to immediately work together while still getting to know each other, and while some of them were still tripping over their own childhood memories of residential school. They were selected through a process negotiated between the federal government, the Assembly of First Nations, and Inuit Tapiriit Kanatami. The committee had seven First Nations members, two Inuit, and one Métis, roughly reflecting the proportion of Survivors from each of those groups and the diversity within them. Barney Williams and Terri Brown were from the west and north, Raymond Arcand and Eugene Arcand from the Prairies, Doris Young and Gordon Williams from central Canada, and Lottie May Johnson from the Maritimes. Inuit members were John Banksland from the western Arctic of the Northwest Territories and Rebekah Uki Williams from the eastern Arctic in Nunavut. John Morrisseau reflected the Manitoba Métis homeland.

The Commissioners received the Survivors Committee membership a couple of months after we started our jobs. We immediately spotted a hole—there was no voice from Quebec. We asked for an eleventh member, but the government held firm at ten. Then, sad news shook the committee almost before it got started. Ray Arcand from Alberta passed quite suddenly. So, Commissioner Littlechild agreed to sit with his fellow Survivors on their committee to maintain the Alberta perspective and strengthen internal communications between Commissioner and Survivor teams. That also freed up a spot for us to insist on a replacement—someone from Quebec. Madeleine Basile joined soon after. She and Eugene (known as Big Bird) were the youngest and sometimes referred to affectionately within the group as "the babies." Gordon Williams became the committee chair, and Barney Williams, our Commission Elder. He continues to play that cherished role in my personal life. The TRC Survivors Committee provided invaluable advice on key activities such as Survivor sharing circles, Expressions of Reconciliation, National Events, and commemoration.

Part of the Settlement Agreement included a $20 million fund for commemoration. Part of our TRC Mandate was to recommend to government how to distribute that money. It would never be enough for the hundreds of proposals we received from all over the country—one of the reasons why we later included commemoration in our TRC Calls to Action. In the meantime, we worked with the Survivors Committee to establish criteria to evaluate the many competing requests for commemoration dollars. We decided projects could be local, regional, or national in scope, with specific dollar amounts for each category. Also, a big part of our assessment centred on reconciliation. How would this proposal contribute to education, healing, and ongoing reconciliation between Indigenous and non-Indigenous peoples? All communities needed the healing benefits of commemoration, yet some would have to be turned down. It was painful work. We couldn't have done it without the Survivors Committee.

The TRC Mandate also specified seven National Events. Canada is a country with thirteen jurisdictions, three distinct Indigenous Peoples, dozens of diverse nations within those groups, and hundreds of Indigenous communities. Many are in some of the most geographically and logistically remote parts of Canada, with people who can't easily or affordably get to a more centralized event. How were we going to decide where to hold *seven* National Events?

Here again, call in the Survivors Committee. First, they recommended the TRC National Events be spread out as follows: British Columbia, Alberta, Saskatchewan, Manitoba, Quebec, the Maritimes, and the North. Ontario, with the biggest population, would not get a National Event, but both the opening and closing ceremonies would be held there, with many of the same program elements.

Then the committee debated specific locations. Former school sites were early suggestions, especially in those places where schools had only closed within the last fifteen years. But many were in remote locations. The Commissioners weighed in with a reminder that the TRC was not limited to Survivors. It was about wide societal impact. Our Mandate said we had to educate Canadians and inspire ongoing reconciliation. To do that, we needed to engage citizens and institutions, including educators, all levels of government, churches, and other faith communities—all sectors of civil society. Relatively central locations for National Events would allow as many as possible to get there. A transportation hub with available accommodations would be ideal. To ensure wide reach beyond the event itself, we also needed media outlets and reliable internet service. The Survivors Committee concluded that TRC National Events be in Vancouver, Edmonton, Saskatoon, Winnipeg, Montreal, Halifax, and Inuvik.

Finally, they assigned the theme for each National Event based on the seven sacred teachings of the logo. As these events unfolded, each carefully chosen theme seemed perfectly matched to the place, the stories, and the moment. I shall forever honour the essential contributions of the TRC Survivors Committee to the work of the Commission. They were our advisors. Some were Elders. They became our cherished friends. They gave us their best. Several have since joined the Ancestors.

But for now, they were expert guides on the TRC journey, following a path of national milestones we charted together:

2009: Ottawa, Opening
2010: Winnipeg, Respect
2011: Inuvik, Courage
2011: Halifax, Love
2012: Saskatoon, Truth
2012: Montreal, Humility
2013: Vancouver, Honesty
2014: Edmonton, Wisdom
2015: Ottawa, Closing

As I reflect on those early weeks of the TRC, including the two magical days in Edmonton in June 2009 when three new Commissioners met for the very first time, I notice something more clearly than before. We built ourselves a firm foundation of overlapping circles. We were a circle of Commissioners within a circle of support. Our circle of Survivors encircled all parts of the country. We planned a circuitous journey, following the flames of a circular logo. All our careful intentions aimed for spiritual healing. Overlapping circles spiralling upwards—gyres. With fires and gyres, we strengthened ourselves for a national journey of reckoning. We had already come full circle: mind, body, heart, and spirit—and we had just begun.

CHAPTER 2

Witnessing the Future

ONE OF OUR earliest pieces of formal correspondence as new TRC Commissioners was an invitation from Her Excellency the Right Honourable Michaëlle Jean, the twenty-seventh Governor General of Canada. It was to hold the opening ceremony of the Truth and Reconciliation Commission at Rideau Hall. Her willingness to host, and to take on a special role we asked of her, helped us settle on the theme for that Opening Event: Witnessing the Future.

Rideau Hall is both residence and workplace for the Governor General in Ottawa. Years ago, I got a deluxe tour of the historic building and its expansive, park-like grounds. The French word *rideau* means "curtain." The name refers to the curtain of water seen by French explorer Samuel de Champlain at the point where what became known as the Rideau River flows into the Ottawa River. The name caught on widely with those who put themselves in charge of naming landmarks in and around Ottawa, erasing many original Indigenous names.

Long before the corduroy logging roads that my grandparents remembered, or the dirt roads, or the railways that political promises built, or the trains where politicians staged their platforms, or the pavement and the planes, there were curtains of water, highways of water, ribbons of water tying us all together as a country. We needed to remember that now. At the heart of our Commission's job was the responsibility to help everyone in this country remember what Mother Earth had long ago provided—an interwoven cord of winding water binding us together from coast to coast to coast, to connect, support, and nurture us all. We were each born from a burst of life-sustaining water from the wombs of our mothers. Remembering the gifts and symbolism of water could help with unifying, cleansing, healing, and new beginnings. No wonder so many treaties between the Crown and Indigenous nations include the phrasing "As long as the river flows." It is a binding commitment to time immemorial, an enduring recognition of the relationship between people and place and our interdependence with the natural world.

A river runs through it—I knew that was true of just about any place in Canada. I spent most of my early life in various parts of Ontario and Quebec, along the Great Lakes watershed. That's the international water boundary that defines about a third of the Canada-US border, as the massive inland lakes feed the St. Lawrence River on its easterly run toward the Atlantic Ocean. And I've spent most of my adult life in the Canadian northwest, in the watershed of the mighty Mackenzie, the great river known here as Dehcho, with two more great lakes and countless rivers, creeks, and streams that feed into it on its northerly run to the Arctic Ocean.

Auntie Dora was my relative through marriage and my next-door neighbour in Fort Good Hope in the early 1980s. We lived in adjacent little log houses built by previous generations of kin: an interrelationship of families and homes, huddled together in this tiny speck of a community tucked along the banks of that massive river.

In my early days in Fort Good Hope, I would hear the words for sugar, salt, chocolate, fork, cup, table, long john underwear, thank you, and my ear would recognize the French-language roots in colloquial Dene vocabulary. I grew up with English as my mother tongue, but at school I had to learn Latin and French. That insight into how those two languages were structured has helped me understand the meaning and origin of many English words, as well as some words in Indigenous languages. That's especially true when Indigenous words have been influenced by the overlay of colonial tongues and trade. So many Dene learned their English from francophones—French-speaking missionaries in residential schools who forced Indigenous kids to forget their own languages and learn to speak English.

Auntie Dora's English was that kind of second language—forced upon her, never fully embraced. Dora had a colourful way of speaking, weaving together as many words as she could muster to make the strongest possible point. Once, while explaining where another place was in relation to Fort Good Hope, she said, "You have to go way up down north."

I hid my smile at first, not wanting to be disrespectful yet utterly amused by what seemed to be a contradiction—up, down, and north, all in the same mouthful. But slowly, I grasped her real meaning. The Mackenzie flows downstream past Fort Good Hope and crosses the nearby Arctic Circle as it heads "up north" for several hundred more kilometres, eventually spilling into the Beaufort Sea and the Arctic Ocean. Auntie Dora's meaning was clear and accurate: up north, downstream, northward—*way up down north*. Her sense of direction, her sense of place, her sense of relationship with the land and water were all interconnected with the defining flow of the river.

With all that symbolic river connection, Rideau Hall felt perfect to me for launching our TRC work. But there were also lots of good strategic reasons for the Commissioners' decision to hold the Opening Event there. This neutral location would not suggest that any one group of Survivors, any one residential school, region, or Indigenous nation, was more important than any other.

Many Indigenous people see the Governor General, the monarch's representative in Canada, as the one with the responsibility to uphold and safeguard the spirit of treaties signed between Indigenous nations and the government, in the name of the Crown. They refer to their "special relationship" with the Governor General, expressed more officially by Indigenous leaders and legal scholars as "the Honour of the Crown." My husband, Stephen, tells of Dene Elders back home who talk about the late queen "Lizabeh" and her son "Chali" and wife "Ghamila" as if they were personal acquaintances. That's why Indigenous leaders have sometimes taken their treaty grievances directly to the Governor General. Rideau Hall was a setting that belonged to all the people of Canada, with particular ties to Indigenous Peoples.

By definition and obligation of the role, the Governor General must remain non-political and non-partisan. That fit very well with the way we had already begun to frame the idea of reconciliation: it wasn't about political parties; it was about the people of Canada. Also, this particular Governor General, Madame Michaëlle Jean, had stated her special interest in matters affecting children and Indigenous Peoples. That priority was reflected in the unprecedented artwork she had chosen to display in the Rideau Hall ballroom. The conventional portrait of the Queen was replaced by a magnificent four-panel tableau by the late Anishinaabe artist Norval Morrisseau called *Androgyny*. The painting is the master work of a residential school Survivor, though he is much more widely known as a world-class artist. In 1983, Morrisseau offered *Androgyny* to the people of Canada in his own gesture of reconciliation. In brilliant primary colours, it depicts the interconnectedness and fluidity of life and gender, people and nature, humanity and spirit. The four-panelled structure mirrors ancient teachings about the sanctity of four: the four elements, the four directions, and the four dimensions of human life—mind, body, heart, and spirit. It would be the perfect backdrop for the launch of our TRC journey toward understanding and healing of the one, the many, and the whole.

~

On October 15, 2009, the big day started with a ceremonial cleansing of the Rideau Hall ballroom. Elders arrived early with burning sage and other traditional medicines to prepare both the space and the Commissioners for what lay ahead. The ballroom was set up differently on this day. The chairs were placed in circles to capture the worldwide Indigenous perspective of the inseparable relationship between the individual and the collective, and so that each person would feel fully and equally part of a shared experience. Even the flowers sat in a circle, a distinctly colourful flow of red, yellow, black, and white, ribboned together in a singular display on a bed of lacy green sprays of cedar. The four colours and the cedar are key aspects of traditional Indigenous healing—a finishing touch as we marked the beginning of a national healing journey.

Official events at Rideau Hall begin in a particular way. Guests are seated, the ensemble known as the Canadian Armed Forces Serenade of Strings begins to play, and everyone rises in respect and anticipation. The Governor General enters from the back in a formal procession, preceded by a military attaché and followed by all other dignitaries for the day.

Official First Nations events also begin with an entrance rich in protocol. It is known as the Grand Entry. Guests are seated, traditional drummers begin, and everyone rises in respect and anticipation. The highest-ranking chiefs enter from the back of the meeting space, preceded by eagle staff carriers, and sometimes Indigenous veterans, and followed by all other dignitaries for the day.

The processional for the Opening Event of the Truth and Reconciliation Commission of Canada was a combination of the two. There was an ensemble, and there were Indigenous drums. There was a military attaché, and there was Indigenous representation from the Canadian Rangers unit of the Canadian Armed Forces Army Reserve. There was the Governor General, and—walking beside her, not behind—there was the Chair of the Truth and Reconciliation Commission. Behind them were two more Commissioners, one Indigenous and one non-Indigenous, also walking side by side. For my first formal processional into Rideau Hall, I wore a dress with turquoise embroidered eagles designed by West Coast artist Dorothy Grant. My northern garments would have been far too hot for this southern weather, and in the heat of this day's many profound moments, they would have done me in.

The other dignitaries in this processional were not elected leaders of governments, Indigenous organizations, or the national churches. They were already seated as guests. The dignitaries were the ten members of the newly named TRC Survivors Committee. They represented a 150-year history of 150,000 Survivors from some 150 schools throughout the land. I could sense the collective anger, impatience, and expectation vibrating from the Survivors at our backs, a live wire of hope igniting the entire room.

And there were children. Rideau Hall is typically the setting for the public business of state, the quiet dialogue of diplomacy, and the ceremonial rituals of international relations. Not exactly kid stuff. But we needed children here, especially if we were going to be talking about their future. Several came with their residential school Survivor grandparents. For others, both Indigenous and non-Indigenous, this was the finale of a two-day workshop learning about residential schools and each other, many for the first time. The TRC's breathtaking Bentwood Box was on display in front of the Morrisseau painting. Coast Salish artist Luke Marston had lovingly carved its four sides to depict the range of ages and cultures of residential school Survivors. Very soon these young people, also diverse in age and culture, would be offering their symbolic gifts in cross-cultural teams of two, shy and proud. Their gifts would be the first Expressions of Reconciliation for the Bentwood Box to receive. Hundreds of others would come from all sectors of society over the years ahead.

Survivors and their grandchildren were front and centre, reminding everyone just how young Survivors had been when they were taken away to residential school, their lives turned upside down. The contrast of ages also emphasized how long Survivors had been waiting for the truth of their experiences to be acknowledged and finally put right so that their grandchildren could know a different kind of life and future. To bring these points into sharper focus, I assigned and scripted the production of four video vignettes. We selected Survivors from four directions of Canada representing First Nations, Inuit, Métis, and francophone experiences. We chose excerpts of each Survivor talking about their experiences at residential school, intercut with reactions from their own grandchild. The sequence of these four Elder-child conversations created an emotional picture to introduce some basic, gut-punching facts about the Survivors: how young they were, where they went, how many others were taken, how long they were gone, how homesick they felt, how they lost their language, how they were afraid, how they felt ashamed, how they'd felt lost ever since—the ongoing struggle of the residential school Survivor. With most of those Survivors now elderly, this was an overdue reflection of the harms Canada had done to little children. The physical, emotional, and spiritual scars from residential school days had left marks still visible today.

When it was time for the speeches, the Governor General spoke first to the Elders: "You represent the former residential school students from all regions of our country. You are here because you went to one of those schools. You are the little children of yesterday ... By listening and learning, we may also begin to bear witness to how we might, together, make things better for the future."

Our Chair, Murray Sinclair, then reflected on the historic significance and purpose of a TRC, and what made ours so special, from legal, political, and societal points of view. He concluded: "Today, the Truth and Reconciliation Commission is that opportunity to speak up. We want to know what you know, and how you feel about it. The sadness but also the triumphs, the courage, the friendships, the accomplishments, and the joys."

Chief Wilton Littlechild always wore two hats: as one of the three Commissioners and as one of the eighty thousand residential school Survivors still alive when we began. In response to the video, he said, "Thank you for your strength and courage in sharing your stories with your grandchildren, and with all of us today ... There are also non-Aboriginal children here today ... Witnesses are asked to store and care for the things they see and experience. A very important part of that is to share it with their own people. So, when you go back home, if you share what you have learned with your family and friends and classmates, you will also be helping the Truth and Reconciliation Commission."

Lastly, there was me, the non-Indigenous Commissioner: "The history of Indian Residential Schools in this country, and what needs to be done to address the legacy of them, is not just something for and about Aboriginal people. As a country, this history belongs to all of us. As its citizens, we *all* own our past, just as we will *all* own its future. It is the same with our theme today: we are *all* called to Witness the Future."

And so, the stage was set for the very first of what was to become a signature Commission activity: the induction of a TRC Honorary Witness.

I was the lead Commissioner for TRC Honorary Witnesses. We each brought forward names for consideration, with final decisions made as a Commissioner team. It was uplifting to identify and recruit influential Canadian individuals and groups, as well as some international collaborators of common cause, willing to help advance our work by associating their good names with it.

Madame Michaëlle Jean, a non-Indigenous Canadian of Haitian heritage, was our first inductee as an Honorary Witness of the Truth and Reconciliation Commission of Canada. The Governor General, as part of their job celebrating Canada, regularly welcomes outstanding Canadians into the stately ballroom of Rideau Hall to honour and recognize their great achievements before a gathering of family and friends, and pin them with one of several meritorious medals. This time, the Governor General was going to be pinned. Unlike other insignia handed out in this grand room, ours was not really a pin for achievement so much as an acknowledgement of Canada's historic *under*achievement. To become a TRC Honorary Witness was to make a public pledge of commitment to helping the country reach what it had failed to achieve: respectful relations between Indigenous and non-Indigenous people.

First, I explained the meaning of the term *Honorary Witness* and the importance of the designation to our Commission. Next, I called up and introduced the person or agency we were about to induct, highlighting their accomplishments and influence. Then I called up my fellow Commissioners so we could do the final three steps as a team.

Commissioner Sinclair presented them with a small hide pouch embroidered with our TRC logo and explained the meaning of the tokens inside. Commissioner Littlechild offered them tobacco, a sacred acknowledgement that we were asking for their help. After a few dropped pins and onstage scrambles, we agreed that, as the Commissioner with the smallest fingers, I would always do the finishing touch and pin each TRC Honorary Witness with a specially made pewter version of our own TRC pin, further adorned by a single hide fringe.

By the end of the Opening Event, Her Excellency the Right Honourable Michaëlle Jean was wearing the first official Honorary Witness pin on the lapel of her bright blue suit jacket. That day, she paved the way for close to a hundred other prominent influencers who followed her lead over the years of the TRC. Each Honorary Witness participated in at least one of our major events, listened to Survivor statements, and spoke publicly at the end of the day to the full gathering, often thousands of people. They bore witness to what they had heard and learned, shared the personal impact it had on them, and made a public promise to use their influence, networks, and opportunities to enlarge the circle of residential school awareness and the commitment to ongoing reconciliation.

The opening ceremony ended with a massive traditional Dene drum dance. It filled the expanse of the converted indoor tennis court of Rideau Hall, now commonly known as the Tent Room. But on this day, beneath the candy-pink-striped cloth awnings, it became the TRC community hall. Everyone in the circle, young and old, from far and near, with all our many differing steps and styles, dancing to the same beat for this precious encounter of possibility—we were a moving image of reconciliation.

As for me, amid all the grandeur, symbolism, and ceremony of that day, some memories remain privately poignant, uplifting, and amusing. I can still hear the quiet reverence of the Prayer for the Children—multiple voices from diverse cultures and faith traditions united in a single prayer, beginning with an Elder and ending with a child. I can still see the sheer, contrasting freedom of a little boy *not* in residential school, happy to run around the rim of the old fountain outside Rideau Hall, and do the inevitable—fall in and get soaked! And when all the officialdom was over, the lone Survivor who found himself locked out of the building, taking a necessary leak in the bushes off the front driveway of the grand old building—a new river running through it!

The TRC would soon be fanning out to all the overlapping homelands and waterways of the country. We could expect many emotional stumbles as residential school Survivors struggled to choose the right words. Auntie Dora had shown me long before that even when language is fractured, with patience and careful listening, deeper meaning becomes clear and precise. That was my hope for our TRC. My attachment to her, and her attachment to the river, had somehow flowed into my thinking about Rideau Hall as the right fit for our start. That connection felt right as we launched the Truth and Reconciliation Commission of Canada on our nationwide river-run of hope and healing through the many rapids and waterfalls ahead.

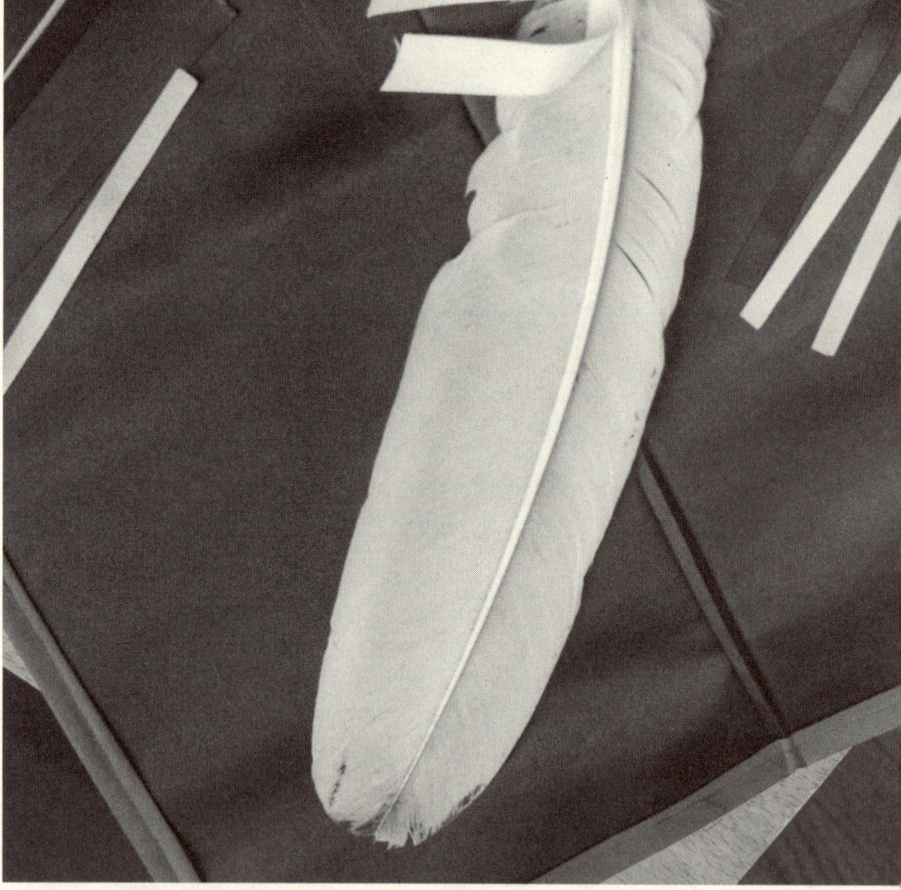

TRC Commissioner Marie Wilson's white eagle feather gifted with a teaching. Photo: Tessa Macintosh

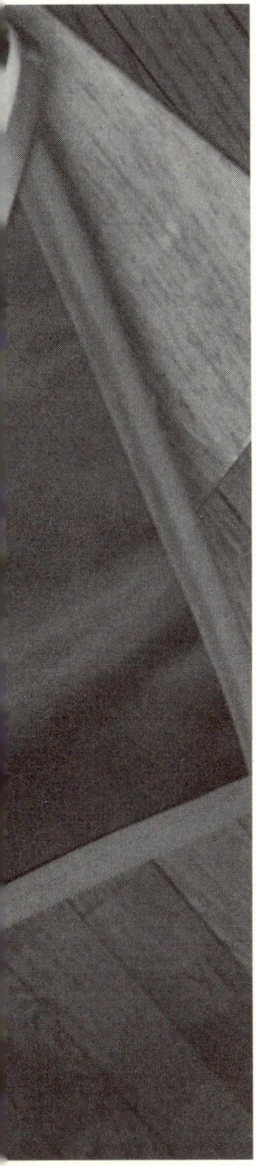

PART II

RESPECT

MANITOBA

Respect is about giving and sharing, which is one of the greatest secrets to a good life ... The greatest gift you can give ... is yourself, being a model and example.

—Elder Dr. David Courchene,
A Story of the Seven Sacred Laws

CHAPTER 3

A Grand Entrance

"IT ALL STARTS with respect. It all begins with respect. It's all about respect."

Among Commissioner Murray Sinclair's many fine qualities is his compelling voice. I can't tell you how many times I heard our Chair say variations of these words, especially in the first year of the TRC, when we were spending most of our time together, three Commissioners still sizing each other up, still getting the lay of the land and a feel for the work. By the time the Survivors Committee agreed that the first National Event should be in Winnipeg, home of our new TRC offices, home of our Chair, it almost felt preordained that our first theme would be Respect.

Leading up to that first National Event, we spread ourselves throughout the province and the country in something like a national speaking tour: a strategy for getting the word out about what to expect from us over the next five years, letting Survivors know their TRC was back and on the job, telling governments and churches what we needed from them, and asking international partners, educators, businesses, and philanthropists for their help. Later, we would settle into a pattern of several weeks or months of community hearings in a region, culminating in the National Event. This two-staged approach helped spread the word to smaller communities and build momentum ahead of the bigger event. It also allowed time for local fundraising and planning, and for Survivors to become familiar with the look and feel of our events, and with the various ways they could share their statements with the Commission.

There did not appear to be any concerted effort by the Government of Canada to explain to all Canadians their shared responsibilities for reconciliation. It fell to us as Commissioners on the front lines to explain over and over again how the TRC came to be, how it fit into the overall Settlement Agreement, how the TRC part of that agreement was not about any financial compensation, how our work was about documenting history—including Survivors' stories—and healing and reconciliation, and how all "the people of Canada" play a part.

Those early outreach events smothered me with emotions and shrouded me with a cloak of new blessings. Take Oromocto, New Brunswick, for example. Oromocto was where I first saw in action Commissioner Littlechild's perpetual hunger for well-cooked ribs! We still laugh about the incredible serving size—a stack of two slabs, both wider than the serving plate and too delicious for any leftovers.

Oromocto was also an early introduction to the wide range of residential school legacies—how behaviours and alliances formed at school could affect later realities. "The people who were bullies in residential school are the same ones who are bullies back home in our communities today," we were told. "They control everything. They decide who gets what, for jobs, opportunities, even houses." We were shown pictures of tents as winter homes for Survivors desperate to get permanent shelter while also battling serious illness.

Such was the terrible, intangible gift of Oromocto. The material gift, though, was two traditionally crafted ash baskets with differently shaped handles for men and women. We received them wrapped in teachings about the sacred importance of the ash tree to Mi'kmaq and Maliseet people.

In Alberta, Commissioner Littlechild's spiritual advisor, Elder Rick Lightning, prepared us in his ceremonial ways. It was my first time in a sweat lodge. The sacred ceremony is not for me to describe or explain, but I can share my memory of an overwhelming feeling of peace and cleansing. Unexpectedly, I was given a beautiful Nehiyawak spirit name and instructed to learn to say it in the language of my northern Dene family.

A different kind of naming took place farther west. Nuu-chah-nulth Elder and Survivors Committee member Barney Williams invited the Commissioners to his home on Vancouver Island. We gathered in a wooden community hall in Errington for a ceremony and feast. In front of witnesses from his family, Barney adopted us. He gifted us with seven cobalt-blue glass trading beads, prized among West Coast nations. The name he gave me came with a teaching: "Your name is Chukwasakwithlem. It refers to the dorsal fin of the humpback whale. It is essential for balance, strength, and endurance. You will need that for the work you are doing for Survivors and for the country. It is also the name of my grandmother and the name given to my wife, Trina. You have become one of the women in my family."

Barney has since told me that adoption in his tradition goes beyond giving a spirit name. It is the extension of family with new bonds of inclusion. Since my adoption, I have been invited as family to attend other special ceremonies: the transfer of responsibilities to his son as hereditary beach-keeper, and the conveyance of Barney's honorary doctor of laws from the University of Victoria. My adopted grandfather, naniiqsu, is now Dr. Barney Williams.

Back in central Canada, I received not a name but a feather. It was rare for me to attend an event alone with Murray. We were in Manitoba, his home turf. I treasure those few times for the one-on-one conversations that came with them. Murray's a great storyteller, and I'm a professionally trained question-asker, so our discussions were rich, meaningful, and fun.

After a warm welcome, a short visit, a shared meal, and general remarks from both of us about the TRC, we received generous gifts in the final moments of an afternoon event under an outdoor arbour. Mine came from the weathered hands of a shy, elderly woman with plump, round facial features and magnetic eyes. She looked straight into mine as she handed me two priceless treasures: a fragrant braid of sweetgrass and a hand-stitched, bright blue and red satin folder holding an eagle feather. Pure white. So beautiful. She held my gaze as she handed it to me, speaking softly: "This one, of course, is for you, the woman, the mother. It is white and pure and most sacred, because you are woman and we are the life-givers. Now you are the mother watching out for all our children." Her quiet words sent a shiver through me. As stirred as I was by the moment, I was slow to embrace the importance and reverence of the unique perspective I was bringing to the Commission. I could not foresee that this Elder would eventually find her way back to me, reminding me of her message.

My own mother was a model of curiosity and stubborn determination. I have inherited both traits. She enjoyed meeting new people, experiencing new places, and practising new skills, even going back to school to start a new career in her late fifties. Not much could defeat her. She never gave up, and she faced any obstacle as a challenge to be solved. "This too will pass," she would say.

She would also say, "Count your blessings, Marie." She taught me that counting your blessings was much more than a Sunday school teaching. It was a good spiritual practice for everyday living: to ground yourself and reframe any challenge positively, to tackle it from a place of strength. I have a folk-art wall hanging strategically placed in our home to help me remember her lesson. It features three little hand-painted wooden figures decorated with the names of my beloved children: Kyla, Daylyn, Keenan. They are designed to swing beneath a banner that reads *Count Your Blessings*: a daily greeting; this mother's daily prayer. Over the years of the TRC ahead that maternal perspective would keep calling out to me and would eventually lead to some of my deepest reflections.

~

By the time of the first National Event in 2010, I was enriched and strengthened by a new name, a new family, and new insights about residential schools, my fellow Commissioners, and myself. After many months of small-group preparations, it was finally time to face the big crowds in Winnipeg, the geographic centre of North America. I was full of hope as we gathered in the light of the first flame of our TRC logo, the grandfather teaching of Respect. The core meaning of the word is "re-spectre": to see again. We were convening a national public encounter, an invitation to move beyond the haunting of the past, to begin to see each other anew.

We had decided to make our TRC National Events four days long for maximum exposure. People came in droves from far and wide, an estimated forty thousand over the course of this first one. It took place outdoors at The Forks in downtown Winnipeg, where the Red and Assiniboine Rivers join. This is the heart of the homeland for several First Nations and Métis, a historical gathering and trading centre, and a modern-day meeting place. It offered a beautiful natural site to draw and hold thousands of people, and a captivating backdrop to grab the attention of thousands more through the media.

Several intersecting walkways criss-cross the expansive grounds at The Forks along the river. For our event, about twenty small, canvas-covered information and retail booths lined the edges of one lengthy walkway leading to a couple of much larger tents. The adjacent field was speckled with large white tipis decorated in the gold and orange of our TRC symbols. The tipis hosted outdoor public sharing circles with residential school Survivors and related programming. Private statements from Survivors were heard in various rooms on designated, protected floors of the nearby hotel. Educational activities, especially those where the Governor General took part, were at the nearby Manitoba Theatre for Young People.

The day before this first big event started, the Chair and I met with a delegation of the United Church of Canada. This Protestant denomination ran about 10 percent of residential schools. In 1986, it became the first church to apologize for its role in colonialism, generally. It followed up in the 1990s with another apology, this time specific to residential schools.

The church representatives set up the meeting as a sharing circle. Some very well-known residential school Survivors were part of it, such as Alvin Dixon and Chief Robert "Bobby" Joseph, who were instrumental in the work leading up to the Settlement Agreement. They had already spent years fighting their cause for justice at national negotiating tables, within this church, and within wider society. The meeting also included a few ordained Indigenous ministers and some non-Indigenous, including Rev. James Scott. Jamie Scott had been involved in reconciliation efforts well before his role at the negotiating table for the Settlement Agreement, and he remained consistently involved throughout the implementation of it, including the six and a half years of the TRC. We all benefited from his respectful voice of reason and his skill and expertise as a professional conflict resolution mediator. Another person in the circle was the Honourable Reverend David MacDonald, the United Church's special advisor on intergovernmental relations. This highly accomplished circle was also where I had the surprise and honour of meeting my new auntie, Geraldine.

Geraldine Robertson spent the defining years of her childhood in Mt. Elgin Industrial School, near Muncey, southwest of London, Ontario. Like most children who attended residential school, she was from a place more than a hundred kilometres away, on the St. Clair River, near the top end of its run from Lake Huron, down and around through the shared Canada-US waterway that eventually flows into Lake Erie. I spent the second half of my childhood in Sarnia, just a few kilometres farther upstream, and grew up knowing Geraldine's home community by the name that still shows up on maps: the Sarnia Indian Reserve. I have since learned that its Indigenous name is Aamjiwnaang, meaning "up on the hill where she belongs"—beyond ironic, given the circumstances of Geraldine and many others being taken away from there to a place of *not* belonging.

Geraldine came up to me after the church circle with a personal message: "I know your aunt Eva. She was my neighbour for years, and she is my friend. We still get together every week. She wanted me to tell you hi, that she loves you, and that she sends you a big hug."

The feel of that hug was such a comfort as we headed into the unknowns of this first National Event. When I told Geraldine that, and how I wished I had family near me during this hard work, she said, "I'll be your auntie, Marie." I would experience the gift of that promise many times over the years to come when Geraldine would seek me out amid large TRC crowds, always to give me the loving hug of a cherished auntie. Today, I cherish her memory as another of the many Survivors since departed.

The Commissioners were also honoured by host Indigenous nations in Winnipeg. Following a welcoming dinner, they bestowed on us a specially made TRC eagle staff. We danced that staff around the huge banquet hall to the beat of an Honour Song, for all to see, for all to honour.

We received countless gifts from many others, including the gift of music. It was 2010, and I was thrilled to learn that the Commissioners would be having lunch with a small group of notable musicians including Buffy Sainte-Marie. Buffy brought back cherished and defining memories of my early teens, when my older brother introduced our family to her famous war protest song "Universal Soldier." Her music immediately took over the airwaves of our home. Her songs gave me my first lessons in social justice activism. Buffy was my first female superhero. My own exploration of human rights took me on an international journey that eventually led me to this new role as a TRC Commissioner, and now landed me face to face with Buffy here in Winnipeg.

She and other musicians played important roles at this event as headliners for the evening showcase performance. A massive outdoor stage took up the biggest section of our TRC event field, specially set up for that concert as a way to draw in even more people from the wider community. Music was good medicine to lift everyone's spirits after the hard work we did together, whether sharing residential school experiences, or learning about them for the first time.

We were all there to listen, to learn, to bear witness: three Commissioners and their spouses, old and new staff, national and international guests, more than sixty specially trained health support workers, dozens of statement-takers, and thousands of others from churches, governments, universities, and the public. The sun welcomed us as we proceeded behind the flags and staffs carried by our spiritual advisors to the ceremonial Oodena Circle. This Grand Entry was the first time our new TRC eagle staff was raised and presented in a public, ceremonial way.

Chief Littlechild was the one Commissioner missing from that first entry procession. He made his own grand entrance a few minutes later—on horseback! A group of riders had travelled to Winnipeg from Saskatchewan, culminating in a dramatic arrival in the Oodena Circle. Willie told us the ride helped complete the circle of his own residential school experiences because when he was taken away for school, he was also taken away from his best friend—his horse. To arrive at this first Truth and Reconciliation National Event on horseback reclaimed a piece of his own lost childhood.

Over the next four days, and for the first time ever in this country, thousands of Indigenous and non-Indigenous people gathered in a shared purpose: truth-telling of history; healing of mind, body, and spirit; and reconciliation of relationships, all under the theme of Respect.

Our theme encouraged the many voices we had drawn together, especially the previously unspoken or unheard voices of residential school Survivors. Out of respect for their varying needs, we created several different types of safe space for them to give and share their statements in public or privately. When sharing publicly, they were modelling to others the courage it took for them to do so. Because of the respectful nature of our approach to these sessions, many more Survivors would often then come forward to also share.

Each Survivor shared their truth as they had lived it. We didn't interview them. There was no second-guessing, no cross-examining, no doubting from the Commissioners. We had no reason to. No one had forced them to come. The process was entirely voluntary, and there was no financial incentive for anyone to fabricate their stories.

And in any case, we reasoned, why would any Survivor willingly put themselves through the emotional turmoil of remembering things they had spent much of their lifetime trying to forget, except for a sincere wish to finally be heard, and for the burden and weight of their long-buried truth to be lifted?

Instead, we reminded them of the core educational purpose of the Truth and Reconciliation Commission. We made sure they understood that we were an independent Commission, not government, and that they themselves, through their own legal representatives, had fought to have this TRC, and had agreed to pay for it out of monies from the court settlement they had won. Then, we told them how much time they had—usually fifteen to twenty minutes, depending on how many others were signed up to speak. After that, the Commissioners listened intently.

It was a process that allowed Survivors to dominate the airtime of hearing days, each in their own way. Some were surrounded by family. Some sat alone with their health support. But throughout, recurring themes emerged. The overall narrative began to take a familiar form: rupture from home, the first day of school, the traumatic events, the emotional scars, and life in the aftermath.

The theme also drove all our efforts and decisions to reflect and incorporate diversity and inclusion. We respected linguistic diversity with simultaneous translation services as needed. Out of respect for distinct Indigenous nations, we scheduled a rotation of traditional songs and drums. We also respected spiritual diversity by including several modes and languages of prayer from multiple faith traditions.

We tried to model the kind of reconciliation we were asking of others by creating spaces for them to inspire each other. We hosted public Gestures of Reconciliation to allow individuals and groups from all parts of society to state their intentions to contribute toward ongoing education and reconciliation. For example, the Royal Winnipeg Ballet pledged to commission an original dance and musical score entirely devoted to interpreting the devastation of the residential school experience.

We enlarged our family of Honorary Witnesses, too. Out of respect for the international interest in our work as the first TRC of its kind, we inducted an Australian agency working on behalf of Indigenous Australians and Torres Strait Islanders who had lived through their own version of child displacement. We also inducted a New Zealand cultural scholar and Indigenous champion of the Māori language. As the list of TRC Honorary Witnesses grew, so did the expectations of them from the TRC Survivors Committee. One of them put it like this: "We are Survivors for life. And so, we expect you to be Witnesses for life."

Respect was on full display at the outdoor evening concert stage. It showcased a multi-nation powerhouse of musicians who had devoted much of their professional craft to singing out the pains of the people and the enduring beauty and potential of the country: Jim Cuddy and Greg Keelor with Blue Rodeo, Murray Porter, and Buffy Sainte-Marie, among others. Susan Aglukark sang her finale in sweet harmony with international Apache guest Robby Romero, a musical advocate on Indigenous and environmental rights at the United Nations. Like thousands of others, he came to Winnipeg in solidarity and out of respect for what the TRC was setting out to do.

The final, nighttime gathering brought us back to the Oodena Circle. The huge numbers from day one had held and even grown. We crowded together, draped in the intimacy and superb acoustics of warm darkness. Each Commissioner was to offer closing reflections to the crowd, but after three days of many powerful words from many Survivors, what more really needed to be said? In an inspired spur-of-the-moment decision, I gave my spot to someone I knew could offer a far more beautiful, haunting, and hopeful memory to take away than any of my own words could possibly convey. I called on the amazing and unassuming Tracey Brown. This former child TV performer had been singing all her life, much of it with her kin, the Family Brown, and in professional partnership with her multi-award-winning music-producer husband, Randall Prescott. Together, they had nurtured, mentored, and produced a long list of Indigenous artists. Several had gone on to their own award-winning careers, including Susan Aglukark. Tracey has the deep, rich, perfectly controlled voice of a natural tenor in the angel choir. With no other instrument but her velvet-coated voice, she filled the air of the Oodena amphitheatre with all the loss, defiance, and promise embedded in Stephen Foster's spiritual of pain and emancipation "Hard Times Come Again No More." It was a perfect summary of the range and tone of our days.

On that last day, we returned to our first TRC sacred fire. It had been carefully tended since day one. Here, we began the tradition we would carry throughout the Commission: we burned the tissues holding all the tears shed during the event by those who had spoken or witnessed. In this symbolic way, such tears were gathered, honoured, and finally released.

After so many powerful moments and gestures, what could possibly be left? As if on cue, an eagle circled the fire, high overhead. More than one! Three eagles suddenly soaring high above us. Willie had taught me that an eagle is a special blessing. Perhaps it was a benediction for the three Commissioners far below, contemplating the final embers of their first TRC National Event, and the lingering flame of Respect they had ignited.

CHAPTER 4

Riding Out the Storm

OVER THE DAYS in between that dramatic mounted-horse beginning of our first National Event and that quiet, reverent closing, I experienced commotion on all fronts, both inner and outer. Even the skies were in on it.

Day one of the National Event had started off sunny and clear, both the dispositions and weather. I remember the sharing circles most of all. Three of them, in particular. The first was called a Circle of Reconciliation. It was the most high-profile, with about twenty-five people in the middle of the largest tent. Representatives of all the parties to the Indian Residential Schools Settlement Agreement sat in that circle, including then minister of Aboriginal Affairs, the Honourable Chuck Strahl, the leadership of a couple of the national churches, and others involved in running or supporting the residential schools. Survivors from diverse organizations, cultural backgrounds, and school contexts brought our purpose for being there into sharp focus. The weight, grief, outrage, outpouring, and incredulity of their words slowly compounded on the rest of the circle as we moved around it, spilling out and penetrating the hundreds of others surrounding us.

Gasps and sniffles, sobs and wails. An airplane pilot shared how he stumbled into transporting children from their home communities to faraway schools, how devastating it was, and how he quit his job over it. A deaf Survivor talked about the particular abuses they suffered as a child with disabilities, with no way to tell or ask for help. A representative of the RCMP talked about his regrets as a much younger cop, rounding up kids as school runaways and taking them back without knowing or thinking to ask them what they were running away from. A former teacher talked about the shame of learning too late about what had been happening to children at her school under her blind eyes, the pain of wondering why the children didn't ask her for help, and the torment of learning that they chose to suffer in silence rather than tell her, afraid that the one kind person in their lives would be sent away for speaking out on their behalf. She also talked about the unfolding joy of reuniting with a former student to piece together the facts of the past and reconnect in meaningful adult friendship.

One of the last Survivors to speak was Charlene Belleau, who cried out her family's desperation. They did not know what had happened to their relative, a great-uncle also referred to, in the Indigenous way of acknowledging departed Ancestors, as a grandfather. He never returned from residential school. They later learned he had been part of a suicide pact among children at his school. The family still didn't know where he was buried. Looking straight at us, Charlene sobbed out her request: "I want you to find him. Find our grandpa." This unforgotten and still-loved uncle's story would be one of thousands we would tally in our TRC Final Report six years later. Within its first two pages, Volume IV included a clear message that many more children were still missing, beyond the numbers we could already confirm.

The three Commissioners completed the circle. By the time it was our turn, the circle and the entire tent were awash in emotion.

We spoke in sequence of how we were sitting: Commissioner-Chair Sinclair, Commissioner Littlechild, and me. Whenever I was the last to speak, I would call on my live-broadcasting skills, listening intently to find what value I could add to what had already been well said by my colleagues. We had been sitting in this circle for a long, emotional time. Our bodies, our hearts, and our bladders needed a break. I knew there was little capacity to hear much more, so I acknowledged and honoured the truth and courage we had all witnessed. And then I ended with simple words that came from wherever such words come, in the moment of need: "I see you, I hear you, I believe you. And"—did I actually say it, or did I just feel it so intensely, still too self-conscious to speak the words out loud?—"I love you."

The circle ended, and a lineup formed in front of me immediately. I was surprised by the response and by the many variations of the same message spoken to me through hugs and tears:

"Thank you for your words, and for finally hearing us."

"It's the first time I have ever heard anyone say they believed me."

"It is so healing to hear you say you see me and believe me."

"I have waited my whole life to hear that—to hear those words."

That was the first Circle of Reconciliation, but there would be many more truths to hear, with countless variations of these stories, over the years ahead.

~

The second circle that left a deep mark on me was designated for women only. As the only female Commissioner, it fell to me to lead it. In writing these words, I recognize for the first time that the anxiety I felt at that moment may have been heightened and possibly even triggered by earlier highly stressful moments in my life when I had felt like I was on my own, fending for myself. It happened as a child when my two older brothers shared a room and I was alone in mine. I was six years old, sick with whooping cough and quarantined for more than three months. My condition silenced my calls for help. I had faced illness, isolation, and nightmares, alone and afraid.

I felt this way again as a journalism trainer in South Africa, in April 1993, in the dangerous time before the first post-apartheid election a year later. I was at a wildlife park northeast of Johannesburg with fellow trainers Bob Culbert and Norm Bolen, our lead and designated driver. We had travelled there for an Easter weekend break from training, staying in two separate canvas tents mounted on wooden frames. It was comfortable and cozy enough, until nightfall. Darkness comes early in that part of Africa, and that night, it seemed like it would never end. Our camp was perched a short distance above a watering hole—at first, we heard the soothing splash and slurp of large animals on water. Then, suddenly, the rustle and roar of the hunt! The terrified and terrifying screech, shriek, rip of the attack! The grunt and gulp and belch of the feast! In a brief lull, I thought of running over to join the men in their tent a couple hundred feet away, but then it started up again, sounding even closer, right between the two tents. Fear froze me in place.

But that was minor compared to the next day as we drove back toward Johannesburg. There had been a political assassination overnight, and the whole country was on alert. Recalling the rifts and riots of recent civil upheaval back in his native Ireland, Bobby Culbert captured the fear we all felt when he blurted, "Jaysus, it was never this fucking scary in Belfast!" We laughed ourselves back to calm, but my focus had changed. Human beings terrorizing a whole society was far more frightening and unpredictable than the natural commotion of animals outside our tents the night before.

Back in Winnipeg, the dramatic events of 2010 unfolded under a tent of a very different kind. I was the lead for this women's circle that kept expanding as more and more Survivors dragged chairs forward to squeeze in. By the time the shuffling ended, the circle was about four times the size our events team intended, with some fifty or sixty people. How could each one possibly speak in the time scheduled before the next event? Would I have to cut people off? And could I even sit still that long? Would I have to get up and leave the circle for my own needs? I knew that both cutting people off and leaving would be a breach of sacred circle protocols.

There was nothing to do but begin, pointing out the great numbers and encouraging everyone to manage their time out of respect for the others wanting their chance, too. We were only about a quarter of the way around the circle and already rapidly running out of time. Once the Survivors started talking, it was a kind of tsunamic eruption. They had been holding back for a long, long time. There was no holding them back now.

I was listening so intently, so moved, I barely registered that even the tipi was moving, the sunny skies shifting. That's when I got word that we were in the throes of a major storm, with hurricane-force winds mounting around us. We urgently needed to take shelter indoors. There was so much exposure in that tent, so much raw vulnerability; we needed, somehow, to hold our circle together, to close it respectfully, with strength, and especially with support for one another.

Of all the people to enter my mind at that moment, in came Mrs. McCracken. Doris McCracken had marked my life as my Brownie leader and later my Girl Guide leader. She was patient, kind, and caring. She taught us "the Brownie Squeeze." It was how we ended every meeting, always in a circle. As a final gesture, we would hold hands, Brown Owl would ask someone to start the squeeze, and we would all stand there watching it make its way around the circle, one set of little-girl hands at a time, until it arrived back to the one who sent it out. We were all connected, safe to leave the circle on our many ways home.

The inspiration came as suddenly as the storm itself. I felt so out of my cultural depth, so completely small-town Ontario, but I stuck my neck way out, inspired by my childhood memory. "We cannot close this circle as we would have liked, but it doesn't feel right to just abandon it and each other," I said. "Let me tell you about the Brownie Squeeze, and let me suggest we quickly do that together, so that we will know we are not alone as we leave this circle. I'll start."

I braced myself for disdain or derision. Instead, I saw my squeeze make its rhythmic way around that huge circle of little-girl Survivors turned grown women. That squeeze of energy and spirit connected us all and landed back at me. I let go of the hands beside me to wipe away tears. Outside, it was pouring. Then, we were all on the rapid move, including the tent, which collapsed soon after we all made it out.

~

The third circle was inside a nearby building. This space was quickly revamped to reconfigure the women's circle after the storm. Everyone arrived wind-swept, some soaking wet from the hasty run from the collapsed tipi. All eyes were looking at me, waiting to begin again. I noticed a quiet movement across the room. Someone was stepping silently into my direct line of vision. It was Charlie Tobac from Fort Good Hope. Such a welcome sight—a face from home! I had known Charlie for decades. The last time I had seen him was two years before, on the day Prime Minister Stephen Harper apologized to all Survivors.

The apology that happened on June 11, 2008, was part of the settlement of the residential schools lawsuit. Hearing Canada and its politicians acknowledge the deep harms residential schools had caused Survivors, their families, and communities, and publicly apologize for it, was seen as an essential step in clearing the way for individual and national healing to begin. Survivors and national Indigenous leaders had also worked hard to make the moment as public as possible, a critical step in beginning to educate the people of Canada about this part of the country's history, and a practical effort to connect Survivors throughout the land so they could experience some support and comfort in knowing they were not alone. Across the country, arrangements were made for big-screen viewing circles where people could gather to witness the apology together, with specially trained health support workers on hand.

Prime Minister Stephen Harper of the Conservative Party had inherited the Indian Residential Schools Settlement Agreement from the Liberal prime minister before him, Paul Martin. But did Prime Minister Harper even believe in the apology? Or was he just doing it out of obligation, as ordered by the court?

"What will he say? How will he say it? How will I hear it? And what if I can't control myself? What if it just makes me angry all over again? What if it makes me fall apart?" These were the questions my residential school Survivor husband was asking in the days beforehand. We were just coming through the first year of our own personal reconciliation journey, on the heels of a two-year separation, on the heels of a residential school legacy meltdown. We were wearing the scars of the emotional harms we had inflicted on each other, still raw from the pain but wiser, in the way that hardship brings wisdom. And we were hope-filled, in the way that words spoken differently can open up new conversations, deeper truths, and new peace with oneself and others.

Now, what was this official apology going to do to that new-found peace? My husband chose to watch the apology from the safety and familiarity of our home. It was one of the most intimate and vulnerable moments of our life as a couple, sitting silently side by side on the couch, holding hands, holding our breath, waiting for some sign of sincerity, some flicker of authenticity. It came partway through, as the prime minister said, "Today, we recognize that this policy of assimilation was wrong, has caused great harm, and has no place in our country." He looked away during the applause that followed that statement, appearing almost teary-eyed. But the actual quiver in his voice and emotional pauses came as he said this: "We now recognize that, in separating children from their families, we undermined the ability of many to adequately parent their own children and sowed the seeds for generations to follow, and we apologize for having done this … The Government of Canada sincerely apologizes and asks the forgiveness of the Aboriginal peoples of this country for failing them so profoundly."

Stephen and I were both in tears. And we had an immediate need to be with our children and in community with other Survivor families. Our kids met us at the Tree of Peace Friendship Centre in Yellowknife. The hall was overflowing with people, comfort, and palpable emotional release. There were several local speakers, but I only remember one—Charlie Tobac.

Charlie was one of the local guys around town when we lived in Fort Good Hope in the early 1980s. Fort Good Hope is a typical Dene community, with a very high percentage of residential school Survivors. Charlie was one of them. He coped with his trauma as best he could in a remote town without any professional supports. Alcohol was and, for many, continues to be the self-medication of choice. But in more recent years, Charlie had found sobriety and embraced traditional spiritual practices, and he and his wife were beginning to work in healing circles as Traditional Knowledge Keepers. The day of the apology was the first time I got to see him in this healthy new role, fully present and electric in his impact.

Charlie stepped lightly in his moccasins to the microphone and aimed his piercing eyes straight at a woman seated in the front row. The room was hushed as he gently said, without preamble, "I'd like to apologize to my wife, Laura. I beat my wife. I beat the one I love most."

Charlie went on to acknowledge his failings as a husband, as a father, and as a violent man. Rather than evaluating the worth or sincerity of the apology from Ottawa, he paid it forward, offering his own apology to the one who mattered most to him, admitting to the things he had done and could not undo, and promising to continue to change in the ways that he could.

I burst into tears, grateful for my husband's shoulder beside me to bury my quiet sobbing. And as I cried, something suddenly seemed so clear to me. I blubbered, "That's what I *need.*" I was thinking, *That's what we both need—a ceremony to offer our apologies to each other, and to recommit to each other, with our children there, to help them understand better what has happened.* That private family ceremony happened a few months later.

And two years later, amid the high emotions of this sharing circle in Winnipeg, Charlie made the moment for me again. From across the circle he caught my eye and looked right at me with a sliver of a smile and the slightest nod of his head, as if to say, *Yes, you can.* Charlie was wearing his moccasins, as always. I noticed he was also wearing a special vest, the one identifying him as part of the health support team specially set up to keep everyone safe. Sadly, Charlie Tobac is another friend who has since passed.

That was the day I truly began to appreciate the breadth and value of the health supports in our midst. The wise negotiators and authors of the Indian Residential Schools Settlement Agreement had included a clause obliging the Government of Canada to provide "culturally appropriate health supports" for all aspects of implementing the agreement. The TRC was just one part of the Settlement Agreement, but we benefited tremendously from its health support provisions. Indeed, one of the principles listed in our TRC Mandate to guide our work said plainly, "Do No Harm." The health support teams played an essential role in making it possible for us to fulfill that obligation.

At this first National Event, everything those teams had to offer was on quiet display. They led us in morning prayer ceremonies in multiple traditions. They drummed us out of moments of extreme tension with prayer songs. They sat ahead of time with every Survivor who was signed up, waiting to speak to the Commission, to ground and reassure them. They made sure no one sat alone while sharing their school experiences, placing themselves discreetly beside or behind the Survivor as requested, always equipped with water, tissues, and reassuring words and touch as needed. They debriefed with Survivors afterwards, to release and relieve energy and assess the need for follow-up care. They moved quietly about our circles, keeping an eye on Survivors first and foremost, but also on all the others drawn to TRC events. This included family members, who were often hearing horrific stories from their siblings, spouses, parents, or grandparents for the very first time. At the end of each day, the health supports would then sit together, giving each other the same caring attention they had offered to so many others throughout the day.

They were also fully attentive to the Commissioners, as Charlie was from across the room, and as Brenda Reynolds was at my side, handing me a blanket, a drink, and directions to the nearest washroom, should I need it. Almost everyone else in our sharing circles came and went over the course of a TRC event, or at least were free to. But the Commissioners received every public statement at close range, with full emotional impact, for hours on end, one statement after another, and often for two to four days at a time. A private, end-of-day debrief with an increasingly trusted and cherished health support became a steady limb to cling to, to help pull me out of the rush of the day's emotional flood. This day, it was Brenda who was there for me, just as Suzy Goodleaf, Liz Oscroft, Maggie Hodgson, Vina Robinson, and many others would be over the events, regions, and years to come.

By the time the third circle ended, the storm was over. Everybody felt it. We had entered the day from a comfortable place of sunny security. But every new revelation of residential school truth had whipped the skies into an increasingly whirling rage. Every sob and burst of pent-up tears had been met by sheets of natural downpour. And the repeated reassurance of no longer being alone had brought a new kind of calm, even as the skies opened up and cleared, extending the arms of a brilliant rainbow.

Marie and Stephen's married life begins in Fort Good Hope, Northwest Territories.
Family Album

PART III

COURAGE

THE NORTH

To walk in courage is to do the right thing—to always take the high moral road. You will need courage to live your true spirit.

—Elder Dr. David Courchene,
A Story of the Seven Sacred Laws

CHAPTER 5

My Home on Native Land

THE HOME OF my earliest memories was humble and basic. Still, or perhaps because of limited means, we were raised to always think of others worse off than ourselves. Apparently, most of them lived in Africa, based on what our parents told us: "Don't waste food. Think of all the starving people in Africa. What do you mean, you don't like it? The little kids in Africa would love to have something like that."

My parents' admonitions were not worldly, well-informed, or sophisticated. The goal was to teach us to be grateful for what we had. Still, they were not wrong about the price of waste, the importance of gratitude, and the fact of poverty in Africa, even to this day. But if they had been taught a more truthful history of Canada—if all of us had been—they might have known that we didn't have to cross the ocean of our minds to imagine examples of greater need. There were, and are, plenty of examples right here in this country. I would see this for myself later, but first, I had to go to Africa.

My parents' mealtime lessons instilled in me a sense of wonder and curiosity about a much bigger world than my little corner, which was limited to the nearby towns and villages where all our relatives lived.

I longed to experience Africa for myself. That longing eventually landed me in West Africa as a young university graduate, teaching English in Burkina Faso. I was naive to the ironies of English as a mandatory school subject in a place claimed by its colonial history to be francophone, naive also to the imposition of both English and French, despite the prior existence of about a dozen major Indigenous African languages throughout the country, with some fifty distinct dialects.

Nor had anything in my education equipped me to immediately spot the Canadian parallels to this African language reality. The same two languages—English and French—had been superimposed over a comparable number of Indigenous languages in Canada. I would later learn that eradication of those languages had been one of the core purposes and practices of residential schools. At this time, the mid-1970s, the schools were still operating in many regions of Canada, but I, like most Canadians, wasn't aware of that yet.

I had been captivated by the name of the place where I'd be living: Ouagadougou. I later learned that the French-influenced spelling originated from a much older Indigenous African word: *wogodogo*, meaning "where people get honour and respect." But it was the music of the name that got to me first—Ouagadougou. The sweet sound was superficial, though; everyday realities were more dissonant. At that time, Burkina Faso was still called La Haute-Volta, or Upper Volta, and it was the second-poorest country in the world, in a continent that was facing all the acute pressures of rapidly modernizing economies: industrial development, unstable governments, environmental impacts, displaced people, and rampant poverty.

I taught children who came to school in bare feet, who couldn't grasp the distinction between *ground* and *floor*. Other words in the few textbooks we had, all produced in faraway France, seemed beyond translation. *Refrigerator* and *vacuum cleaner* and similar notions of modern European living were completely foreign, irrelevant to the everyday lives of most of my students. What schools used to call a blackboard was a single piece of pitted plywood, painted black. The chalk for writing on it had to be signed out, rationed each day from the school office, one piece at a time.

Similarly, deep, multigenerational poverty is part of Indigenous reality in Canada. Poverty, with its many associated negative social indicators, has been a reality for years and in some places is getting worse, not better.

Our TRC work sometimes took us to the glaring centre of entire communities full of residential school Survivors. In the lead-up to our Northern National Event facilities for one such community hearing were more threadbare than usual: folding tables topped with pitted plywood in a dingy hall. Modest and rundown on the outside, the building was defaced and derelict on the inside. Angry, violent, vulgar graffiti shouted from its walls. The room's focal point was a five-foot area halfway down the right side that was partially blocked off with a caution ribbon but protected only by a battered old wooden chair sitting in front of it. It was an open hole in the floor! A mere twenty feet away from where I was installed to preside over hearings that day. Out of the corner of my eye, it was a constant distraction, an unsafe eyesore in our midst. The historic Truth and Reconciliation Commission of Canada was about to hold a community hearing in this sad and dilapidated room. It was the town's only public gathering space.

Early in my marriage I had lived in a community that had spaces like this. Over my years as a reporter I saw other such places, all stamped by poverty, especially in more northern and remote parts of Canada. Precisely because of that remoteness, many of these communities have experienced some of the most acute residential school impacts. Not just a few children but the majority of today's adult population was taken far away for school, often for years at a time.

Sooner or later in a long day of hearings, you just have to go. I walked cautiously past the hole and turned into the women's washroom. Three stalls. Not a door in sight. There were hinges all right, but whatever doors had once been there had long since left the room.

I am not a bathroom snob. I enjoy one of Yellowknife's iconic old restaurants, its washroom with plywood doors from the mid-twentieth century repainted every decade or so. Even more modest, our first home farther north featured no indoor plumbing. We had an outhouse for finer weather and, for the long cold winter, an indoor "honey bucket." And then there are the many times over the years I have been in outdoor bush settings with no structured facilities at all. As a woman, you learn discreet ways to do your business with as much dignity as possible.

But on this day, in this little eastern Arctic community, the privy was truly deprived. It didn't bother me so much as an individual; my outrage was at the deprivation of this entire community. The revered pacifist Mahatma Gandhi once said, "Poverty is the worst form of violence." For Canada to be a truly peaceful nation means, in part, to set down the violent arms of poverty in Indigenous communities.

Still, nature calls. I was adjusting my clothes, trying to make do, when it suddenly got darker in my stall. I looked up to a wall of cobalt blue. And then it spoke: "I'll make a door for you."

The door was a parka. The contrast could not have been starker between the state of the facilities and this beautiful, handmade wonder of temporary cover. The bottom trim was an interplay of embroidered floral and geometric designs, contrasting material, and rickrack. The crowning detail was the white-fox trim of the hood, dramatically offsetting the brilliant blue of the parka. What a gesture of generosity by my faceless, unnamed donor. My embarrassing moment had become a picture of stunning blue beauty, within a frame of abject poverty.

Suddenly, I was back in Africa. Back within the memory of another poverty-riddled moment, also wrapped up in blue. It was at a truck stop in the middle of the desert. Not really a stop. We were stuck. Again! I was hitchhiking across the Sahara Desert as I circled back from Casablanca for another school year. I had hooked up with two other young Canadian women as we headed south from Algeria. We piled high onto the back of a big-wheeled transport truck with a dozen or so male strangers from various African countries, each tucked into our various perches between undulating, shifting sacks of dried macaroni. The truck was overloaded and top-heavy. The driver was sullen, gruff, and careless. We never tipped, but we did get stuck. More than once. We were unpaid crew, essential for all the digging out. Everybody climbed down, dug, pushed, piled back on. That part, at least, was like back home in Canada, but with sand, not snow.

On that truck was an elderly man wearing a boubou, a long flowing robe designed to create a breeze rather than cling to the skin, intricately embroidered for grander occasions. Somewhere in the front folds of a boubou is a pocket that serves as a built-in wallet. Maybe it was all the climbing up and down from the truck and the perpetual adjusting of the cloth up over his shoulders to keep from tripping while he did his aged share of the grunt work. One way or another, the old man's money got away from him. A sudden gust of Saharan wind scattered it far and wide toward an endless horizon. And off he went, wildly chasing his precious bills, now skipping ahead of him across the surface of the sands. Then his boubou took flight, also whipped up by the winds. It soared ahead of the man, a magnificent unfolding of brilliant blue cloth with rippling white embroidery, a perfect match for an equally blue sky and gusting white clouds overhead. My eyes watered from the sprays of sand—or were my tears for the runner, zigzagging in all directions, knowing he'd never reclaim his meagre wealth, and knowing, as we all did by now, that our angry driver would just as likely leave him behind. Forced to settle for less, the old man made it back just in time before the big truck rolled on.

My bathroom reverie shifted from the hot African desert of the past to the cold Arctic desert of the present: two scenes of having to make do with less. In each one, determined dignity faced off with glaring poverty, defiant of surrounding realities, dressed in blue, trimmed in white. As I noted these common threads, I grasped more fully how the one scene had helped prepare me for the other. I made my way back to the Commissioners' table, dodging the hole in the floor, and still wearing the invisible cloak of kindness and respect that had been wrapped up in that blue parka.

The day I left Ouagadougou I cried. I had met and worked with so many fine people, generous well beyond any material capacity, and dignified, even in poverty. I was a rarity, a woman on my own and thousands of miles from home. I was completely taken in by the community and given introductions to traditional foods, invitations to family celebrations, and countless marriage proposals, all aimed at saving me from what was seen as my sad, unnatural solitude in this place of communal living and widely extended family. It was two years full of curiosity, care, and acceptance. Several families and former students came to the airport to cry with me. We all knew we might never meet again, but I did not leave empty-handed. In addition to spices, colourfully embroidered cloths, photos, and other markers of the place, the more lasting gifts were the invisible ones—my experiences themselves. They had equipped me and toughened me, as my spiritual advisor, Peter Short, observed years later, for my life and eventual work ahead. But in the short term, these experiences lingered with me in ways that were not easy to explain, or to bear. My greatest culture shock was in returning to the comparative affluence of North America.

Once I was home, as I switched my career path from teaching to journalism, I began immersing myself in Indigenous issues in Canada. These were the stories I recognized as variations of what I had seen and experienced in Africa, and they were the stories I felt called to tell. I could see how much Canada had to learn about itself. I, too, had much to learn. I spent the first several months of my new life as a budding journalist working my way northward. On November 11, 1977, I became a reporter for CBC Northern Services based in Yellowknife.

My personal and professional worlds unfolded from there, as I became a radio news reporter, a wife, mother, television reporter, TV program host, international trainer, and eventually, regional director for all the public broadcaster's radio and television services throughout northern Canada, the first one based in the North. Through the combined forces of love and luck, I have experienced the breadth, depth, and complexity of this part of Canada during the years when it has most reshaped, redefined, and even renamed itself.

For the first fifteen years of our life together, my husband hid the stories from his time at residential school. For most of his life he also hid them from himself, from his own consciousness, smouldering below the surface. It took many years and many crises to figure out there was more harm in burying them inside—the inner corrosion of his secrets, the outer ravages of his life, and the hard-wire between the two. Over the years, between and amid alcoholic breakdowns, emotional shutdowns, and counselling, I gradually heard sporadic accounts of a boyhood interrupted. They helped me piece together a fuller picture of that child's frightening brush with heavenly hell.

Fighting back my own tears, I listened to the deep memories of a nine-year-old boy:

> They came and took me and my older brother and sister. Picked us up from residential school in a small plane. Didn't know where we were going. Didn't tell us anything. We're flying through all these clouds. Can't see anything. They took us to this place in a building with a funny smell. Left us all alone in this room. After a while these strange bodies walk in. Looks like my grandfather, my father, and my other big sister. But they don't look right. They don't have clothes on. They have these funny robes. My brother and sister run over to them, but I just stand there, frozen. I turn my back to them. Can't look at them. I'm afraid to. I'm staring out the window. Terrified. All this fog. Where am I? Is this heaven? I think they are ghosts. Maybe we are all dead. All I can do is cry.

I wanted to scream at all the invisible adults. How could they?! And every motherly instinct in my body wanted to reach out to the child, to comfort and reassure. But that child was no longer within reach. He was now a man. He was my husband. And he was lying beside me as this story seeped out of him more than forty years later. Drip, drip, drip …

There was no turning back for me. I would never see him the same way again. This scene of Stephen as a small child melted away so much of my anger from past letdowns—the sequels of rage and silence, the physical and emotional disappearing acts of our life together. This moving image offered me the gift of kinder eyes for seeing the whole man. It helped me see anew those extraordinary things about him that are, in fact, miraculous. How he grew up to become a teacher, a leader of the Dene Nation, the national host on behalf of all Indigenous Peoples for two papal visits to Canada, a government minister and premier, a singer-songwriter, a storyteller and author. In that moment, together, amid resurrected scenes from a long-abandoned building, we both wept.

This moment is just one close-up in the great unfolding that has been my life married to a residential school Survivor. Like many children, especially in northern Canada, my husband landed in residential school because of tuberculosis. His mother was sick and in hospital "down south" in faraway Edmonton. That's a long way from home on the Arctic Circle. In those days, a single father was not seen as equipped to raise kids alone, and everybody else in the family eventually got TB, too, until there was no one left at home. Three of the kids—Stephen, his older brother, Everett, and sister Cathy—were sent farther north, to Inuvik, and the Catholic residence known as Grollier Hall. It's a place that has earned its reputation as a pit of child sexual abuse. The TRC revealed that for more than twenty years, a continuous string of pedophiles lived or worked at Grollier. Little Stephen was only in that place for a year, but that was long enough to experience it all—repeated emotional and physical injury, overnight lock-ups in dark rooms, and sexual abuse. By the time of the mystery flight through the clouds that he thought might take him to heaven, he was already disoriented and deeply confused about what was real. Whether he was a "bad boy" or "the devil," as he had been told so many times. Whether he deserved to be alive.

In fact, he was a long way from heaven. He was visiting the primitive Aklavik hospital, a place also previously home to one of the oldest residential schools in the country. His ehseh (grandfather), betá (father), and bedare (sister) Jeanne were not the ghosts he feared but patients, now struck with tuberculosis like his amá (mother). For whatever reason, they were flown farther north rather than south like her. Stephen learned later that his áhson (grandmother) and beshileh (little brother) Tommy were also somewhere in that hospital. But they weren't there for that reunion, as ruptured as it was. In the mind of little Stephen, no one was where they were supposed to be. The entire family was blown apart and scattered. A safe memory of "home" had been the only escape from the hell he was living back at Grollier Hall. Now, that was gone, too. The nine-year-old had lost all his bearings.

I've often wondered if the grandfather chartered that plane. I never got to meet Gabriel Kakfwi but have never stopped hearing about him. The same old man who had to bear watching his little grandson turn his back on him was an accomplished and well-travelled man outside that Aklavik hospital room, even worldly by the northern standards of the day. In the shadow of the dominant Hudson's Bay Company, he had opened his own fur-trading post: Kakfwi General Store. He paid a hefty price for defying the norms of the time. The federal government had passed the Indian Act in the 1870s to give itself access to, and assume ownership of, as much land as possible all over Canada. It took control of the people they renamed "Indians" by designating the tiny "reserve" lands where they could live, and making them official wards of the state. The government then protected itself from any associated financial, social, legal, or political risks by making it illegal for Indigenous people to vote, go to university, gather in large numbers, hire a lawyer, or borrow money. As "wards," they now had the same legal status as children. So, the government, as their official guardian, would have been on the financial hook if anyone borrowed or made promises of money, goods, or services and didn't pay back. The only way around that for a business-minded "Indian" was to stop being one in the eyes of the law.

Gabriel Kakfwi had to give up his official identity as a status Indian so that he could have access to money, credit, and supply contracts, just like every other businessperson in Canada. And he made a successful go of it. His strong legs and wide-ranging travels on foot, snowshoe, and by dog-team as far north as the Arctic coast and as far south as Edmonton were stories of legend in the family and community

I married into. Ehseh Gabriel would have had connections, maybe some favours or promises due, and maybe some money set aside. Maybe enough to pay for a flight for three grandchildren.

Whoever paid for the plane, the littlest boy paid for the experience. He carried the heavy memory of that trip as one of so many others he would drag into our marriage. He set them down as unnamed, unwanted, invisible dead weights in our home and in our family. We tripped over them for years, still in the dark about so much of how they got there.

Eventually, everything seemed to shatter at once. Stephen moved out. Our kids struggled, each in their own way, to find themselves. Close friends died or moved south. Cherished colleagues moved on. My father got increasingly ill on the other side of the country. It was a dark time.

The longest night of the year is always exaggerated in this part of Canada—"North of 60," as we call it, north of the Earth's sixtieth parallel. Daytime hours shrink shorter and shorter in our long winter season. Then, there is a sigh of relief every December 21. We mark it with reverence because—as if just in time—Mother Nature dramatically reminds us of the promise of new light going forward. Days start to grow longer by up to six minutes a day. For Stephen and me, new light emerged much more tentatively. But it did come, slowly and tenderly, with much work, honesty, and humility. It wasn't quick or easy, but what came next was an eventual recommitment to our marriage and family.

Coincidentally—though Elders would later tell me it was Creator's plan all along—while the first Truth and Reconciliation Commission was collapsing, our family was restabilizing. We received the gift of another grandchild. We moved back under the same roof. We supported my mom, our kids, and ourselves through the passing of my beloved dad. We gathered in ceremony to exchange our apologies and regrets with each other and our children. And they, in turn, offered us their forgiveness and love, as they witnessed the renewal of our vows.

We were two years into our new relationship when news broke that there would be a call for three new Commissioners for a Truth and Reconciliation Commission. I consulted with many people whose thoughtful opinions mattered about whether to apply. By the time I was done, after weeks of discernment and careful wording, I felt a deep sense of peace. Preparing my application had allowed me to stand back from the many disparate chapters of my life and recognize how they added up as a whole. I could see myself, perhaps for the first time, as someone I was happy to know. The process had already brought its own reward, whether I got the job or not.

I did the application. The multi-party committee did the interview. The minister did the job offer. And I was the lucky one who got to say yes. When Minister Strahl shared the names of the other two Commissioners, I gave an even more enthusiastic yes!

Then he told me to keep it all confidential. He hadn't reached all the Commissioners yet, and the public announcement wouldn't be made for more than a week, to coincide with the first anniversary of the official apology. I promised to keep it quiet, with one obvious exception.

Stephen was out of town at a Dene Assembly but would be touching down in Yellowknife that afternoon on his way to other meetings. I sent him a message to get off the plane in Yellowknife, even though it meant he would have to go back through security. The sun shone down on us as I whispered him the news right there by the taxi stand.

Stephen called me later that night for a less rushed exchange of excitement, encouragement, and expectations. He signed off the call with a plea I never forgot: "Make sure they understand the enormity of it."

Hard-learned skills, a lot of forgiveness, and the passage of several years had readied me for the work of truth and reconciliation beyond our immediate family and on a national scale. I had been trained and tested by my upbringing, professional experiences, motherhood, my spiritual seeking, and my life with a residential school Survivor husband. I had also been prepared for this work by the family I was welcomed into—my thirty-thousand-year-old Dene family, my home on Native land.

CHAPTER 6

The Tender Touch of Outreach

AS WE PREPARED for the Northern National Event in Inuvik, we had to face the limitations. A remote community of just over three thousand people, Inuvik lacked the wide range of infrastructure and facilities of Winnipeg, a well-equipped city with a population approaching one million. Its remoteness also meant that we couldn't count on reaching the same huge numbers of Survivors through the National Event alone. Vast distances and exorbitant travel costs would make that impossible, no matter where in the North we decided to hold it. So, we needed to take the Commission on the road to reach as many northern Survivors as possible. The North is where we began the pattern of holding a number of statement-gathering events in smaller communities throughout the region in the months leading up to the larger National Event. This was a particularly good place to start this approach, as the North is also where the late Justice Thomas Berger pioneered the way to successfully go about community consultation, setting an internationally acclaimed high bar for us to follow.

In the late 1970s, Tom Berger conducted a two-year Royal Commission of Inquiry into a proposed natural gas pipeline stretching from offshore Alaska, across northern Yukon, down the Mackenzie Valley of the Northwest Territories, and on through to Alberta and beyond to markets in the United States. It would have been the largest pipeline ever built and the largest industrial project in North America. Big money, big geography, and big questions were being asked about jobs, profits, social impacts, and environmental risks to an ancient Indigenous homeland.

Tom Berger guided that inquiry by creating time and public space for all voices to be heard, from the centres of power to the people on the ground. He listened to engineers and scientific experts on the complexities and safety of Arctic pipeline construction in the modern economy. And he listened to Dene and Inuvialuit on their expert knowledge gained from a lifetime of interdependency with the wildlife, lands, and waters along the proposed pipeline route, grounded in their traditional economies, with their own visions for the future.

Justice Berger listened to their own voices, in their own languages.

Now, some thirty-five years later, the TRC had to figure out how to amass an unprecedented oral history of the residential school experience in Canada. We had easy consensus on the approach we would use—the Berger process. I had seen it in action and knew the galvanizing community impact it could have.

Some of my best years in television reporting were from remote places that most Canadians never get to. The Canadian Arctic is one such region—Inuit Nunangat. The vast homeland of the Inuit is a place of breathtaking beauty, above the treeline, defined by rock. It is a source of infinite inspiration for all kinds of artists; most famously, perhaps, it is a carver's haven. The abundance and variety of Arctic stone have made master carvers of some Inuit, famous throughout the country and around the world.

I can't tell you whether the carver I stumbled upon was one of those masters. That's not what interested me that day in the 1980s, when I noticed him huddled into an outdoor space between his little house and even smaller work shed. I was wandering around a town on Baffin Island, getting a sense of the place, thinking about what pictures and personalities I could reflect in the story I was working on. The carver was covered in fine powder from his hair to his heels; even the glasses halfway down his nose were layered in it. Power tools droned as his dusty grey hands brought to life a delicate little stone animal.

"How do you choose your rock?" I asked him. "And how do you know what to carve?"

Such transformative power, turning a piece of rock into a piece of art. He was just as masterful in answering me: "I get close to it. Touch it. Get a feel for it. See how rough it is or how smooth. What tools I need to get at it, without breaking it all apart. See how big a piece I need. See how it will look when I hold it up to the light. I try to see what's hidden inside. Then, I just sit with it. And keep looking. And keep listening. Waiting for the animal to appear."

A year or so later, on the opposite coastal waters of the Arctic, in another remote village, Justice Thomas Berger said something that took me right back to that Baffin Island carver: "I can't wait to see how this turns out."

Tom Berger was leading the Alaska Native Review Commission, and I was working on a documentary for CBC national television about lessons from Alaska, as constitutional talks between first ministers and Indigenous leaders were getting underway in Canada. I saw first-hand how Berger approached the several public inquiries and commissions he led over the years, within Canada and internationally. He set out with a preoccupation for the people who would be most directly affected by his conclusions. He anchored his work in a process that allowed them—their voices, concerns, and wisdom—to be heard as experts in their own right, along with all the other experts. He got close, going where they were. Then—like that old carver—he sat, he watched, and he listened, waiting for the essence to appear. What I witnessed in Alaska was the same patient process he'd perfected the decade before in the Mackenzie Valley territory that soon after became my home.

Our TRC Commission Chair also supported the Berger approach. Murray revealed that he was so impressed with the strong voices that emerged from the Canadian Berger Inquiry that he named one of his daughters a variation of the Dene people at the heart of it: Dené. For Commissioner Littlechild, the Berger process fit right in with his relentless personal efforts at the United Nations, pushing for decades toward the UN Declaration on the Rights of Indigenous Peoples and the provisions within it for the duty to consult, ensuring Indigenous voices are heard directly on matters that affect them.

As a former journalist, I pushed two other Berger lessons that also helped our Commission: get the media onside early, and provide translation services. A key to the Berger Inquiry's lasting impact was the daily radio and TV coverage by Indigenous-language broadcasters Joe Tobie, Louie Blondin, Abe Okpik, and Jim Sittichinli, an unprecedented multi-language team championed and led by then CBC reporter Whit Fraser. He much later became the viceregal consort as spouse to Governor General Mary Simon.

Now, as our TRC journey continued, we were once again about to listen to, and learn from, the peoples of the North through a vast round of community hearings, beginning in Nunavik, heading on to Nunavut, and then visiting several communities in Yukon and the Northwest Territories, all leading to the National Event in Inuvik several months later. For many Survivors, this was their first time sharing, and the only time anyone had come to listen to their stories of immeasurable childhood bravery and adult resiliency, revealing individual, collective, and systemic human rights violations. In the North, we would hear and witness first-hand some of the most extreme examples of isolation, deprivation, and poverty.

~

One of our first TRC community hearings was in a tiny village in the High Arctic. My two fellow Commissioners were with me, along with our small team of northern staff and a modest team of health supports, mostly non-Inuit from other parts of Canada. Northern media were also there, both English- and Inuktitut-language programmers. I had once been their boss when I was the regional director for CBC North. The majority of people packed into this old, one-room community hall were local Inuit. Through my work as a journalist, I had known several of them personally for many years. The senior classes from the local school and their teachers were also there, at the encouragement of our TRC Chair. We saw the public sharing of residential school experiences as an opportunity for wider community education and understanding.

There were prayers, introductions, and explanations of how the day would unfold, and then the first few speakers. We had barely begun when it started. The wailing. Quiet sobbing that grew steadily louder, gradually morphing into primal keening, loud and relentless, expanding in waves around the room, ignited by the telling of residential school secrets that reverberated in the memory cells of so many who had joined us, fuelled from the depths of pain, shame, and loss.

There is always something behind the howling. I first learned that in our small home community of Fort Good Hope, just below the Arctic Circle in the Mackenzie Valley of the Northwest Territories. When I moved there in 1981 as a newlywed, many hunter-trapper families still lived on the land in traditional economies. To this day, there is no permanent road into that community, though there is now a short-seasoned winter ice-road for the ever-growing number of vehicles—mostly trucks with sturdy suspension! But back then, many Dene families kept dog teams as working animals, reliable transport, and supply carriers that could travel hundreds of kilometres into the bush. A large, healthy dog team was a highly valued asset that guaranteed a family's food supply and livelihood.

When something is happening, the dogs know it first, and they talk about it loudly. The arrival of food, the appearance of harnesses before a run, an approaching stranger, a lurking predator, the unveiling of the full moon are all events that will set them howling, sometimes a noisy nuisance, sometimes a lifesaver. In the dark night of winter months, the sound can invade an entire community—haunting, eerie. It used to terrify me as I walked home from my mother-in-law's place across town, protective arms clinging to the baby daughter snuggled in front of me. I wasn't afraid of the dogs' howl; it was the potential danger of whatever they were howling about that always got to me, heightened by knowing a wolf had entered a house and attacked a grandmother who was saved only by the bravery of her grandson.

Almost thirty years later, I was flooded with similar terror as I looked out into that overcrowded community hall. Like most places in this region of the country, where the last residential schools were still operating in the 1990s, the vast majority of the older adult population are Survivors, and every major family group has been affected by residential school trauma. As one of their members spoke, the others joined in their outpouring. Hearing this grief from one of their own relatives at such close range, and evoking their own school experiences, the interpreters also broke down. Instead of translation, we heard the amplification of their stifled sobs through the microphones as they tried to find the words. Several at the media table were also faltering. Many of them, too, had been to residential school. Our TRC staff, still so new in this very first round of community hearings, were also bereft. Most revealing and concerning of all, the health support team, those who were there to watch over the well-being of Survivors and others, were overwhelmed and under-resourced. None of them, and no one among us, was prepared for the enormous outpouring of this community-wide wail. The piercing, agonizing din, so much thicker than anyone knew to predict. My guts tightened with every mounting decibel.

Peter Irniq returned us to calm. This Inuk Elder and former politician had been a leader in residential school Survivor advocacy. He stepped forward to tend to the wounds, binding the room together in a circle, hands held, prayers spoken in two languages. He reminded the Survivors of the courage they had shown in getting this far, to a public opportunity to speak their truth. He pointed out their strength in numbers and their common purpose. He reminded everyone that this difficult work was for the sake of the children. And he invited us to pause, take a deep breath, take care of one another, and sit down together to eat in the simultaneous nurturing of mind, body, heart, and spirit.

As I think back, it is clear to me now that the common link between the wailing humans in this community hall and the howling dogs back in my husband's hometown years before was fear. In that case, I feared for the safety of my baby and wondered whether I would be able to protect her from unseen lurking dangers; in this moment, I was fearing for my *own* emotional well-being and wondering whether I would be able to protect *myself*. In this dramatic early TRC moment, I knew that I would have to take care of myself somehow in order to do the job expected of me as a Commissioner.

Beyond fear, these two scenes also demonstrate courage. The

courage of action and the courage of leadership. Courage in the actions of that young Dene teen back in Fort Good Hope, running headlong into danger in order to save the life of his grandmother from the wolf. And courage in the leadership of an Inuk Elder who spoke so caringly in the aftermath of this room full of broken-hearted crying. In translation, he said, "Residential schools are a very long chapter in the history of Canada ... but they are a very short chapter in our own history, the history of Inuit." His words were a declaration, calling on all Inuit to be strong, reminding them that they had already survived so much in the previous seven thousand years, and that they could now also outlast the residential school devastations of the past one hundred.

I saw resilience and defiant optimism in both, each demonstrating the power of courage, love, and hope to diminish and displace fear. I also felt the strengthening of my own courage, knowing that for thousands of days yet to come, I would bear witness to countless variations of the emotional ruptures and unpredictability of this day, yet I trusted that the days ahead would also be trimmed with moments of shining resilience to uplift us all. I left that community clinging to this hope.

~

There were so many things I never could have imagined I'd hear as a Truth and Reconciliation Commissioner. Welcome to Watson Lake, Yukon, on the western front of the Canadian north. This community hearing in 2011 was held in a newer and larger gymnasium than most of the ones I'd seen in other, poorer regions of the North. The man sitting before me was someone I had known for years. At least, I had known his public self. Whenever I faced a person I already knew from my prior life as a reporter and TV host in my new role as Commissioner, I felt a particular tenderness and hoped that my familiarity and previous dealings with them would contribute to a foundation of trust, given the personal risks they were surely taking in sharing their story.

He started with the recurring residential school storylines about rupture from home, land, and family; loneliness; loss of language; imposed religious practices; and restrictive rules. I had heard countless times that this included the separation of children by gender and by age, and the routine separation of siblings within the same school. In the case of a brother and a sister, there were sometimes restrictions against, and punishments for, even looking at each other, even in church. But this man's sibling story went far beyond that. He said he never knew what his younger brother had done wrong, if anything, and he wasn't sure his brother did either. All he knew was that he, the big brother, was forced to participate in meting out the punishment, while the little boy he knew and loved ran the gauntlet.

Historically, to run the gauntlet was to be on the receiving end of a brutal form of physical punishment, forced to run between two rows of soldiers lined up to strike as the guilty one ran by. The practice dates back to the early fourteenth century in Europe. In modern times, in the case recounted this TRC day, the guilty party was a small boy. Through tears, the big brother remembered how he had failed at the very job he had been taught to do—protect his little brother. He desperately wanted to. "If they'd just told me that if I refused, *I* would get punished instead, I would have taken it. But that's not what they said. No, they said my little brother would get it *worse*. So, the only way I could protect him from *that* was to help beat him up. I tried not to hit him too hard. But I hit him. And he never understood why. He never knew what had happened. And we've never been close since. All our lives."

The room shifted, flooded with unspent emotion from those who had lived it, or their own version of it, and those of us called to bear witness to it. I held myself back until the privacy of my own end-of-day. After all, this was not the only Survivor statement I was to hear that morning, and the next person on the list was already at the table and waiting. But one of the health support workers later told me that the emotional outpouring did not end in that gymnasium. They had accompanied the man outside to get some fresh air, where he was joined by another man who had also been in the room. The younger brother had heard it all. Everything he had not known as a child. That day, he finally understood. The two brothers could not let go of each other.

I learned important lessons that day. When I saw the power of humble truth to transform—we need more truth. When I witnessed the power of forgiveness to redeem, to breathe life into depleted spirits and seemingly dead relationships—we need more forgiveness. When I felt the power of facing up to ourselves and our histories, allowing new meaning into the events of our lives and deeper understanding of the words we use to describe them, however sordid or foreign their origins—we need resilience in our lives, resilience in our language.

Like the word *gauntlet*. Its meaning does not need to remain frozen in time, stuck in the past, or attached to painful recollections. It can have beautiful new meaning sewn into it. I have a pair of Dene gauntlet gloves with vibrant orange and green floral beadwork and beaver trim on smoked moosehide. They are magnificent. Those gauntlets spent too much time carefully tucked away in a drawer. When I wear them now, I honour the little boys from Yukon and remember the lessons they taught us all that day.

~

What I experienced as a Commissioner was at very close range because of how we set up the rooms. Generally, however modest the facility, it became a reverent, hushed space. The physical setup was a circle of imagination within a circle of intention. Picture the Survivor at a table toward the front of any room, always at the centre of attention, the centre of our purpose. Picture the community seated in semicircles of chairs gathered behind the Survivor, a kind of human blanketing of support. Together, they made up one side of the circle. Now see the Commissioner table. It's right across from the Survivor, facing them, just a couple of metres away. Also imagine all those tens of thousands of people from countries around the world, all gathered via the internet, all encircled, virtually, behind the Commissioners. Together, they formed the other side of the circle. Filling in the spaces between and around those two halves, connecting them all, were the health supports, the media, and the translators. By design and purpose, we were all in it together.

Occasionally, we met Survivors who did not feel right about that setup, having their backs to other community members. They wanted to speak directly to the crowd instead. We never said no. We built our plans on flexibility, adjusted on the fly, and did whatever made Survivors feel most comfortable. But it did change the tone of things. It placed the Survivor at the front of the room instead of within the circle of support. Invariably, with the additional pressure of all eyes on them, those Survivor statements came across more as speeches from the head rather than sharing from the heart.

Our typical TRC setup seemed to give more support to the Survivor, especially the many nervous ones who had no prior experience speaking in front of large groups. From their vantage point at the Survivors table, there were no other visible onlookers to distract them. That helped them stay focused, as most struggled with the weight of so many emotional memories. And it offered them the intimacy of direct eye contact with one nearby person who was listening to their every word—the Commissioner. That is why, on the day of the nosebleed, I was the first to see what no one else could see, not even the person bleeding. It must be hard to detect a new source of dampness on a face already soaked with tears as the story of a brutal childhood pours out.

I was the lone Commissioner at that hearing. *What should I do?* Was the person in serious medical distress? Would calling for help make things better or worse? What good would it do to interrupt? Or what harm, not knowing the impact of pulling them out of that deep, trance-like place of bloody remembering? All I knew for sure was that I didn't want to pile on more trauma by embarrassing them in front of the whole room.

The health support worker sitting beside the Survivor was looking down at that moment, listening carefully. But then, as if hearing my silent call, they glanced up. I caught their eye, made a subtle gesture with my head, a tissue in my own hand, and directed their attention to the Survivor. Not a word was exchanged between us. Just a quiet moment for wiping and water and comfort. The deep breath. The swallow. The bleeding stopped, and the Survivor carried on. I did, too, but the moment has stayed with me.

I know how *not* to cry. It doesn't mean I can't; it doesn't mean I don't. It means I've learned how not to. My professional training in journalism equipped me to function in the face of tragedy, loss, aggression, heated debate, conflict, and even war zones. I learned and practised how to cope, how to do my job of staying present to the unfolding story, keeping my eyes and ears open, keeping myself safe, intact, carrying on.

Each of the nearly seven thousand residential school stories we recorded had the power to bring anyone to tears, with their recurring themes of childhood violence and violation, family breakdown, and personal devastation. I teared up many times, but I almost always composed myself because I could see the impact my tears could have on someone sharing. It happened once, early on.

I can still hear the raspy voice of that tiny Elder describing what could only be called a pedophilia ring in the isolated community where they and so many other children were captive to the adults around them. Priests and nuns at the school, the person running the store, the one in charge of all the community's external telecommunications—all the vital lifelines supposedly there to help—were tied in an intertwined knot of complicity and silence.

Watching the frail, almost child-sized body of that Elder seize up with fear as they spoke, I let my motherly heart wander into their story of powerlessness, enraging me, heating me up. My eyes started to leak; the Survivor stopped talking. Their sudden silence jarred me back to my control centre. I could *not* be the cause of a Survivor shutting down and holding back, swallowing what their courage had brought them there to spit out that day, all to protect me.

I fought back the tears, cooling down. Maybe that's what my spiritual advisor, Peter Short, had meant when he told me the story of tempering: hardening the hands, strengthening the metal, fortifying the body as a whole. TRC hearings called on strength for the moment, and flexibility for whatever was coming next.

It wasn't always so torturous. Occasionally, there was sheer delight. Throughout the previous weeks, several Survivors had told us how their love of music began at residential school. That's where they first learned to play an instrument, to read music, to enjoy school dances, however tightly monitored—a ruler length between boys and girls, regularly measured by hovering nuns. One of the first Inuit rock groups—the Harpoons—came out of the school in Churchill, Manitoba. The Harpoons kicked off the long musical career of the legendary Inuk singer-songwriter and guitarist William Tagoona, and the band rocked to the steady beat of another great Inuk—drummer Jose Kusugak. For the rest of his life, Jose drummed out the cause of Inuit identity and language, proclaiming in the 1970s that Inuit would one day have their own territory. (And, yes, Nunavut came into being as the thirteenth jurisdiction in Canada on April 1, 1999.) Similarly, after touring Canada and the United States with his Dene rock bank the Chieftones, Albert Canadien returned to the Northwest Territories to become an educational champion for Dene language and culture, and write one of the first Dene memoirs, *From Lishamie*. And Johnny Landry's legacy is the song that became an unofficial Dene anthem and the rhythm of the final dance at countless gatherings—"Hina Na Ho." Juno Award–winning Inuk artist Susan Aglukark brought the song's uplifting power to wider audiences with her rendition.

In the North, we also heard much about one exceptional residential school, with one particular priest: Father Jean Pochat. He was the Oblate priest assigned to oversee Grandin College, a residence set up with the goal of forming future leaders for the Catholic Church. The church never got any priests or nuns out of Grandin College, but Grandin did become one of the residential schools with a reputation for leadership. It churned out several chiefs, a couple of premiers, a member of parliament, several teachers and members of the legislative assembly, and at least one language commissioner. It also earned Father Pochat the highest civilian recognition in the country, the Order of Canada; he was nominated by his former students. Many Survivors said that he always encouraged them to be themselves, to speak their languages, and to be the best they could be; that he was the one Father who treated them like a father. Father Pochat's leadership demonstrated the stark difference between brutality and benevolence.

And then there was this day in another northern community. It began, like most others, with a sacred fire. It was a day to hold in awe the capacity of the Dene to make fire in adverse conditions. There was fresh, heavy snowfall overnight. All the wood, soggy. All the ground, wet. All those gathered, damp. Still, the fire roared for us, and the prayers carried us through another long day as Survivors brought forward their courage and their painful memories.

Yet, eventually, as with so many other hearing days, there was a breakthrough. This day, it came with the community chief's closing remarks: "I've known all of you my whole life, but with all that you shared today, I feel like I'm really just getting to know some of you for the first time. Even my own brothers and sisters. I never really heard you talk about it before. We are family, but I haven't always understood you. Because of the schools, we haven't really got to know each other before today."

It was May 10, 2011. My birthday. Far from home, without my family, I took in the chief's words as a special birthday gift, a gift of hope. It was an early indication that our efforts, wherever they might lead Canada in the future, were already making a positive difference, if only for those participating in the present moment. Things could shift: one person, one family, and one community at a time.

Maybe it was that boost of hope that made the caribou stew, fish, and bannock taste all the better at the community feast that followed. And then, literally—the icing on the cake! Willie had snuck away to the one and only store in town and bought the one and only cake. Out it came, with candles and singing. Chocolate through and through. There must have been close to a hundred people in that hall, but the cake was no bigger than a dinner plate. Miraculously, there was a small bite for everyone. It was communal sharing in the familiar Dene way I cherish. That day, we all shared the sweet taste of hope.

CHAPTER 7

Courage on the Home Front

AFTER MONTHS CRISS-CROSSING the Arctic and sub-Arctic regions of Canada, we were ready to light our second TRC National Event thematic flame—Courage. It was the end of June 2011 in Inuvik, Northwest Territories. The NWT sits between Yukon to the west and Nunavut to the east. The Mackenzie River valley runs the length of the territory, south to north, a defining feature. The Dene Nation call this homeland Denendeh, the Land of the People. It has also become home to me. Our Dene children and grandchildren were born here and still live in our midst.

There were unforgettable examples of Courage on display at the Northern National Event, just as there had been throughout the community events leading up to it. At a hearing in the eastern Arctic, an intergenerational Survivor had talked about her residential school parents: an early departed mother and an emotionally damaged father. She talked about her father's harsh physical discipline, about how she and her siblings were forced to line up after his beatings and say, "Thank you, Daddy." She talked about how she had further suffered after his death, how angry she had been because she was unable to face up to him as an adult, to tell him how much harm he had caused. Finally, she shared that she had recently gained new insight into her father's traumas as a child; she now understood that he had raised her and her siblings the same way he had been raised in residential school—with extreme violence. Digging deep into her well of courage, she told us how she had gone to his gravesite to sob out what she needed to say to her father because she could no longer tell him in person: "I forgive you, Dad."

In a transcendent role reversal from one intergenerational story to another, now in Inuvik in the western Arctic, I witnessed the equally courageous words of a father speaking to his daughter, the two of them also devastated by raging anger. In this case, there was still hope for their relationship, as both parent and child were still alive. Side by side at the sharing table before me, the Survivor worked his way up to a long-suffocated message for his child: "I'm so sorry for how I raised you." Then came the daughter's courageous response to her heartbroken, aging parent: "I love you, Dad."

If such outpourings echoed from opposite ends of the North, it is because not a single community is unaffected. The North is the only region of Canada where, in most areas, Indigenous people still make up the majority of the population, so the per capita impact of residential schools is higher here than anywhere else in the country. Some of Canada's earliest residential schools began in the western regions of the North in the 1800s, with some of the last schools closing more than a hundred years later in the late 1990s. At the other end of the timeline, some of the most recent schools were also in the North, in the eastern regions, started in the 1950s and '60s, at a time when many schools in southern Canada were closing. Memories of residential school are still raw for multigenerational Survivors in the west and for first-generation Survivors in the east. Without exception, they all lived thousands of miles away from the government and churches that made rupturing decisions about their fates: moving families from seasonally migrating camps on the land into government-run communities; and moving children from familiar cultural nesting grounds to live with strangers in foreign-imposed realities, including the unfamiliar confines of huge permanent buildings.

Until the late 1960s, the Northwest Territories was still run from Ottawa. In 1967, in a symbolic Canadian Centennial project, the government bureaucracy finally moved north. The administration settled into the recently declared territorial capital city of Yellowknife. Even so, for several years to come, the NWT was run by unelected officials who still reported to a federal government minister in faraway Ottawa. This imported governance structure completely disregarded and overrode age-old leadership roles and norms of Indigenous nations who were, and remain, the majority of the permanent population of the North. Today's Indigenous leaders continue their efforts to reclaim that self-governing autonomy.

The town of Inuvik is another example of faraway decision-making. It was designated and built up in the early 1960s to take over as the regional centre. Aklavik, the long-established mission and fur-trading centre nearby, was a natural meeting place defined by Indigenous relationships with surrounding lands and waters, relationships captured in the name itself—Aklavik: "place of the barren-land grizzly"—and in one of its nicknames: the muskrat capital of the world. Although Aklavik was the senior community, it was soon overshadowed in size and prominence by the man-made town of Inuvik. Inuvik is not the territorial capital. It sits more than a thousand kilometres north of Yellowknife. Yet this was where our Survivors Committee had guided us to hold the Northern National Event—Inuvik. The Place of Man.

As we refined our approach to events, we reached out months in advance to form a community-based cultural advisory committee. We aimed to recognize and respect the distinct Indigenous nations wherever we were in the country, and to ensure that local knowledge and appropriate cultural protocols guided our programming. In this case, this central part of the Far North is neither exclusively Inuit nor exclusively First Nations, so we worked with both. For months, we planned and prepared with Inuvik-based Inuvialuit and Gwich'in host organizations and with the town itself. We also engaged with neighbouring Indigenous organizations in the Northwest Territories, Yukon, and Nunavut, and with Anglican and Catholic churches that had run schools throughout northern Canada.

We knew in advance that Inuvik would be the smallest of all the National Events, given the cost and distance of getting there and the limitations of a community of a little more than three thousand. Even so, we also knew that Inuvik would bulge with the arrival of about a thousand more people from both Inuit and First Nations backgrounds, most of them residential school Survivors travelling in from all three northern territories: by truck from Yukon, by plane from Nunavut, and both plane and boat from the NWT. They had all been fundraising for months. As I had seen so many times before, without the material means or access of southern Canadians, Northerners knew how to step up, pitch in, and punch far above their weight. With populations of just forty thousand to forty-five thousand per territory, and many communities of less than a thousand, the same few people are constantly called upon, and they consistently deliver. The North is a tight community within a vast geography. It knows how to improvise, to work with what's available, and to take care of each other. The bursting town and the cultural crossroads of this Mackenzie Delta–Beaufort Sea region, well above the Arctic Circle, just below the seventieth parallel, set the scene for an extraordinary four-day National Event.

June 28, 2011. I clearly remember how the first day of the TRC Northern National Event began for me—sitting on a toilet. Not for the reasons you may think. My computer was balanced across my knees, and I was writing notes for opening remarks later that morning. It was still in the wee hours, though broad daylight. This was Inuvik, Land of the Midnight Sun. The bathroom setup was not to escape the light, but to claim peace and quiet. My crowded hotel room was filled with the restless tossing and snoring of three grown men: husband Stephen, brother-in-law Everett, and cousin Peter. It didn't matter how many demands lay before me as a Commissioner, and how much privacy I might have wanted for my own needs over the four days. This was our family. With a big bed, a flat couch, and a large enough floor, we made do.

My brother-in-law was very ill, in the last weeks of a losing battle with a treatable cancer. It had been dismissed for too long as something much more minor, no matter how many times he'd gone back to his hometown nursing station. It's a familiar northern story, with essential services and medical expertise too far away and Indigenous complaints too frequently ignored. In his weakened state, he needed his cousin's help to get on the little airplane and manage the 320-kilometre flight northward. Everett never gave a statement to the TRC; that was more than he could handle. But he found great joy and peace in being there with Peter, Stephen, and me, and in brief reunions with some old friends from residential school days. Peter also had personal reasons for getting to Inuvik. His older sister in hospital had asked him to come to her before she passed. Both Everett and Peter had flown to Inuvik on the wings of courage.

This National Event put extra demands on me as the one northern Commissioner. Most were emotional ones, as I learned new and horrible secrets from family, friends, and community members I cared about deeply. Other demands came with familiarity. I'd been a radio and television reporter and TV program host for many years, so I was widely known and recognized. Sometimes people I had never actually met reached out as if we were old friends. Such familiarity also brought advantages. I knew people to call upon for various parts of our TRC programming. That's how we ended up with my long-time CBC colleague and friend Les Carpenter as a flawless emcee for several of the public events. Les was from Sachs Harbour and Inuvik, of mixed Inuvialuit and Gwich'in ancestry. He was a gifted broadcaster but had moved off-air to work in management for affiliates of the Aboriginal Peoples Television Network. He had also served on various national and international committees for the Inuit. And he had gone to residential school. He guided us seamlessly through our opening ceremony.

As always, we began with invocation and inspiration. The drummers had travelled to Inuvik by boat from our family's home community of Fort Good Hope (Radilik'o) hundreds of kilometres upstream. I was happy to hear their familiar voices sing an ancient Dene prayer song. After prayers, each Commissioner introduced themselves, acknowledged our host nations, and explained our own role as hosts of the event itself. This was our time to recap the context of our TRC and to stress that we were an independent Commission. This was always important, a fundamentally crucial aspect of our work. We were *not* a government Commission. Canada had been ordered to make the Commission happen by the Supreme Court of Canada. Canada only had a TRC because the Survivors fought to make it happen. Otherwise, they would not agree to an out-of-court settlement, and the Canadian courts would have been clogged up for decades dealing with tens of thousands of residential school claims. We also explained that Survivors had helped finance the Commission through their decision to set aside a specific portion of their settlement monies for the costs of running a TRC. And, as always, we recalled our core purposes and intentions: to dig deeper into the truth of the schools, to further educate the public by doing our work publicly, and to inspire each other to ongoing healing and reconciliation.

That was our pattern, always followed by brief remarks from the local Indigenous, territorial or provincial, and municipal leadership, and by each of the parties to the Residential Schools Settlement Agreement: the national Indigenous organizations, the federal government, four national churches, and, most essential of all, the Survivors themselves. They are the ones I remember most fondly from that day, represented by two beloved members of the TRC Survivors Committee. The late John Banksland, at home in this Inuvialuit region, had been a long-time advocate for residential schools' recognition and was seen as one of the Elders on the committee. Terri Brown, a matriarch in her Tahltan Nation in what is now known as northern British Columbia, went to residential school in Whitehorse, Yukon, and was now working for the Dene Nation out of Yellowknife. She had reached out to me with particular kindness when I first became a Commissioner. Now, two years later, Terri and John were extending that encouragement to everyone gathered in Inuvik.

Then, we were all invited to dance. It was a big, elevated stage. The Commissioners made our awkward best efforts to mimic the skillful Inuvialuit dancers who surrounded us. There would be more dancing to lift us up over the days ahead—and one more grand opportunity to laugh at ourselves!

The Inuvialuit and Gwich'in were exemplary hosts in Inuvik. Nowhere else did we see two former premiers now serving as heads of their respective Indigenous organizations and leading the way through a TRC event with such determination, practical hard work, and cultural energy. Former premier Nellie Cournoyea of the Inuvialuit Regional Corporation (IRC) was literally on her hands and knees, up to her elbows in animal blood, as she helped with the back-breaking work of preparing mounds of wild food. The IRC had arranged for the hunts, and then donated the harvest to feed the thousands of local and out-of-town guests. Former premier Richard Nerysoo of the Gwich'in Tribal Council jigged up a storm to the tunes of local fiddlers at a welcoming dance, feet flashing, beaded moccasins ablur, compelling others to join in.

Several western Arctic Inuit communities, distinguished as Inuvialuit, have their own proud dance troupes. Traditional dancing is done as a group, with no solo parts. Still, the Aklavik dancers came to Inuvik with an outstanding star performer—Philip Elanik. You couldn't take your eyes off him! Watching Philip dance was like watching a shape-shifter in complete transformation: one moment man on a dance floor, the next moment hunter on the prowl, animal on the move, bird in flight, carried away before your eyes. As if his life depended on the frenzied energy of his dance. And then we learned the man's heroic backstory ...

Philip was a young father of six with a couple more adopted children. Just six months earlier, there had been a raging house fire. Philip challenged that burning building, rescued the children, and earned the brutal scars of a severely burned man. Less obvious were the other scars he had already been wearing, as a cancer patient. He rose up, determined in the face of both, clinging to Inuvialuit culture as his lifeline. The bravery of Philip's story inspired courage in everyone around him. His positive, resilient energy poured out from the dance floor, touching all of us gathered in Inuvik.

Culture as healing. Courage in motion.

The impacts of northern residential schools are both multigenerational and multicultural. With no widely established system of "Indian" reserves, many northern schools housed kids from wide cultural backgrounds: Dene, Inuit, Inuvialuit, Métis, and sometimes other Indigenous and even non-Indigenous children. They didn't know each other's cultures, traditions, or languages, yet they were all thrust together to fulfill the homogenized, Christianized dream of Canada's first prime minister, the one who put residential schools in motion: Sir John A. Macdonald. In 1879, he said, "Indian children should be withdrawn as much as possible from the parental influence, and the only way to do that would be to put them in central training industrial schools where they will acquire the habits and modes of thought of white men."

Like the schools, Inuvik is a cultural crossroads of various groups of Inuit, Métis, and Dene, all living alongside non-Indigenous families in a shared community. This is where the TRC heard—not for the last time—about the experiences of children who bore the brunt of their colour, both within the schools and within their own families, where siblings might be different shades of brown. Those who were considered to be too white were frequently rejected and bullied by classmates. Meanwhile, those same lighter-skinned children were often favoured by teachers and other staff. Those perceived as too dark could also be bullied, and frequently berated and targeted by priests, nuns, and others for additional verbal and physical abuse. As I heard northern Survivors describe scrubbing their hands raw, trying to get the darker colour out, I recalled a would-be hockey player we'd heard about a year and a half before at the Rideau Hall opening. Priests had put that boy-athlete into vats of bleach, hoping to lighten his skin so he would qualify to play in the Quebec provincial tournament. Under the glaring light of Courage in Inuvik, it was becoming clearer that variations of such travesties had happened all over the country. Later TRC events would further remind us of that.

Many northern Inuit and First Nations children had been plucked directly from bush camps where they were living traditional lifestyles with their extended families. Extreme distances—hundreds and often thousands of kilometres away from home—made it impossible for parents to visit, and for some, especially unilingual Indigenous parents, impossible to even know where their children had been taken. Remembering through a child's eyes, many Survivors told us they were brought to live in the largest building they had ever seen. They already felt terrified and lost, just due to the school's size, and that was before anything else that was yet to come. The overall experience left its many marks.

The stories of sexual predation and related assaults were graphic and relentless throughout the Inuvik event, as they had been throughout the North, as Survivors disclosed details of shame they had been carrying for decades. Public sharing helped classmates realize how many of them had lived through variations of the same abuses, kept secret until now from each other and from their own families.

No wonder we heard so many times in Inuvik, as in other northern communities, that going back to school at the end of the summer was not something to look forward to. Not for the kids and not for the families and communities they left behind. Who would look forward to walking back into closed walls of loneliness, humiliation, injury, assault, shame, anger, violence, and even death? One Survivor described their residential school days as moving along a steady scale of experiences from bad to worse.

At a gathering on the Yukon-BC border before the Inuvik event, I heard broken, haunting words as an elderly woman described what returning to school felt like, looked like, sounded like. The season of overwhelming sadness was still fresh in her mind: "September. Everybody-Cry-Month. Back to school. Back of truck. All the kids gone. Everybody cry. Even the dogs cry. September. Everybody-Cry-Month."

This Elder's heart-aching memory would later help inform our TRC call for the establishment of a new statutory holiday in September. In Canada, September 30 is now the National Day for Truth and Reconciliation.

The long, combined stretch of missionary zeal and residential schools in the North has left many communities anchored in Christianity, and not all from the same denomination. The Inuvik National Event portrayed the enduring strength of church-based communities of faith, through prayers, worship services, gospel sing-alongs, and many acts of volunteerism. Through Survivors' stories, Inuvik also revealed particular spiritual abuses, as individuals and families of different denominations became divided, sometimes within communities, sometimes across cultures.

In the details of the Indian Residential Schools Settlement Agreement, including the establishment of a Truth and Reconciliation Commission, the Supreme Court of Canada had ordered specific obligations for the four national churches that ran the schools. It was a clear conclusion by the highest court in the country that the very churches that have built themselves up around core teachings of peace, love, care, forgiveness, and redemption have much continuing work to do to redeem themselves. Inuvik provided an exceptional gesture toward that end made by Anglican and Catholic Church leaders. Inuvik also provided further evidence of the need for it.

I had convinced our emcee, Les Carpenter, to participate in one of our early dialogue circles. He and several other prominent Survivors talked publicly for the first time about their residential school experiences. Among others, the circle included NWT premier Floyd Roland, former premier Richard Nerysoo, and the NWT senator at the time, Nick Sibbeston. The director of the NWT Human Rights Commission, Thérèse Boullard, situated residential schools in the broader context of international human rights violations. And Les Carpenter opened the door to the bigger conversation that followed about the pitted aggressions between Anglican and Catholic residential school children. He described how they heaved rocks at each other across the schoolyard. Les told us that sometimes these religion-based battles between the kids played out while the grown-ups in charge watched. They didn't stop them; they supervised.

Catholics and Anglicans had played a kind of proselytizing hopscotch down the Mackenzie Valley, leaving a trail of predominantly Catholic or Anglican communities or families along the way. Both had landed heavily in this Beaufort-Delta region, where Catholic Grollier Hall and Anglican Stringer Hall had separately housed generations of northern children, but who all went together to Sir Alexander Mackenzie School. Now here we were in 2011, and something unprecedented in the country was about to happen: church leaders from those two Christian denominations were about to apologize to Survivors, and to each other, both for the harms of the schools themselves and for the ruptures they had caused within families, within communities, and between Peoples. It was a powerful moment of exchange, seemingly unscripted, between the head of the Anglican Church in Canada at the time, Rev. Fred Hiltz, and the highly regarded, Dene-speaking Bishop Murray Chatlain of the Mackenzie–Fort Smith diocese of the Roman Catholic Church.

The apology was not a universal crowd-pleaser. Some were immediately critical, including some southern TRC advisors, saying the churches had taken advantage of the Survivors' venue for their own purposes. But many more, especially among the northern Survivors and families who had been directly affected by the denominational divide, welcomed this Catholic-Anglican apology as long overdue. Several told me the gesture was very healing for them to witness.

The churches, or at least their local congregations, played another significant role in Inuvik, with a symbolic gesture of retribution. Many Survivors had mentioned the hurt of never having their birthdays acknowledged throughout their residential school years. Now, the very churches that had deprived so many children of the annual celebration of their birth would make enough cupcakes for the entire Inuvik throng. The little cakes were the first of what would later become a signature TRC closing activity—the birthday party.

Unlike all the others to follow, though, this first one was a surprise party. It was inspired by the people of Tk'emlúps (Kamloops), thirty-five hundred kilometres south. In 2009, one month into my new Commissioner job, I had been invited to a major regional event organized by the Tk'emlúps people and the BC Indian Residential School Survivors Society. The sweetest, most stirring thing I remember from that gathering was the ceremonial arrival of the largest cake I had ever seen. It took several hands on either side of an eight-foot board to carry it in. "Happy Birthday, Dear Survivors" rose up into the open skies of the powwow arbour, and the lineup for a slice of birthday cake circled the entire inner grassy grounds. Never before had I seen so many people crying into their cake. Never before had I shared in such collective tears. Together, we were weeping for the deprived joys of generations of emotionally neglected children.

I carried that memory into planning the Northern National Event. I proposed that we select one Survivor as a way to honour all Survivors gathered in Inuvik—a kind of guest-of-honour, the way you would have a special birthday child at their own party amid all the other invited children. The big secret was that our co-Commissioner and residential school Survivor Chief Wilton Littlechild was to be the honorary birthday boy.

At a prearranged time, just as we called for a break in the afternoon hearings in the main hall, one of the youth volunteers led Willie out of the gymnasium and into a nearby building where hundreds sat in darkened anticipation. In a complete role reversal, Willie, already an Elder, blindly trusted this young one to guide him by the hand along a stone-lined, balloon-decorated path, unknowingly on his way to a surprise birthday party for him and for all Survivors. They entered the room, the lights came on, the tears came down, and the singing erupted—in English, French, Gwich'in and several other Dene dialects, Inuvialuktun, Inuinnaqtun, Inuktitut, and every other surviving Indigenous language available in this northern region. There were candlelit cupcakes for the thousands of Survivors never before honoured, birthdays never before celebrated. It was a room full of bittersweet joy and teary laughter.

After days full of gut-wrenching stories, we needed such ways to lift everyone back up, in keeping with our TRC Mandate obligation to Do No Harm. Survivor stories could hurt so much; we also needed to laugh. For thousands of Survivors who grew up in the enforced silence of residential schools, unsuppressed laughter was still a relatively new freedom.

The people of the North are masters at making their own fun, long ago inventing and practising Arctic sports such as the Inuit one- and two-foot high kicks, the cheek-pull, the knuckle-hop, and the Inuvialuit blanket-toss, and the Dene snow snake and pole push, and snowshoe biathlon. In more contemporary times they have celebrated the change of seasons with competitions that test land skills, such as moose-calling, fire-making, tea-boiling, rabbit-skinning, and canoe racing. Throughout the North, talent shows have grown into the perfect showcase for traditional music such as Inuit throat singing and Dene love songs, and sometimes for Métis fiddling and jigging contests. They have also proved to be a great platform for country-and-western cover tunes, Celine Dion wannabes, Elvis impersonators, and rock-and-roll wailers.

We realized that nothing could bring more fun to our TRC events than a talent show. Peals of contagious laughter rippled through the room in response to our headliners: Tim O'Loan as a crooning Dene Elvis, and the dynamic wailing duo of Barney Williams and Jerry Saddleback. With every opportunity, these two lifted themselves from their respective roles of Survivors Committee member and spiritual advisor—to step onto the stage and become crowd favourites in the TRC's own Rock and Roll Hall of Fame. Chief Ed John, inducted as a TRC Honorary Witness earlier that day, was completely doubled over beside me, struggling to catch his breath. Hurt 'til you laugh; laugh 'til you hurt. Laughter was great medicine for all of us.

The fashion show brought a similar gift of laughter, with the three Commissioners of the Truth and Reconciliation Commission as the show's finale! Murray, Willie, and I each wore special garments gifted to us backstage before the show. It was time, once again, for us to demonstrate our own courage. Nothing to do but laugh, I figured, ham it up, and hope the room would laugh, too. I was first out, strutting and turning with as much exaggerated facial pouting as I could manage without cracking up, to model my new backless, stylized, maroon wool vest, trimmed with hide-fringed yoke panels and bone buttons down the front. Willie was next, with a sort of fancy, prancing jig-step to show off his new beaded Dene moccasins. Murray brought the house down in a made-to-measure anorak, a traditional men's pullover shirt in the style of the Inuvialuit. The three of us stood together at the T of the stage, laughing at ourselves along with the crowd, a fashion show hit!

Staged at the top of the world, and seared into my memory, the Northern National Event was transformative. So many people I knew had set down intimate burdens from the past, while others prepared themselves for what was looming head. I was among those who had come to Inuvik carrying the weight of loss. Still fresh in my heart was the passing of my beloved mother, Ellen Wilson, just a few months earlier. The demands of the TRC left little time for personal grief. My mind returned to the prophetic advice we had received from Sheila-Marie Cook in the earliest days—to be prepared for everything that would happen in the lifetime of our TRC, including deaths along the way.

The Northern National Event was Philip Elanik's last dance. Perhaps, with his gifted dancer's wings, he had been preparing for his final flight. He died within the month, at just thirty-three years old. Two weeks after that, my brother-in-law Everett passed. When I first met him, he was still running a dog team, reclaiming his life on the land after residential school, later becoming a chief and an accomplished fiddler. He had come to Inuvik to say final farewells to his residential school family, those friends who understood better than anyone else ever could the hidden folds of his life that he took with him to his grave.

We have also since said goodbye to our beloved Survivors Committee Elder and friend John Banksland. He had been so proud to welcome us all to Inuvik in his homeland. When the Commissioners handed over our final report in December 2015, John Banksland was one of the three designated committee members to receive it on behalf of all Survivors. He wore his traditional Inuvialuit anorak jacket proudly and defiantly. "It's a symbol not to be ashamed of who you are," he said, as he boldly challenged the newly elected prime minister Justin Trudeau, reminding him that "this country is made of people, not paper." More recently, we lost another cherished Survivors Committee member. Rebekah Uki Williams from the eastern Arctic was one of the first Inuit to serve as a deputy minister in the new territory of Nunavut. And Les Carpenter, the Inuvik emcee I first knew at the CBC as the young man with the gifted voice, has spoken his last word. Following his death in 2018, mutual friend Dave Kellett and I were comforted to arrange for Les to receive the Order of the Northwest Territories posthumously.

With the loss of so many people who played huge roles, both on the stages of Inuvik and within my heart, the TRC theme of the Northern National Event now resonates with me even more strongly: Courage on the Home Front. That flame of Courage burned so brightly under the northern Midnight Sun, that great eternal flame. As for the town itself, I can never again think of Inuvik as the Place of Man. Forevermore, I shall think of Inuvik as the Courage of Survivors.

Survivors Committee chair, Gordon Williams, embracing fellow Survivors at a TRC gathering. Credit: NCTR

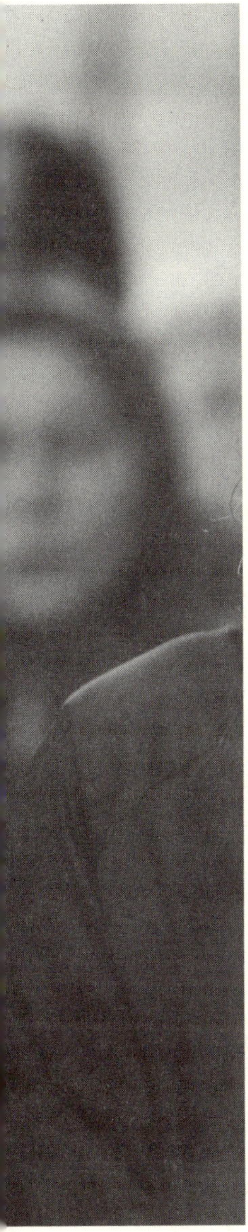

PART IV

LOVE

THE ATLANTIC

We all need love to heal properly. In love, you will defeat all that is evil in your world ...
Love is the essence of the Great Spirit ... Love is the essence of your spirit.

—Elder Dr. David Courchene,
A Story of the Seven Sacred Laws

CHAPTER 8

The Big Red School

FOR MANY RESIDENTIAL SCHOOL Survivors, the next flame of our TRC National Event circle would be the hardest theme of all—Love.

One Survivor used these words to capture the core truth of his story: "That's when the love-bond was cut. When I was taken away from home, the love-bond was cut from my family. It still is today."

That single sentence floored me with its wallop of sadness, loss, and longing. Like so many Survivors, he began his TRC statement with the very first traumatic day of rupture from home. And then the days that followed, as it became more and more clear to him that no parent was coming to save him from the fears of his new life in residential school. Throughout the TRC, Survivors told us about feeling afraid, unprotected, abandoned, cut off from parents and siblings, and left to believe what so many of them were told—that their parents didn't want them and didn't love them, that their parents were worthless in any case, and that they themselves were good for nothing and would never amount to anything.

The TRC Survivors Committee had deliberated over which of the seven sacred teachings to assign to which of their home regions for the seven National Events, several wanted to host Truth. They all wanted the truth to finally get out. They wanted the whole world to know exactly what the government and churches had allowed to happen to them as children.

Love was something else. No one wanted to host that theme, not at first. Many remembered their residential schools as loveless places. Love was missing from their childhoods. As adults, many had found love to be difficult, elusive, broken, or even impossible. As one Survivor said, "Living without love for so many years left its mark on me, and often the negative repercussions are passed on from generation to generation. Some residential school students looked for love in the wrong places."

In the end, the Survivors Committee agreed that Love would settle in the east, daily birthplace of the first light and its dawnland people, the Mi'kmaq, part of the Wabanaki Confederacy of nations that overlaps four provinces and two countries: Canada and the United States. It was also the home territory of Mi'kmaq Elder and committee member Lottie May Johnson.

And it was where the lingering legacy of the only residential school in the entire Atlantic region still looms large—Shubenacadie, also known as "Shubie." Some Survivors were so young when they went there, they simply remembered it as the "big red school": "Once we got locked up behind those closed doors of the big red school, there was no turning back, no running away."

Shubenacadie cast a long shadow, one that stretched well beyond its Nova Scotia location. Children were also brought to that school from New Brunswick, Prince Edward Island, eastern parts of Quebec, and even parts of Newfoundland, from the Labrador region. Northern Labrador, now recognized as Nunatsiavut, is part of the Canadian Arctic landscape. It is physically attached to the land mass northeast of Quebec but oddly attached by geopolitics to another province—the island jurisdiction of Newfoundland. For legal technicalities related to when Newfoundland officially joined Canada in 1949, long after all other regions, Labrador got left out of the Residential Schools Settlement Agreement. For different reasons, several Métis communities in other parts of Canada got left out, too. In contrast, the terms of our Truth and Reconciliation Commission spoke of "all those who have been affected by the residential school experience." We decided to hear from *anyone* who wanted to talk to us, whether or not their school was officially recognized in the agreement. Later, in both the 2012 interim and the 2015 final TRC reports, we specifically called on the government to settle fairly with those excluded from Labrador, as well as the Métis in the west. Meanwhile, in the lead-up to the TRC Atlantic National Event, we included parts of Labrador, some of the smallest communities in this regional tour.

In Nova Scotia, Eskasoni was just the opposite, the largest Indigenous community in eastern Canada and among the largest in the country, where Survivors recalled their Shubie days in accounts that fly in the face of love as we imagine it:

> There was no love in that place.
>
> We watched the priests and nuns eat eggs and fruit, while we ate watery porridge and gruel and sometimes rotten fish. When it made us gag and throw up, they forced us to eat our own vomit. We were always so hungry.
>
> I learned to steal in that place ... I tried to work in the kitchen so I could steal pieces of bread and apples to share with the others. Just like we were a family. Brothers. We were all helping each other.
>
> We were left outside in the cold ... didn't matter how cold it got, and we didn't have the right clothes for it. The little ones would be

> so cold they'd be crying. We'd get them to stand in a corner of the outside building, and us bigger ones would huddle around them to protect them from the wind, trying to keep them warm.

Of all the strange places for me to think of them, here come the muskoxen! This was no place for an Arctic animal, but it was that image of children trying to protect the smallest in their midst that brought the unique ancient beast to mind. Muskoxen wear thick fur coats; coarse outer hairs fight the frost, guarding an underwool as soft and warm as any fibre on the planet, the rare and luxurious qiviut of exclusive yarns and knitwear. For muskoxen it's a natural adaptation for warmth in the extreme cold of the Arctic. It's also a visual deception, part of their defence. It makes them look much bigger than they are.

And muskoxen form that same kind of defensive circle, the adult animals standing shoulder to shoulder in the face of predators, heads and horns facing the outward threat, with their young gathered inside the circle, behind their shield of protection. I asked myself how these Survivor children had so instinctively known to do what the muskox does naturally. And I wondered, yet again on this TRC journey, why children were left to protect themselves. Why the adult protectors had abandoned the circle.

Humans have much to learn from muskoxen. It's one of the reasons I treasured a small stone carving the Commissioners had received from the Inuvialuit Regional Corporation during the Northern National Event in Inuvik—three little muskoxen huddled together in a circle. Throughout our term, the carving sat in humble prominence in a glass case at the entrance to the TRC head office in Winnipeg. Whenever I was there, I would pause to acknowledge its intricate, powerful imagery—the natural world offering a teaching to humanity: to recognize itself, to reform itself, and to remember its inborn responsibilities to each other.

For many Survivors, the road to residential school was by train, where their heartaches began: "There were lots of stops. At every station there were a lot of kids crying. Didn't know where they were going. No families. No clothes. No farewells. No anything. Next station to next station to next station. Last stop: Shubenacadie. Get ready."

The man sitting in front of me was not just speaking for himself. Like many who gave statements to the Commission, he was speaking for family who had not lived to share their own stories, saying, "I am their voice today." He was speaking for his mother and her two older sisters, four, six and eight years old, and especially for the middle child, his auntie. This was the residential school story *she* had shared with *him* about the love of siblings, about unconditional love, and about the train ride that haunted her for years.

In his auntie's voice, the man said, "This was during World War II, and the parents were both in hospital. We were all told my parents were dead when I was seven, and that no one loved us. There were always rumours of Sisters molesting girls. My older sister was beaten all the time. She had a broken arm. The Sister kept punching my stomach when I started my periods, accused me of having sex with boys. My uterus was misshaped as a result of beatings. I was not able to carry babies. X-rays show that I have several broken bones on my body. Then there was the death of my older sister Mary. She was vomiting and there was no doctor and no one was helping her. I snuck upstairs and tried to help her, but Sister strapped me. At four a.m. Sister told me to get dressed and she took my younger sister and me to the railway station. It was a [military] troop train. The soldiers carried on a casket. I asked what was in the casket, and they said, my sister. She was lying in that box there beside me. I kept quiet about this for years.

I cannot speak Mi'kmaq. I couldn't talk to my dad. I was unable to trust anyone."

Then the nephew added his *own* story as an intergenerational Survivor, son of the youngest sister, but raised by others. His mom moved on to another life, another family, another country. "When I first got to see my mom she was in Maine, with two little girls and a boy. The little blond girl sister was scared of me and my dark skin. My mom never told us anything about Shubie, so I didn't know. She got sick and we gathered together around her. We wanted her to say I love you, but she never did. But I know she did in her heart. In our language we never say goodbye. We say we'll see you again. One day we'll all meet again. It doesn't matter—Native, non-Native, we are all one."

My memory of the next speaker tightens my heart. Benji. He overwhelmed the room with his story of self-loathing that he transformed into self-love. It hadn't come easily.

> I did not understand why they took us away from our parents. A policeman in a uniform and a guy with a hat and tie. What did we do wrong? They put me and my brothers and sisters on a bus to the train station. Nobody came to say goodbye to us. No hugs. I was six years old.
>
> Nuns took girls to one side. Priest took boys to the other side. Stripped us. Took our clothes. Washed us. Touched our bodies. Scrubbed so hard they tried to take the Indian away from us. Lots of little boys crying. They shaved our heads. I still have a scar from that. Then this brown bottle that smelled funny to take the Native stuff away. No more Indian. No more talking Mi'kmaq. No birthday party—nothing. When winter came, nobody told us my mom died.
>
> We had a hard time with that person who was supposed to look after us in a right way, but he looked after us in a wrong way. He

strapped us almost every night. Take your pants down. Bend over. Strapped across bare buttocks. We all got punished for things we never said. Don't speak your language. You'll get strapped.

I used to wet the bed. We cannot use the washroom after ten o'clock. The Brother called me "pissy-potter." I had to carry the wet blanket over my head and walk in front of the girls in the cafeteria. So ashamed! Girls looking and laughing. So scared to get punished again. Strapping. Locked you up. Put you in your cell. Lock you under the steps.

Our freedom was ended when I was a child.

Benji told us his family and friends all went their separate ways after residential school. He carved out his own trail of turmoil: no counsellors, no support, drinking, jail every weekend, violence, wrongful arrest, wrongful conviction—for murder—more jail, joblessness, hard times with women, suicidal thoughts, shame. He thought he was a freak, but he was not alone. Other Survivors shared loveless scenes from school days at Shubie:

"We did not celebrate Christmas. I remember streamers for decorating, but Santa never found us there. The Sister said our parents sent packages. Then the nuns would take everything back and say they would send it to orphanages."

"I was four years old. My chore was to dust the baseboard of the corridors and the chapel. I used a duster cloth to make my doll, my toy."

"I've seen a lot of abuse. They picked on people that had darker skin. One girl they abused was very dark. I asked why one girl was so dark and they said she came from an orphanage that burned."

"I grew up thinking that people with darker skin didn't have any feelings."

"This other girl her eyes were all bluish. She was blind. She couldn't see so she couldn't read. She was strapped for that. Another guy was told to read. He couldn't because he stuttered. The nun put a piece of wood in his mouth all day. When she took it out she asked him again to read, but he still couldn't."

"A little girl spilled milk. She was strapped 'til her hands turned blue. She was smaller than me. I was four or five."

"One guy got picked on by nuns. They put a dress on him and a ribbon on his head."

"There was a lot of abuse in the bathrooms at night."

"I wanted to run away back home. Thank God I never ran away or I would have been bald. They shaved the heads of kids that did."

"A few years ago, a boy who got shaved as a kid told me he didn't even run away. He fell asleep and when he woke up everyone was gone and the doors were locked."

Years later, there was some kind of divine intervention—at least for Benji.

I got adopted by an elderly couple. They took me to live with my sister. I graduated. I went back home to my community, where I belong, where I can speak my language, where I could be with my family, my aunties, my uncles, my friends. That's where I want to be. I became a traditional dancer. I have more respect for my people than the Roman Catholic Church. More respect for Elders. That's where I learned my culture. I like the sound of that drum. The sound of the people singing.

Everything changed for me. I got married, have six children, never punish them. This is my life story. Who I was, and who I am today. I am a Survivor, and I am a traditional person. I am strong and

> I'm still here, helping others to get up on their feet. I respect myself. I honour myself. If I need help, I know where to go. Nobody can stop me. I love myself for who I am today.

If only one residential school story could serve to tell them all, that might have simplified the many conclusions we would eventually have to make. But on this day, as with almost every other day over the course of our five years of hearings, something became very clear: there could never be a one-size-fits-all description of residential school experiences, nor of their aftermath. And there could never be one simple prescription for what to do about it now.

~

We heard many accounts of kids learning to fight at Shubenacadie, a school run by the Roman Catholic Church:

> "A strong Catholic religion is supposed to be a safe space. We were challenged to many fights. We were fighters. Residential school made us that way."
>
> "They set up a boxing ring and made us fight each other."
>
> "We'd give our desserts to the big boys so they would protect us from the fights."
>
> "The nuns said, 'You Natives won't end up being anybody. The only good Indian is a dead Indian.'"
>
> "The nun said, 'Speak English so I can understand you,' so we couldn't even tell our parents what was going on. I tried to write them a letter but had to copy from what they wrote on the blackboard."
>
> "We were afraid of them and sometimes afraid of each other. Every man for himself."

From adult children who survived the school, we also heard about a different kind of fight—the fight over faith itself:

> "I don't want to go to church. I don't want to listen to priests. I hate them. I don't want to listen to them anymore. No more nuns. No more priests. No more punishments."
>
> "I will never forgive the church for what they did to me. They should apologize to *us*!"
>
> "At school I had to learn to pray in English and in Latin. Today I am still relearning prayers in Mi'kmaq. I am also a strong Christian. I've got nothing against religion itself. I don't blame the church. I blame the people who were at residential school, the priests and the nuns."
>
> "It hurts me when people put down Christianity. I am a strong, proud Christian. My church has been important to my healing. Now I also get stronger when I talk, thanks to this eagle feather. What they did to us was so bad, they even turned God into a victim."

I couldn't forget those words, spoken so quietly, sorrowfully, almost prayerfully by one of the Atlantic Survivors. Increasingly, the Church wasn't easy for me, either. I was a Protestant, but that was no defence. Other regions of the country were already making clear that atrocities had happened at Protestant-run schools, too. Our TRC work was rattling my faith. What in God's name were we thinking? Everything I was hearing was so contrary to my own spiritual beliefs and the Christian teachings that fed me as I grew up—"God Is Love" at the heart of it. Now, day after day, I was witnessing accounts of atrocities perpetrated by the supposed servants of God. Amid so many graphic examples of lovelessness, selfishness, racism, blatant immorality, and blind criminality, all committed by those on the payroll of the church, this was the only conclusion that approached making any sense to me—even God was a victim. I carried anguish and shame as a member of the faith that inflicted so much harm on generations of children. Unsupervised, unaccountable front-line workers got away with repeated deviant behaviours that have continued to tarnish the reputation of the largest religious institution in the world, built and billed as the standard-bearer of goodness and kindness ... *Even God was a victim.*

The Church had imposed itself on Indigenous societies and spiritual practices that were much older than Christianity itself. These days, many Indigenous people have reclaimed ancient traditional ceremonies that were forced underground, outlawed by the federal government, with the supporting influence of the Church. Many others continue to follow Christian practices.

We had already noted this blending of spiritual practices in the North. In some regions, for example, Dene drummers commonly introduce and conclude a prayer song with the sign of the Cross. Our TRC aimed always to be respectful of local cultural protocols and spiritual practices, including Christianity, but it was a fine line to walk. For many Survivors, as we heard again in the Atlantic region, reclaiming traditional practices was key to reclaiming their identity and healing. For others, the Church was still essential to their lives. It held deep and sacred family memories of marriages, weddings, baptisms, and funerals.

The Commissioners had agreed on spiritual practices for our own strengthening and well-being. For each of us, that included personal practices as well as more communal, traditional protocols we had agreed to for the Commission as a whole. Before each National Event, we prepared ourselves with early-morning private prayers around a sacred fire that burned continuously throughout the four days. The rooms for our public Commissioner hearings were smudged in advance, and so were we. Smudging was available again throughout statement-gathering sessions, especially in moments of highly traumatic sharing. It worked for us, but not for everybody.

The practice of smudging is not universal to all Indigenous Peoples. We had seen this in Inuvik, where it was neither familiar nor comfortable to some. We later learned that after we left town, some devout Indigenous Christians had used soap and water to scrub down the walls of rooms that we had smudged for TRC purposes. It was evidence of something that was true for all aspects of our work—people are not all in the same place in their spiritual beliefs, or their healing pathways.

~

Although Shubenacadie was a loveless place, for many, finally returning home was no warm embrace either. Over and over, Survivors told us how they were forbidden to speak their Indigenous language at residential school, and then were teased back home for talking funny. So they just stopped trying.

> "I never understood why I got punished so much. But I did do something wrong—I went to residential school. They took away our language, culture, our beliefs. The legacy is that I am barely able to speak my own language."
>
> "Today I understand why I speak English and am still afraid to speak Mi'kmaq. I understand people around me, but when I go to say something, I'm still waiting for that strap. My cousin had to feed me, my hands were so swollen from that strap."

From no love at school to rejection back home. Survivors returned with strange haircuts and clothes—and were laughed at for looking funny. Some kids came home to younger siblings they had never met before—and now felt like they had become one too many. There was no longer space for them; they didn't fit in.

> "We weren't even welcomed back into our own communities. We were outcast."
>
> "Things were so violent at home we couldn't be together as a family even when we got out of there."
>
> "After school I went to Navy boot camp. It was really easy compared to res. school."
>
> "At that time there were no counsellors. We were alone and not accepted by our own people. I've been put down and ostracized in this community ever since."
>
> "I spent a lot of time on the streets with drugs, drinking and angry, mad at the world, not feeling like I belonged anywhere."
>
> "We were different. We were like strangers."

All day at the hearings in Eskasoni, we heard what life at the big red school had been like—and the realities of returning from it. We heard several times that the Catholic Church should apologize for its role, but this day ended with another kind of apology.

Leroy Denny was among those sitting in that crowded hall, listening for hours. What is the immeasurable value of sharing long-held secrets in a public space? Eskasoni showed us what can happen when you finally understand something you did not know. Leroy was the last to speak and the first to respond to all the others. "Today is a historic event toward healing our Nation," he said. "When I went to school, nothing was taught about this. Today we have some answers. It was criminal. Today we have learned why my friends and cousins were so different and why they didn't want to share their stories. I want not just our people but everyone in the world to know that five-year-olds had to take the physical, spiritual, sexual, and emotional abuse inside the walls of Shubenacadie."

Leroy Denny was their chief. Nobody was expecting his wavering voice, nor his personal apology. "I was one of those who gave you a hard time when you came home. We used to tease you," he admitted. "What I heard you say today about your time at school, that just saddened my heart. Forgive me. And I'm sorry. I can't stay for the feast—I just have to leave. I'm going to go home early today, and I'm going to hug my children."

That day had taken us deep inside the walls of the big red school. Driving back toward Sydney for flights homeward, our hearts were still bursting from all we had taken in. Such a day was often when we most needed an infusion of laughter. At a pit stop with Wilton and our senior health support Brenda Reynolds, we found everything we were craving: washrooms, coffee—and miraculous T-shirts! There was only one decision to be made. Not whether to buy them, but which Commissioner should hold up which shirt? The answer was obvious.

Willie's said *The beatings will continue until morale improves.*

Mine said *Am I the good sister or the mean sister?*

The three of us laughed so hard, we were crying. Knowing it was sacrilegious. Believing it was heaven-sent …

CHAPTER 9

Love: A Many-Splintered Thing

IN THE QUIET HUSH of a cool, dewy October morning in 2011, in the earliest hours of the Atlantic National Event in Halifax, I was standing on holy ground. A Traditional Knowledge Keeper was preparing a sacred fire to receive the Commissioners' tobacco offerings and private reflections. This ritual was how we centred ourselves, steadied ourselves for the work of the days ahead. There was something about the way Elder Earl Sack moved—slowly, focused, humbling his body—that added reverence to the prayerful place. We would be back here in four days for a different kind of prayer.

The evening before, members of the local organizing committee had started things off with another ceremony—an honouring event in the name of a revered residential school Survivor, the late Nora Bernard. Judging by the heartfelt tributes offered to her memory, to know Nora was to love her for all that she stood for: strength, justice, and hope. Her name had come up several times in community hearings over the preceding weeks. Survivors had talked about the heroism she exhibited while they were students together at Shubenacadie. The purpose of this night was to further acknowledge that, as well as to remember her beloved place in a large extended family. But it was especially meant to honour her memory for the long and relentless leadership role she had played in getting residential school grievances before the courts. Survivors talked about the humble beginnings of her work in 1986, collecting names in an old band hall in Indian Brook, Nova Scotia. They told of the backlash of accusations, name-calling, and threats she endured. They spoke of her warrior spirit and her relentless dream. Nora's dream transformed into a regional lawsuit, which eventually joined eight others from throughout Canada, into the largest national class action in the history of this country, possibly the largest in the world. Nora Bernard had left her mark and would not soon be forgotten.

TRC Survivors Committee member Lottie May Johnson credited Nora for her own ability to finally start speaking out and healing: "It all started for me with Nora back in 1995, meeting at her home. People were afraid to sign, and she said, maybe someday people will hear our stories. I can still hear her at times, urging me to go on. She told me, 'You can be a Survivor, a victim, or a messenger.'"

"That's what I want to be," Lottie told us. "A messenger."

To celebrate Nora was to celebrate courage, leadership, and resistance. Her commemorative evening set a tone of inspiration and resilience that would permeate much of what was to follow over the next few days, offering new insights into the presence of love in our midst. But not immediately.

On that crisp, sunny October morning, led by eagle staffs and our spiritual advisors, we three Commissioners and our spouses, the Survivors Committee, national and local Indigenous leadership, and representatives of the parties to the IRSSA walked from the sacred fire on the grounds of city hall to the opening ceremony in the convention centre, weaving through the streets of downtown Halifax, smiling and hopeful. It was the first time we had walked through such a busy city centre. The visible public response helped us foresee the walk's potential for even greater impact in the larger urban centres of future events.

After introducing ourselves and the context of the TRC, and recalling our purpose and intentions, we moved into what had become a signature event: the Circle of Reconciliation. This was an opportunity for representatives of all parties to the Settlement Agreement to demonstrate a new spirit of reconciliation by sitting together in a circle. It was entirely different from how they had sat just a few years before—as opponents in that massive court case negotiated behind closed doors. This was a public dialogue, on the main stage, in front of everyone. First, we heard from representatives of the Survivors and Indigenous organizations who had mounted the court case, and then from the Government of Canada and the various churches.

That's when things blew up. The Catholic representative, the church's most senior official in Halifax, said: "This gathering is educating me. I came here just a short while ago. I am hearing about this for the first time."

The room erupted! Boos and shouts of condemnation rolled across the rows of a thousand or more in that huge hall. The Commission had been unfolding on a national scale with a lot of publicity for a year and a half. His church was not a disinterested party. It wasn't right for him to be—or claim to be—so surprised by all this "new information." The wave of outrage, shock, and anger was not going to die down on its own.

But this was a TRC gathering. We had a specific obligation in our Mandate to Do No Harm. That included this Catholic archbishop who was being verbally battered before our eyes. As the leaders of the TRC, it was the Commissioners' responsibility to model the reconciliation we were advocating, and to hold the room together in a way that would ensure it was a safe space for all. Otherwise, why would anyone choose to come, much less speak up? And we needed people to come. If we were going to succeed in educating the country, we needed the public to show up and participate. Even uninformed church leaders.

I leaned over to Murray and whispered that we needed to reel it in, and that he was the only one who could do that.

Our Chair took to the podium and spoke clearly, purposefully, maybe even brutally to some ears, as forcefully as I have ever heard him speak. But his booming voice quieted the room and reclaimed the calm needed for the archbishop to complete his thoughts: "The experiences of today are moving. You have touched my heart ... I have inherited the burden of a black mark on our reputation and the damage it has done in your lives ... What can I do?"

It was a moment that tested our leadership as Commissioners. And it was a moment that made plain both the importance and challenge of our job of educating Canadians. It was becoming increasingly clear that not all the parties to the Settlement Agreement had taken their responsibilities equally to heart: educating their members, adherents, and constituents about their institution's history and their accountability for the story unfolding before our eyes.

However, other activities at the Atlantic National Event did take us several strides forward on the education front. Although the Commissioners always devoted most of our time to hearing from Survivors, at this event we also broadened out to universities and schools. We hosted scholarly discussion panels on specific aspects of residential school histories; we commissioned and received academic papers on original new research; and we introduced Youth Witnesses to the proceedings. One of them, sadly, now the late Patrick Etherington Jr., had spent the better part of a month walking from Ontario with his Survivor father to this event thousands of kilometres away in Nova

Scotia. This was no one-time feat for Patrick. We'd be seeing him at subsequent events, educating and inspiring others by walking.

Another Youth Witness was Tamara Cremo. I'd met her a few months earlier, during one of the TRC student gatherings I'd proposed and helped lead with Virginie Ladisch and others from the New York–based International Center for Transitional Justice (ICTJ). The non-profit organization specializes in age-appropriate education around truth, memory, and reconciliation—just what we needed to reach out safely to young people. Later, ICTJ was the first organization to become a TRC Honorary Witness. With confidence and enthusiasm from that workshop, Tamara came to the Atlantic National Event with her teacher and classmates from the Mi'kmaq community of Whycocomagh, Nova Scotia. They listened, went home to interview family and other community Survivors, and made a compelling video of all they had learned.

But, as always, it was Survivor stories that opened the widest windows onto so much of what this country has either not been able or willing to see clearly. Not just the facts of what happened to individuals but also the lasting and ever-widening legacy of what has happened to generations of families, communities, and entire nations: "They took away my songs, ceremonies, language, and culture. What happens to a people when you take away everything from them? Why did the government and churches feel the need to change us? We were fine as Mi'kmaq people. This was cultural genocide against my people."

Here and elsewhere, we heard many Survivors call what happened to them "genocide." Over the years ahead, the Commissioners would have many internal discussions about how to reflect that truth in our findings. It was a legally imposed dilemma. Our TRC was part of a post-judicial process, meaning that, in the eyes of Canadian law, Survivors had already been dealt with by the courts. Because we, the TRC, were part of their agreed settlement, it was not up to us—or even within our powers—to draw any new conclusions about broken laws or to name any new charges. But we also knew, for the sake of our credibility in the eyes of Survivors, that we couldn't ignore what so many of them had called out as a crime. I kept thinking about an imperative we had heard in Indian Brook, Nova Scotia, and other places: "Let the Commission put out the truth. Do not be afraid to put the truth out."

Given how often we heard the word *genocide*, it would have been inaccurate for us to leave that out of what we eventually reported in our summaries and conclusions. A major part of our TRC job was to listen to Survivor statements—the largest record of oral history ever gathered in this country; to record, document, and preserve all that we heard; and to accurately synthesize it for the broadest possible public. Reflecting this Survivor's statement and others like it would later allow us in our final reports to conclude that the Indian residential school system in Canada amounted to cultural genocide.

The testimony at our hearings reflected a wide range of violations, from the personal to the collective: harms to the child, the family, and the community, across generations; and harms to an entire country as a breach of international laws, declarations, and covenants. But repeatedly and relentlessly, from multiple speakers, we heard about the biggest loss of all—the loss of love, with its brutal companions of fear, violence, and all the related beliefs and behaviours:

> "'I love you'—never to have your parents tell you that. Love is a very strong emotion. We all need love. Our bond with our communities and parents was broken."
>
> "I went to Shubie and so did my parents and grandparents. The impacts started before I was even born. There was a lot of violence in our home. They had lost their power as parents. What they had gone through in residential school, we were taught these things. Life

outside residential school was bad enough that [my mother] felt it was better for us to be in there without them, than outside with them. We were safer there, in her eyes, than at home. You could see my father change into somebody else when he used that belt. You saw an uncontrollable rage. You could see why she felt we were better off there. But at school we also used to get beaten and strapped for crying, talking, lying down with our own sister, peeing the bed, hating the food—just being a kid. I followed in my mom's footsteps and was a battered woman from the age of fourteen, angry, hurt, and broken when I came out of there."

"Fear is a very strong emotion. I couldn't concentrate and I couldn't learn because of fear. Seems like I was in grade two forever. When I went back home two years later, I was still in grade two. All I knew was rules, regulations, religion, and the belt. I got hit across the head with a Bible. I lived in fear of going to hell. We had no protection. The nuns used to say if we told anyone, God would strike us down dead."

"I felt deserted, abandoned, and forgotten as a child. I still live with intense loneliness. I never saw my older or younger sister. We couldn't talk. I had to make an appointment to see my brothers. How sick is that? My parents only lived five miles away. They were not allowed to visit."

"What bothers me is how our beautiful community has been affected. Today there are a lot of drugs and alcohol and pills. Why is it we still have these suicides? We can't even get rid of the ones that are pushing the drugs and alcohol. Some of that lies heavy on me. I did drink through my pregnancies. We had no proper upbringing. Many Native communities are like that ... how we still are and shouldn't be. Somebody has got to be listening ... there's a lot more that could be done. We are supposed to be a better nation."

> "I didn't hear my dad speak Mi'kmaq until two weeks before he died. I cried. It was another loss. He could speak it, but he didn't teach us. They didn't beat the language out of him. They beat the *value* of the language out of him. And that he could have passed that on to us ..."
>
> "I was still ashamed of being an Indian until Rita Joe started writing her poems. She made me proud to be an Indian because *she* was proud to be an Indian, and today I thank Rita Joe."

Just as the community activist Nora Bernard had encouraged other Survivors to speak up about what had happened to them at residential school, the poet Rita Joe had used her words to inspire fellow Mi'kmaq to be proud of their identity. In her famous poem "I Lost My Talk," she wrote about what she suffered at Shubenacadie. Her poetry led her to receive the Order of Canada and grew into a commemorative play, dance, and symphony.

Rita Joe, like Nora Bernard, never got to speak directly to the TRC. Their voices came through the words of others. But another influential woman of words, the late Dr. Isabelle Knockwood, addressed the TRC at the age of eighty, first at a mid-October 2011 community hearing in Indian Brook, and again a few weeks later at the National Event in Halifax. "In our ceremony for reconciliation, both the perpetrator and the victim come together to forgive each other," she said. "Our experience is *our* Truth. The abusers haven't told us *their* Truth. When church people found out about the book I was writing, they threatened to shoot my house. Chief and Council hired a lawyer to get me off the reserve, but my descendants wouldn't let me quit. The young people."

Out of the Depths is Dr. Knockwood's powerful account of what she experienced and witnessed as a little girl in the 1940s and '50s at Shubenacadie school. The book came out twenty years before our

Commission, but it was clear from what she told the TRC that she had never stopped thinking about the bigger story behind her childhood:

> Our world views were changed in all areas of our lives, in ways that were sudden, unexpected, traumatic, violent, and permanent. Everything about the schools was different. Different sounds, different food, different smells. We became objects, the spoils of war. All culture is land-based. The schools were a joint venture in which each party expects to benefit: the government expected to benefit from our lands; the Church expected to benefit from our souls. Non-Aboriginal people, how they benefited from our loss ... They have the ocean views and the sea coasts, and we have the rock piles. The government did not honour the treaties, so how are they going to honour our stories? Access to resources is what we need to rebuild our nations. The Indian residential school story is all about the land. My biggest fear is that our stories will not be heard.

Dr. Knockwood's final comment brought the house down: "Today I only want my story to help other Survivors. My happiness is my revenge!"

Her triumphant and defiant survival story of self-love, and service to others, reminded me of Benji, one of the first Survivors we'd heard in this region. "Today I love me," he had said.

It also reminded me of an earlier statement we heard in Nunatsiavut, where a visibly nervous Survivor described a very scary incident from when she was a little girl. She was crossing an open field when she stumbled upon a menacing cat, hunched and hissing. She froze in her tracks. There, facing off with the cat, was a tiny mouse, eyes alert, ears flared, standing up on its hind feet. *That could be me*, she had thought. Remembering the fearlessness of that little mouse standing up to that big, terrifying cat had helped her push through the challenges of residential school with defiance and determination. It also helped her get through reliving them, as she told them to me.

For all the wretched declarations about the lack of love at Shubenacadie, we had also heard much about its presence in many forms: love of siblings, love of res school family, love of culture, love of self, and love of community. Shubie has disappeared from the physical landscape of this region, like so many other residential schools across the country—wiped out by intentional demolition, suspicious fire, or abandoned decay. But it is bound to linger longer on the emotional landscape as things slowly change—language is reclaimed, history is rewritten, culture is honoured and embraced, and hope merges into poetry, as also expressed at this Atlantic National Event:

> I am from peace of mind, loving and sharing. Being a grandmother and loving it every day.
>
> It doesn't cost anything to show anybody love, to listen to them, to pray for them, to treat our people like human beings. That's what we have to take away from this. It doesn't cost anything to love our people.
>
> I learned how to drum at residential school support meetings. When I drive by the hill where the big red school used to be, that hill seems to be getting smaller.
>
> We live in the ripple effect of what happened. We can't miss the child right in front of us, my child, their child. It took me about fifty years to realize I live in a loving community.

At the end of Day Four, one final ceremony concluded this gathering of Love. It was time to head back to our sacred fire, to release and let go to the extent that we could. Every day of this National Event, just as we had done in Winnipeg and Inuvik, and would do at all future National Events, the health support teams had distributed brown paper bags throughout the public and private hearing rooms to collect the tissues full of tears brought on by the retelling and witnessing of traumatic residential school experiences. The bags of tissues were gathered and brought together on the final day for the sacred ceremony.

After four days of continuous burning, the fire was now low, deep with tobacco ash, wood cinders, and red-hot coals, ready to complete its last transformation. Elder Earl Sack was kneeling on the ground beside the sacred fire, practically embracing it. He was hunched over in humble reverence, oblivious to the rest of us, his attention completely absorbed in his hushed prayers and the quiet rhythm of his hands. Teary-eyed, with sweat pouring from his brow, he reached out and, one by one, placed each and every tissue into the fire and paused until it was consumed. Thousands of them. To be received, as if a lament. To be transformed, as in a prayer.

Today, as I think about that impossible TRC theme of Love, I remember this final scene of loving defiance: a kneeling human frame bent over an all-consuming flame, shedding tears and prayers, transforming ashes of sorrow into rising gusts of healing. I recognize what I am feeling as my mind revisits this holy scene in the Mi'kmaq homeland: Kesalul. I love you. Je vous aime. Neghǫdı́deʔǫ.

Marie Wilson with older brothers, Bob and Thom.
Family Album

PART V

TRUTH

SASKATCHEWAN

Truth is walking with all the Laws ... the ways of your ancestors ... There is so much suffering today because people have forgotten the Laws. They walk another path that has taken them into darkness. When human beings walk with the Seven Sacred Laws, there will be peace.

—Elder Dr. David Courchene,
A Story of the Seven Sacred Laws

CHAPTER 10

If Truth Be Told

WE WERE FAR from the stormy Atlantic now, with its bittersweet theme of Love, yet the hope-filled words from a Survivor there lingered in my mind: "Reconciliation can happen in an atmosphere of love, hope, and joy." That bold statement left me with a big question as we headed into our next theme. Could reconciliation *also* happen in an atmosphere of Truth?

The central purpose of the TRC was mass education as a pathway to healing and reconciliation. The TRC was a forum for Survivors and others to put the truth of their lived experiences on the record, with a promise that their statements would help inform a more honest and inclusive account of Canadian history. Beyond correcting the historical record, this was also the chance to lay down burdensome secrets carried for a lifetime. The very first paragraph of our Mandate emphasized the connection between speaking the truth and healing the spirit: *"There is an emerging and compelling desire to put the events of the past behind us so that we can work towards a stronger and healthier future ... The truth of our common experiences will help set our spirits free and pave the way to reconciliation."*

In Saskatchewan—home of the greatest number of living residential school Survivors in the country—the chosen theme again rang true. The glaring flame of Truth revealed, released, and restored throughout this province, in stories shared along the rugged path to our fourth TRC National Event.

Occasionally, mercifully, truth came wrapped in laughter. My first TRC outing in Saskatchewan had been much earlier, in the first months of the Commission. It was a huge indoor gathering on the edge of Prince Albert, not far from the infamous Saskatchewan Penitentiary—a place that would come up many times in Survivor statements over the years. The Commissioners had walked into a storm of apprehension, tension, and hostility. Survivors were fed up, impatient, and angry. They'd been waiting more than a year while a first Commission collapsed, a second batch of Commissioners was named, and we got up and running. They were also upset about the financial parts of the Settlement Agreement, the way their lawyers were treating them, the missing school records that were leaving some of them disqualified for compensation, and the lack of emotional supports during stressful months waiting for the outcome of abuse claims. None of these grievances was part of our TRC Mandate, but we were the ones showing up in person in their communities, so we got the full blast of their frustration, confusion, and mistrust. This experience made plain the emotional climate we'd be facing over the years to come and how important it would be for us to keep explaining the specific purpose of our TRC and how it fit into the overall Settlement Agreement. So we made it a standard part of our introductions at every hearing to follow.

Meanwhile, the temperature in this room kept rising as Survivor after Survivor voiced complaints and concerns. Then, one tiny, powerful speaker shifted everything. The short, hunched elderly woman spoke only in Cree. Although I didn't understand, I could see and hear the power of her storytelling. Sudden laughter erupted all around me, including from my co-Commissioner Willie.

"What did she say?" I whispered.

"I'll tell you later," he managed, still laughing.

As we drove back toward Alberta, Willie began retelling her story, laughing so hard again that I asked him to pull over for our safety.

"Well, it's a sad story, really," he said. "She was talking about when she was in residential school, and how she got hit on the head so often and severely that it caused permanent hearing loss. So ever since, she has struggled with that. But along the way, she realized that her faulty hearing could also be funny."

Willie continued with an English version of the woman's story:

> I'll tell you something that happened recently with my daughter. One day, she came to me and said, "Mom, have you seen my panties?" I was thinking, *Gee, my girl is all grown up. Why is she asking me about that?*
>
> "Well, where did you leave them?" I ask her.
>
> "I don't know," she says. So, I'm thinking, *Oh my goodness! What kind of girl do I have? Doesn't even know where she left them!*
>
> "Well, where did you have them last?" I ask her.
>
> "I don't know." *Goodness sakes! How come she doesn't know that?* I'm thinking.
>
> "Well, what colour are they?"
>
> "Colour?" she says. "I don't know what colour you call it. They're van keys."
>
> "Oh, van keys! I thought you said *panties*!"
>
> And then we both laugh and laugh! So, you see, sometimes I can help people laugh because I don't hear too good!

Her story helped us, too. Willie and I laughed until it hurt, until he was finally fit to drive again. And then we talked some more about how this amazing woman had reframed such a negative residential school loss as a positive. Deafness as the gift of laughter she could give to others. Laughter as the gift of medicine for people hungry for healing.

~

A couple of years later, in 2012, the TRC was back in Saskatchewan for community hearings leading up to the fourth National Event, to be held in Saskatoon. During this time, many personal memories came flooding forward for me. Maybe it was the geography of the place and the overall rural feel. I grew up in small towns with easy access to such open fields. And maybe it was the stories themselves. So many of them took me back to chapters of my own life.

I remember learning about the provinces as a kid in school and deciding that I liked Saskatchewan best. No one bothered to explain the Indigenous meanings of any Canadian place names, including the Cree roots of my favourite—Kisiskatchewanisipi, or "swift-flowing river." But even without knowing that, I still liked it best. To me, Saskatchewan sounded like music, maybe the way water does. Twenty years later, I would be calling the place home.

In 1977, I settled into my first job as a reporter for the *Regina Leader-Post* newspaper. I nailed my first front-page story as the Pépin-Robarts Task Force on Canadian Unity rolled into town. Ironically, residential schools were still operating in this province at that time. While that task force was talking about national unity, just down the way, children were still being abused at Gordon's Indian Residential School, which was among the last in the country to close, in 1996. As a result, a huge number of Survivors who spoke to our Commission were from this province.

Some Saskatchewan Survivors struggled their way to the top, invisibly fuelled by their residential school experiences—people like the late Noel Starblanket. When I'd first met him as a young journalist, he was the sitting president of what was then the National Indian Brotherhood—now known as the Assembly of First Nations. Starblanket's resounding presence back then was as a hard-driving leader, a strong and independent thinker, and a rights advocate. Thirty-five years later, at the first community hearing day in Regina, the former national chief honoured me in my role as a TRC Commissioner by remembering me. I was now seeing a different Noel Starblanket. The public persona the country had come to know was about to reveal the private man marked by eleven years of residential schooling and multiple generations of damages before that.

"My grandfather was the first to be abused," Starblanket said. "They called him 'pagan,' 'heathen.' That was in the late 1800s. We've been dealing with that in my family since then." Starblanket said thirty years of personal healing had helped him recognize the symptoms of those multigenerational impacts. He enumerated a long, wrenching list of telltale signs: Survivors may become heartless, driven, ambitious, and demanding egomaniacs. They may become angry, impatient, intolerant, and perfectionist controllers, or stubborn, unforgiving, and vengeful calculators. They may turn into unkind, hurtful, explosive, and violent aggressors. Maybe they become dishonest, promiscuous, irresponsible, and self-absorbed blamers. Or unaccountable, unpredictable, and noncommittal underachievers. They often become insecure, emotionally unbalanced, spiritually bankrupt alcoholics, drug users, or gamblers. They might struggle with suicidal thoughts. And if they survive, they may become another abuser.

My stomach knotted as his list went on and on. Even my reporter's shorthand couldn't keep up as Starblanket described the way childhood abuse causes adult dysfunction and spreads to the next generation. He finally ended with a gut-punching admission: "I have experienced all of those things in my own life, to one degree or another."

Here was a former national chief publicly laying bare his pains and failings. What a hush of silence in response to such vulnerability. But he had more to say. Noel Starblanket was the first Survivor I heard name the issue of lateral violence. "I asked for forgiveness of those who I have hurt, and to forgive myself. Family and relatives can parrot good words, but still cannot let that go. When will this ever become better? It will become worse before it becomes better. The lateral violence I have suffered at the hands of my own people ... Every day I see effects of this residential school experiment. These people are not well. They will continue to hurt you. Lateral violence is extremely difficult. What do we do? Banishments? Bylaws to forbid drugs and alcohol? We are seeking these answers. They are not easy. I don't lose hope, but I don't see it happening soon. I hope we will be able to find some reconciliation."

In this prairie province, seeking reconciliation at times felt like that elusive search for the needle in a haystack. For where do you find it in the stories we heard in the months that followed? Of a child being tied up outside in sub-zero weather, a leash around his neck as if he were a dog. Of a child forced to run for kilometres on a gravel road, behind a truck, in his bare feet. Of the coffins in the corridor of the school. Of the brother and sister who were in those coffins. Of the mother and father who could not come, who had also died. Of the siblings left in school who never got to grieve any of them or comfort each other. "My brother and I figured out a sign language to send little messages to each other. I lost my innocence, my childhood, my family—my identity."

The issue of identity had come up earlier. I remembered former senator Charlie Watt's blunt message at hearings the year before in Kuujjuaq, Nunavik, in northern Quebec: "I want my identity back. Is that too much to ask?" In Saskatchewan, the same loss came up over and again. Survivors described arriving at school as a child, looking one way, eating one way, dressing one way, and immediately being forced to look, eat, and dress differently. They spoke one language and were immediately expected to understand and speak another. Identity also came up repeatedly as a big challenge upon leaving school as teenagers. Several Survivors said they had no sense of home, sometimes nowhere to go, and often little self-regard.

> "I didn't know where I fit in ..."
>
> "I tried to pass myself off as Italian. It was just easier to get by ..."
>
> "They thought I was Chinese and I went with that because it was easier ..."
>
> "I hated white people. I hated everyone. I hated myself."

Throughout the world, personal identity is to be carefully protected, invaluable to the functioning of family and society. We even treat it as sacred. We begin by marking our children from birth. Imprinting them with a name, an identity, a kinship bond.

Our TRC heard much about how even that most basic of human ties—a name—can be taken. Some of the same religious institutions that gave names in sacred ceremony also took names away in seeming administrative brutality. Children became numbers. But numbers weren't the only way that residential schools marked children through naming. Many with Indigenous names got new Christian names. Siblings, already so often separated from each other, became further estranged when differing names were assigned, or differing spellings. Over the many decades of residential schools, identities were shattered at the whims and literacy levels of changing administrations, staff turnover, varying operational practices, and school transfers.

It's impossible to know how many Indigenous names have been lost over the years as both church and government institutions have replaced them, or denied them altogether. Sometimes our TRC became a forum for grievances beyond residential schools, especially when deep and destructive harms were experienced society-wide. Loss of identity was like that when Inuit all across the Canadian Arctic were issued disc numbers, like dog tags, instead of their names. A loss of relationship. A loss of kinship. A loss of humanity.

Saskatchewan was also where we heard more about a different form of family rupturing, distinct from the residential school policy. The country would eventually acknowledge this policy as the Sixties Scoop, another truth of Canada's history, hidden in plain sight for almost three decades.

I was among the blind. As a child, I had waited anxiously for the Saturday newspaper to arrive. It contained two things of particular interest to this young girl: the comics section and a page with a picture featuring "Today's Child." As far as I could understand, there were little kids available for the claiming. In our family of boys, I was desperate to have a sister. I wondered whatever happened to all those children. Years later, as a TRC Commissioner, I was about to meet some of them in person.

He had a different look about him. A different way of dressing. A different way of speaking English. He had been raised in Europe, taken as a young boy to an entirely new and unfamiliar world on the other side of the ocean, cratering a huge hole in his own sense of identity and belonging. He said his adoptive parents had not been mean or unkind, but he never really felt he fit in. And now he was here as an adult, trying to feel his way back home.

Another introduced himself as an American citizen, adopted as a child to the United States. Some of the adoptees who chose to speak to our TRC had lived their own versions of hell in their adoptive homes. Others were just lost—culturally and spiritually displaced. They had not gone to residential school, but many of their birth parents had. This was further evidence of what we kept hearing from Survivors: that those who went to residential school didn't know how to parent. They had grown up as numbers, in violent institutions, without the example of loving parents. As adults, many of them had their children taken away by child welfare agencies. Those children were then swept away in the Canadian international adoption program that came to be known as the Sixties Scoop. Now, in significant numbers, "scooped" children were finding their way to our Truth and Reconciliation Commission, asking one compelling question: What about us?

We didn't wait until the end of the TRC Mandate to take up their cause. We asked the Indigenous affairs minister and the prime minister if we might expand the terms of our Mandate to include the Sixties Scoop, as well as those Métis and Inuit children not covered by the Settlement Agreement. The request was never acknowledged, so we later included their concerns in our final report and TRC Calls to Action.

Along my TRC journey in Saskatchewan, I met a reporter for the Saskatoon *StarPhoenix* newspaper. Rather than interviewing me for a story, she wanted to tell me one. Betty Ann Adam was a Sixties Scoop kid, the oldest in her birth family. For most of her life, she didn't know much about any of the other children. As a reporter with determination and research skills, she slowly put the family puzzle together. She and three siblings were about to meet each other for the first time. She was planning a newspaper series, but with my television background, I helped her see that it could be much more. "You know that it's a movie, right?" I said. "You realize what a historic moment that will be, and how important it is to the story of what's happened to countless Indigenous children and families in this country? You are so much more than the reporter of that story. It is *your* story. You need help to tell it, so that you can be fully present to experience it."

I connected her with people I knew at the National Film Board. Director Tasha Hubbard brought the documentary to life with skilled coaching and respectful, loving care. But Betty Ann brought the story to life through personal longing and professional determination. *Birth of a Family* has grown into a teaching tool with a beating heart. It cradles the earliest moments of three sisters and a brother coming together for the very first time. It puts a human face to how government policy can rupture a family, and explores the long, hard road to putting one back together again.

Accounts of reclaiming identity often went hand in hand with reclaiming sobriety. By my tally of the statements I heard directly, more than three-quarters of Survivors told us they had used alcohol and drugs to mask the pain in their lives. It was a pile-on of similar stories, from the attraction of alcohol, to its betrayal, to the helping hands that eventually made change possible:

> "For me alcohol was not the problem. It was the medicine. If it weren't for booze, I would have killed myself a long time ago. It worked for me, until it stopped working and became just another problem."
>
> "I was looking for love in bad places. I was so lonely I would buy booze and drink just to try to get friends."
>
> "I had a very special teacher. She asked me not to smoke and drink and drug. So I stopped all of it because that teacher said she cared. It changed my life."
>
> "I drank so much I almost died. I poisoned my whole system. I asked for help. I started talking."

"That nurse helped me ..."

"My aunt helped me ..."

"That co-worker helped me ..."

"My niece helped me ..."

"We're not going to talk about the past. We're going to talk about how we can help."

For many Survivors, reclaiming identity was also tied to reclaiming spirituality. As one Survivor said, "I found out who I was at a Native American church ceremony. Sacred people doctored me. That's what saved me. I remember the hate was gone. And I remember the love I took on for my people. As an Indian Elder, I go as a resource to public school. I am taking me back." Another put it this way: "I can't change the past. The only thing I can change is my life."

One day in Saskatchewan, after my closing remarks, a woman came up to tell me how much she wished we could stay longer. "You are like a visiting angel to us," she told me. I was touched and embarrassed by her kindness. I responded by reminding her that, except for my opening and closing remarks, I had said very little all day. The Survivors were the ones who spoke the most, who inspired, who rekindled belief in invisible helpers and in the hope of the Ages.

Noel Starblanket had shared something similar at the beginning of this tour—that his hope came from more than twenty-five years of healing work, including what he called "every kind of ceremony." "No white psychologist or social worker is able to do what we are able to do in our own spirituality. Thank you for your hearts and minds, hard work, professionalism, understanding, and empathy, and for continuing to pray. I ask you to continue to seek the peace that we need so badly."

Once again, there was that winning combination: truth and spiritual healing. Noel Starblanket told us those two things had made the biggest difference for him: being truthful to himself, and prayer and ceremony. He said that was what eventually helped him live up to the prophecy of his great-grandfather and live into the spirit of his own name.

"My name means 'he has a star for a blanket,'" he said.

A blue blanket swaddles him. It has a flowered cloth print on one side and soft flannelette on the other. Blue tufts of tied wool yarn dot the surface in a pattern of four-inch squares. I recognize this little quilt. I'd made it a couple of years before for an older child. Now my handiwork is returning to me, made all the more beautiful by the tiny sleeping baby within. My niece is handing me my grandnephew, forever after to be held and loved as my own son.

I have tried many times to write my son's story, and each time my tears have ground me to a halt. My memories cry for the baby, for the young mother, for myself, and for the multiple tragedies that brought us to that moment.

It is still early, quiet, my husband warming up the vehicle outside, our little girls still sleeping. Two mothers stand alone in the semi-darkness of a northern winter morning, the younger one too frail and unwell from the traumas of premature birthing to handle the additional demands of this new little one, to give him all he will need. And so, with all the love she feels for the bundle she is still holding, she sacrifices herself. She severs the mother-bond. She entrusts that role to another. To me. She raises the babe to her lips, reaches across the darkness, and hands him to me. No words. What could she possibly say? I respond to her silence with a whispered promise—that I will treasure him, protect him, and love him forever. Then, a reverent hush, attuned to the fragile sound of the baby's breath, as if in a sacred moment of rebirthing.

This beloved young woman, barely more than a teen, had been part of my life since she was small. When she was an infant, her own mother froze to death, and I had been part of the circle that watched over her ever since. This day, our special relationship was fixed for eternity in the shared bonds of motherhood.

Her arms now empty, she quietly crosses the room to the stairs, goes down and out to the airport, homeward, a piece of her heart left behind to my safekeeping. The subtle warmth of a January dawn filters through my living room window from the great frozen lake beyond as I stand there, crying into my new baby boy's quilt, smelling the essence of him, overwhelmed already with love for him. And crying for my niece, and all she has paid to give me this priceless gift.

My son's story is not a short story. Even now, we are still putting together pieces of it as we learn more about our niece's lineage, including the father she did not know growing up, only recently learning of his blood ties to the great Métis politician, orator, and resistance leader Louis Riel. But more important to me is realigning the poignant pieces of my son's life with two families, interdependent and indivisible. As mother and son, we shared the heart-ripping experience of saying goodbye to his younger birth-sister. They looked so alike that even they could see it, affectionately calling each other "my mirror." After two years of exhausting treatments and gruelling travel back and forth to Edmonton, her final months were in Yellowknife. As her closest family, her "mirror" and I visited her daily. I often slept over in her hospital bed, cradling her preteen body to sleep. Her name became my son's first tattoo. Yvonne was Keenan's sister from the other family—and we are all one.

Recently, our niece finally opened up about some things she wanted me and our son to know: how sick she was back then when he was born, how hard it was to give him up, how much she needed my help, and how grateful she is that I have always been there for her. When Bonny first called during her pregnancy to ask if we'd take the new baby, Stephen answered the phone and I overheard the conversation. He told her she'd have to talk to me, that it would be up to me, that I would be the mother. My husband honoured my role as mother through it all.

And friends and colleagues supported me. At the time, the Northwest Territories was the only place in Canada that legally recognized what was then called "Native custom adoption." But it wasn't straightforward. In my case, as a "non-Native" woman, I needed sworn statements from within the Indigenous community to affirm that I was fit to raise a Dene child. It was not proof enough that I was already raising two of my own. By vouching for me to become my son's mother, two people changed and enriched my life forever. Joe Tobie, a beloved long-time CBC colleague, has since passed. Jim Antoine, a colleague, former chief and premier, remains a friend whom I cherish as a brother. I have taught my son to respect them and their names always, as family.

Still, over the years I have at times doubted myself. I've wondered if my son felt disappointed that I am not Indigenous, like his birth mother. These questions resurfaced and sometimes haunted me throughout my Commissioner years as I heard countless former children talk about the harms, and often the horrors, of being torn from their mothers and detached from home.

Today, as I reflect again on all of this, and as I share the story with my son now an adult, it is glaringly obvious to me how his story is so different from the many others I heard from lost children. My son never lost his birth mother. While his older sisters had Auntie Bonny, I made sure that he, and only he, got to have "my special Bonny." To our girls, he is their cherished little brother. But only he also has a big brother, as well as little brothers and sisters of his own. He is known and loved by all of us. My son knows his Dene name. He knows and respects the land—he has even chosen a field of work to help protect it. He knows where he fits in. He knows he belongs.

As I sit here, once again soggy-eyed, I realize that it is because of the more recent memories of words spoken during our TRC hearings in Saskatchewan that these bits and pieces of my son's story—of my story—have come flooding back to me, finally allowing me to put them in writing. Just as Survivors inspired other Survivors to share, they have also encouraged me to dig deeper into my own truth. I honour my son and my niece as a cherished part of my life's journey. And I, too, feel so much lighter after setting down our shared story.

~

Saskatchewan left me with a final extraordinary lift. The northern lights found me there. Once again, Commissioner Littlechild and I were on the road homeward. It was a long, dark drive after two days of emotionally exhausting hearings, and I was half daydreaming, looking out the passenger window.

Yellowknife is renowned internationally as one of the northern lights capitals of the world, yet never before had I seen this! Willie stopped the car. I had to get out to believe my eyes. There, before us, was a swath of milky green lights stretching the full breadth of the northern sky, gently waving back and forth, like the span of enormous wings. And emerging from the middle of the wings was a clear shape—the head of an eagle. I gasped, my eyes welling. We were lifted up on eagles' wings.

CHAPTER 11

Wings beneath Our Feet

ALMOST AS FAR BACK as I can remember, I could skate. I don't remember learning; I just remember always being able to. And I could play hockey, too. In my childhood, southern Ontario winters regularly delivered three-foot snowfalls and a few days of cancelled school. I remember skating to school when roads were clear enough, or trudging through unplowed streets, skates slung over my shoulder, ready for recess on the school's outdoor rink. But my earliest skating memories go back even further, to the years before school, when vehicles were one-to-a-family at best, which left plenty of time between cars for a kids-sized period of street hockey. I was surrounded by brothers, and sometimes cousins and other boys, all part of our unofficial small-town street team. I was usually the youngest, and the only girl, but I was included. Most of the kids in the neighbourhood played, thanks to my father.

He loved to tease our mother with the story of how those kids would knock on our door and ask her if *he* could come out to play! Kids liked him because he was a kid at heart. He made sports fun, whether playing with us or with his own adult gang. I spent countless hours behind his team's bench in so many small-town arenas. I roared along with the crowd at any big moment, whether a goal or misdemeanour, immersed in the excitement, the delicious smell of Juicy Fruit gum, and the fog of my own breath in an unheated rink. I can also picture myself sitting in a snowbank at the side of the road while Dad tied my laces. The skates were brown and black, with a crossover strap on top of the laces—the same skates that my two older brothers had learned on. How old was I, anyway? The skates were so small, and so were my feet!

And with that memory, I caught myself thinking about the feet of the residential school Survivor seated in front of me. It was a community hearing in Prince Albert, Saskatchewan, early 2012. I was trying to picture them on a child-sized version of this man making such an unforgettable statement. Comparing them, in my mind's eye, to my own little feet as I remembered them in skates.

We had just heard about what his grandfather had done to make this little boy fall in love with gliding around an outdoor rink. There was no money for skates, but the grandfather, who could neither hear nor speak, could see well enough that his grandson had a gift. He fashioned him a pair of skates from five layers of socks and traditional hide moccasins. In the frigid air, they would turn hard and slide around easily. Then, with a puck made of frozen cow manure, a willow branch stick, and a cleared patch of ice—the grandchild was on his way to hockey stardom!

That little boy was Fred Sasakamoose, the first status Indian ever to play in the National Hockey League (NHL).

In the earliest months of the TRC, the three Commissioners stuck together as much as possible, but we eventually had to split up and spread out in order to tackle the size of the country and the many parts of our Mandate. That's how I ended up doing so many of the community hearings, often as the sole Commissioner. But for this one it was the "A-Team": Wilson and Littlechild. That's what Willie and I jokingly told Murray we called ourselves if he was missing for any reason.

Most TRC community hearings lasted one or two days, but in Saskatchewan, they sometimes went longer to accommodate all the Survivors. Since some schools ran into the late 1990s, the memories shared with the Commission were widespread and numerous. We were now on Day Three, February 2. Two days before, Commissioner Littlechild had introduced me to Fred Sasakamoose, referring to him as a friend and one of his personal heroes. Chief Littlechild had been a hockey player well before his other accomplishments as a lawyer, honorary doctor, and chief. We chatted casually with Fred before that first day of hearings began. He made it clear he had no intention of making a statement; he was there just to watch and listen.

I'd heard that countless times before, at hearings in other parts of the country. Many Survivors would come into those crowded rooms holding back, clinging to the walls and to their secrets, surveying the landscape of the event, and then—a shift, movement. Someone would eventually come forward to say that although they had not originally intended to speak, they'd changed their mind, inspired by the examples of the preceding speakers and the realization that they, too, had something important to contribute. It was an unfolding. A humble cycle of courage feeding encouragement, and that courage then breeding courage anew. We would sometimes start the day with four or five registered speakers and end up hearing fifteen to twenty, sometimes more.

Fred Sasakamoose was one of those holding back. He wasn't going to speak. And then he did. Seeing him attuned to every second of the first two days, I looked for a quiet moment to talk to him privately. Our TRC had no authority to compel anyone to speak. And unlike some other commissions, there was nothing to gain financially by speaking. Our purpose was to educate Canadians. Anyone who spoke to us did so voluntarily. So, I didn't want to pressure him, but our Commission was also, fundamentally, about healing individuals and families damaged by Canada's residential school system. Repeatedly, we heard Survivors say that speaking to the Commission helped them set down burdens they'd been carrying for decades, or helped them feel lighter, or like they could breathe for the first time in years, or helped them reclaim their voice in a throat that had been constricted. In an attempt at encouragement, I told Fred about how sharing their experiences had already been helpful to so many others. With all the additional weight of prominence and profile that he already carried in his everyday life, I didn't want this hockey legend to miss his own shot at healing.

That afternoon, Fred took his turn coming forward to the table where Survivors sat when they spoke to the Commission. He was just a few feet across from us, wearing a Chicago Blackhawks cap and a sparkling, intricately beaded medallion of the Blackhawks logo hanging on his chest. He told us he'd equipped himself overnight with prayers in traditional ceremony, yet the tears came right away.

"I intended not to cry," he said. "Yesterday, when I heard the testimonies, I cried with them. Does an old man cry? Give me back my life. I want my childhood back. I want my innocence back." This seventy-eight-year-old father, grandfather, and great-grandfather was back to being a scared little kid. "I could hear my mother cry. She had no shoes on. We were poor. One horse. It was white. My older brother was eight. I was six. The Indian agent was escorted by the RCMP. It was a big truck. Kids crying inside. Without any questions or answers, they load me onto that truck. Me and my brother. My grandfather, the one not able to talk, was grabbing at me. He got pushed aside, told, 'If you don't let these kids go, you will go to jail.'"

Fred's story ricocheted between residential school terrors and hockey triumphs. "I have to change my story to hockey to calm myself," he explained.

But eventually, it all came out: his rape by another student; the priest who was nearby, who saw it and did nothing; and the little boy who didn't care if he died, too ashamed to see the other kids, and about to become one of so many residential runaways, fleeing from abuse. He was nine years old and he knew the way: get to the river and home from there. He broke trail through the bush for two days, eighteen miles to reach the Saskatchewan River, and three hundred to four hundred yards across its deep current. He was luckier than many other kids over the years who drowned or froze to death in their efforts to escape, but his luck ran out at the ferry. The school had called ahead, and two of the priests showed up to take him back. The punishment that awaited him was one the TRC had heard about before. Humiliation in front of everyone, in the middle of the dining room. Supper of bread and water. Stripped to the waist and whipped. Head shaved and anointed with coal oil, burning the eyes.

But first, he had to get there. The priests made him walk the eighteen miles back to the school while the Fathers rode in the truck. For the last mile, they took away his shoes and socks. He was barefoot on a gravel road, with brutalized, bloody feet. Residential school was a universe away from the loving grandfather who had swaddled those little feet in socks and moccasins, foreseeing their strength and potential.

From there, Fred went on to talk about the ironies of his story, how the deficiencies and atrocities of his school experiences set him up for hockey success. "I only went to grade seven in ten years of my life in res school. I was an employee ... a slave. That's why my arms and wrists were strong, from milking cows."

As for his legs—the Fathers who made him do that long, bloody trek back to the school saw his stamina. One of them became his school hockey coach. He later got him started in Moose Jaw and onward from there. But it wasn't easy. "After ten years in residential school, I didn't want to be an athlete. I didn't want to be a hockey player. All I wanted was my parents. I think the schools left us so crippled up for life. In that 1949 dressing room, boy, was I ashamed to be an Indian. I sat in that corner. Ashamed. I don't belong in your world."

So different from my dad, who made me and everyone else feel like we *did* belong. He made us all feel like we were part of the game, had a right to be there, and were already winners for that fact alone.

In the hearing room, Fred Sasakamoose recalled the first time he no longer felt alone in the world of hockey. "A Black man came into hockey, Al Leacock from Edmonton. He played right wing. Jimmy Chong came on to play left wing. Now I'm not the only one. I put a black lace on my right skate for the Black man. I put a yellow lace on my left skate for the yellow man. The red man at centre … that was me! What an international flavour! It carried me to realize that the world was not only meant for the white man; that there was a place for me, too. We were one. It didn't matter the colour. We were there for one another. What a dream! What a dream!"

It was a dream that led to Fred Sasakamoose's induction into the Hockey Hall of Fame, news he announced to us as part of his statement. "That is wonderful. The finishing touch of my life! If I end my life today, I will talk to Creator and thank him for all he has done for me. Friends, family. I want to stay positive in my life. That is how Creator has brought me where I am today. Those great scars of residential school, I feel they are gone. I think joy is upon me right now. I have created many friends in my life."

Then, looking straight at me, he added, "Today I have created more. I think I have healed at this moment."

To the Commissioners he said, "I look at you. How long did I think that I was alone? You are there. Today, you uplifted me. I feel your strength. I feel I'm getting better. I feel I can talk about it now."

Looking at Commissioner Littlechild, he said, "You are a Survivor."

Looking at me, he said, "You are strength. Woman is strength that gives life to all of us."

The story of Fred Sasakamoose is one of countless others we heard throughout the country about the role of sports in residential schools. They helped inform five of our TRC Calls to Action. They also helped inform the wording of many of the other Calls to Action that capture the spirit of inclusion, based on nation-to-nation relationships between Canada and Indigenous Peoples.

That day in Prince Albert, Saskatchewan, Fred Sasakamoose, the great NHL hero, inspired yet another crowd. And as with all great athletes and leaders, he spread the credit around. He singled us out, as Commissioners. He made me, personally, feel part of his healing team. And he helped me remember that incomparable feeling of inclusion from my own childhood. How I wanted to call my dad that night to tell him I remembered, to thank him. But he had passed away in 2007, shortly before the TRC began. Ever since Fred's passing in 2020, I like to imagine him in a pick-up game with our dear old street hockey captain—my father, Neil.

~

As the TRC continued its work under the Saskatchewan flame of Truth, Survivors had much to say here, as elsewhere, about what government and church officials had done to them. But they were also beginning to dig deeper. To admit what they had done to themselves, their families, and each other.

In this regional collage of admissions, regrets, and forgiveness, I often think of someone in particular. I call him Three-Parts-Patrick (not his real name). I first met him in January 2012. He had a quiet, gifted way with words, painting vivid pictures of memories from his early days: Of many children, dog teams, and canoes. Of family on the land, "living by the gun," hunting and trapping. Of poverty and hunger, yet also of peace, love, and happiness. And then, of being "dragged into something unknown." Residential school. Of jail for his father if he didn't let him go. Of the long, complex, multi-day journey getting there. Of boats and barges. The feeble horsepower of the engines. Of arriving, and the five-year-old child's first feeling: "This was an evil place."

He remembered the name-calling: "dogs" and "savages." The hard labour: digging and hauling heavy sacks of potatoes, stacks of wheat, cords of wood. The menu that never changed: "I knew every meal for nine years. Breakfast: a lump of oatmeal, hard-crusted bannock, and a little bit of milk. Lunch: soup with morsels of meat or rancid fish and a slice of bread. If you were a good boy, you might also get a carrot. Supper: boiled vegetables, cabbage or turnips, and maybe a little piece of meat. An orange or an apple on the table only on the days when the Indian agent or superintendent visited."

And he remembered other abuses: "Those people taught me to be a Catholic. They talked about a kind-hearted Jesus, but before the day was over, I'd get a licking, or more abuse. Later on, I understood it was them, not the Creator. Yes, I believe in a loving God, but at residential school it was not like that. My dad didn't send me a cent for nine years. He had nothing to send. We were poor. I was an innocent altar boy. When we were dressing up for Mass, I used to masturbate the priest for a five-cent chocolate bar."

I met Patrick for the second time several months later. Same province, different community hearing, a long way from the first. This time, he began his story in adulthood, talking about jobs and leadership positions. Eventually, he said what I'd already recognized, that he'd spoken to me before. Back then, he'd thought he was the only one. He said it felt easier today. He had more stories to get rid of, about life *after* school. "At residential school there was a lot of bullying. Today we still see the effects of that. All the lateral violence that has become the norm. Even the distortion of laughter. There is a big difference between laughing *with* someone and laughing *at* someone."

Other Survivors told us about their post-school suffering, including some who never went to residential school themselves:

> "I thought it was only the white people who could do this to us—put us down, call us names, rape us, beat us. It was worse. We called them brothers, sisters, aunties, uncles, cousins."
>
> "I did everything. Drugs. I joined the street. I was lost. If nobody cares for me, why should I care for myself?"
>
> "I went to the police one day to tell them what was happening in residential school. They locked me in that police cell and told me I should never lie like that again. I'm really angry."
>
> "I got my anger out after twenty-one years in prison."

Other Survivors were moving inward, toward self-reflection, sometimes self-loathing, while admitting their own wrongdoing. That was when I began to see our TRC gatherings as a kind of confessional for many, including Three-Parts-Patrick. "I was taught to be inferior, so I never really applied myself to the outside world 'cause I always thought the white man was better than me. The reason I wanted to tell a second story is because a lot of us fear to tell about ourselves in public. For me, I'll even feel twice as light as the first time. Eventually, I'll be a lot healthier."

Eventually came a month later, when Patrick spoke to me for the third time, in yet another community. He'd been working up to this, still carrying the heaviest parts of his story, desperate to set them down. "When I lived at residential school, he also taught me to be an abuser. Well, I lived as an abuser. Was it my fault? I don't think so. How do you blame a five-year-old?"

A hush followed that confession: the five-year-old child, raised by an abuser, in training to become another abuser. It was the kind of raw admission that could start to feed on itself. More confessions from others followed:

> "I was sick mentally, emotionally, physically, spiritually. Who taught me to be like that? That was all we saw. We were just kids. How were we supposed to know what was normal?"
>
> "I grew up hating 'you people.' Even my own people. Where were you when Indian Affairs, the Roman Catholic priest, and the United Church minister came? Nobody was there for me."
>
> "We were taught to hate the Anglicans because they were all going to hell."
>
> "I was told my parents didn't want me. I hated being Indian. I hated my parents. I hated their brown faces. I hated the smell of their house. I was ashamed of them."
>
> "I was a very bad drunk. I beat my wife and she left me. Drinking was just a symptom of all the monsters I was carrying—anger, jealousy, fear, gossip—all those ugly things that are in our communities."
>
> "My husband fought with me. I took it out on my children. I beat my children. They went to school like that. I was not there for my kids."
>
> "I didn't care who I hurt. Didn't know how to love anyone else. Didn't know how to love me. I became like they wanted me to be. A human being with no emotions."
>
> "I didn't have any gentleness in my voice to be a father. I didn't know too many 'feeling' words to express myself to my children."

"My strong opinions came with fists and guns. I have to watch my mouth. I have caused people deadly harm with my mouth."

"There's a lot of people out there that got hurt by me. I hurt all the wrong people for all the wrong reasons."

"I still have to live with my actions. What I turned out to be. I am ashamed. I didn't get that parental love. It is hard work trying to learn new ways."

Variations of these haunting stories travelled with us throughout the TRC. Sometimes, in my closing remarks after highly emotional days, I'd mention something picked up from various twelve-step fellowships. This one, in my own words, often seemed just right.

What we live with, we learn.
What we learn, we practise.
What we practise, we become.
What we become, we pass on to our children.

And then I would often add: "What we become is not all that we are." The words always resonated. I said them to recognize and honour that what happened to Survivors as children was not their fault, and to offer hope that things could change, could be different, could be better.

In Saskatchewan, the confessional turned out to be big enough for government and churches, too. Ralph Goodale, a long-time Member of Parliament turned diplomat, was a federal Cabinet minister at the time of our work in his home province. He was one of very few elected leaders who chose to register and give a statement to the Commission, waiting his turn in line in Saskatoon the same as everyone else.

The churches were always more visibly present than government at events, whether national or local gatherings. And what did the church have to say for itself? In Saskatchewan, more than anywhere before, I heard confessions from senior clergy members. On one memorable day, several of them, from Protestant and Roman Catholic traditions, signed up to speak, in the spirit of confession and contrition:

> I am ashamed to know that the institution I am a part of has allowed such harm. A blind eye was turned on people that were doing these things. We, as church, bought the whole assimilation thing. There has been psychological, spiritual, sexual, physical abuse.
>
> We are tied to each other in many ways. I am an ambassador of love and try to live out that love. We list our identity as trying to proclaim that love. And we lost our identity the moment we tried to wipe out yours.
>
> I am a child of Europe. My parents and their parents came here with their own ideas and their own plans and they took over, using their laws, their ideas, their treaties, and their police. They divided up the country and they took it. One of the things they brought was their Bible.
>
> At weddings we always end by saying, "What God has joined, let no one separate." I've come to understand that it is not just husband and wife joined by God, but children also. So, separating of children from parents was a separation of what God had brought together through the mother and father. I have learned that we weren't listening to our own Bible. We were separating what God had brought together.

That was the first confession I had ever heard come out of the mouth of a Catholic priest. It came across as humble, honest, and true, piercing the core of one of the deepest sacraments of the church.

Many Survivors talked about their repeated forced confessions while at residential school, saying they had to make sins up in order to have something to say. They couldn't think of any real thing they had done wrong as little kids, other than the guilt and shame they already felt simply for being who they were. Also, the confessional was not a safe place to talk about wrongs done to them—sometimes it was the person on the other side of the screen who had hurt them.

But unlike typical Catholic confession, this TRC hearing day was not going to dole out penance. Instead, I observed the kind of compassionate listening and connection that I tried to model as a Commissioner, in keeping with the principle of our TRC Mandate "to inspire reconciliation." Survivors exchanged words of forgiveness, recognition, and appreciation—a welcome to the circle. I witnessed all possibilities, sometimes spoken through laughter, with tears streaming down:

> "When children are brought up without their parents, that's where it starts. I think if we can learn to forgive, that is where our healing journey starts."
>
> "I know what was missing for me. My spirit. My spirit was raped. I learned to forgive the people who did this to me. I learned to forgive myself."
>
> "It's a long process. It's not easy. You have to remove the shit from you if you want to deal with forgiveness. You have to wash with good water, the good spirit."
>
> "Our strength lies in the wisdom of our Elders and in the purity and innocence of our children, because they teach us how to forgive. My children melted the hardness of my heart. Today I thank Creator for what they've taught me. I grew up with them."
>
> "A lot of things in my path were my past tripping me up, weighing me down. Today I'm trying to be proud of who I am. I matter in this circle of life. Creator put me here for a reason. With Creator's help, this is who I am now. I think I am a good Mother now. I am a Survivor."

"Youth crave that spirituality, that pride, and that love that comes with our cultures. I want to be part of that generation that goes to work to rebuild our nations. We need help from outside, too."

"I am not perfect. I am not powerful. I am not holy. I am just a man trying to change my life. That's why I'm here today. I am taking over my life again."

"I am proud of residential school Survivors. This is what the residential schools tried to take away from us. The love we have for one another. That is what will bring us together and will see us through these times."

"What is reconciliation for me? It is my story. The hell I went through and the good people I found along the way among the Indian people and among the white people. There are good people on both sides. They are part of my story and they've helped me."

"The drum says we are all one tribe, just different colours. Everybody has a piece of God, a piece of the Great Spirit in us. We are all the same inside. We all have Spirit. We cannot do our healing without our white brothers. We all belong in that circle. No matter what colour we are."

Allegations, admissions, confessions, forgiveness, and redemption—the TRC heard them all throughout this province, revealing great distances already travelled and greater distances still to go under the naked light of Truth. The Saskatchewan National Event and all the community events leading up to it demonstrated over and again that truth-telling could be so much more than digging down into buried personal pains. Truth could also be lifting up collective spirits, sharing strengths and inspirational examples, invoking the Ancestors, and reaching beyond the limitations of the visible.

The chichigun: recalling the spirits of lost children, still loved.
Photo: Tessa Macintosh

PART VI

HUMILITY

QUEBEC

Walk gently on Mother Earth. Treat everyone as your brother and sister, with humility and kindness.

—Elder Dr. David Courchene,
A Story of the Seven Sacred Laws

CHAPTER 12

Embracing the Mother Load

I WILL ALWAYS associate my time in Quebec with motherhood. That is where I was living when I learned I was carrying a child within me.

> *This is the miracle of birth, and of life—that you are you, and there'll never be another. Your place in life is for you alone. No other can walk in the path that is to be yours. Your birth was intense and painful and wonderful. Your life, if at all like mine, will be the same—intense and, by times, painful and, most often, I pray, wonderful. By the time you are old enough to read and understand this, we may be two quite different people, and this may be quite a different world.*

Those words appear in my strained penmanship in a handmade journal Stephen bought for me from one of Quebec's many gifted leather artists. I wrote them for our baby Kyla in 1981, in the drafty little log house just below the Arctic Circle, where we three began our humble family life together in Fort Good Hope, Northwest Territories.

My new home was a perpetually unfolding demonstration of the extraordinary skill, innovation, and Traditional Knowledge that can sustain life despite harsh realities; and the essential nature of interdependence between people and the environment that feeds, clothes, and provides natural travel routes where paved roads are non-existent. Despite the policies of distant governments that ruptured Indigenous families and provided substandard services; despite the impact of southern lobbyists that crushed Indigenous land-based economies; despite the poverty and isolation; despite and above all that, I lived amid the unimaginable kindness and generosity of those who have so little, who have had so much stolen from them, including that most precious of all things—their children.

I was in my thirties when I first became a mother. That's pretty old by Dene norms. My husband was the same age, both of us seen by our families to be marrying late in life for the times. I had wanted this child for years, never had a sliver of doubt about that, yet I remember the immediate feeling when a doctor confirmed what I already knew deep inside—I was pregnant. Dread. I wanted to feel thrilled, but instead, I felt terrified. I realized that the doubt was not about the child. It was about the adults. Was I fit to be a mother? And had Stephen really meant it a couple of months before, when he'd proposed to me? It was on a bus ride between Quebec City and Montreal as we headed to my family's place in southern Ontario for Christmas. It was an excruciatingly convoluted, tentative, even comical marriage proposal, somehow making it all the more tender and authentic. "I was wondering whether, maybe, we should think about, one day, perhaps considering the possibility of eventually getting married," he stammered. It could not have been more humble, unscripted, and hesitant.

Even though he had followed me from Yellowknife to Quebec City as I took up my new role as a national reporter, Stephen had the brakes on back then, uncertain in recognizing his emotions, holding back from trusting in love, in joy, in his self-worth, and even in life itself, the way I have since seen so many Survivors do. But I didn't see things through these eyes back then.

With the hesitancy of that proposal still fresh in my mind, my concerns were practical and immediate. Were we going to make it as a couple? Could I raise this child on my own, if it came to that? Could we be good parents together? Could we raise a child across two cultures and have them feel secure in who they were? Would our families be able to see the whole child? And, most terrifying of all, would the child love me? Would they see me as too different from their dad, not good enough?

At the time, my beloved aunt Lois offered me words of reassurance that I have cherished and passed on to many others over the years, including my own two daughters: "Oh, Marie, there's nothing to worry about. Babies bring their own love with them." Her wisdom echoed in words I'd heard more recently from an Indigenous Elder in Saskatchewan: "The sacred drum awakens our spirit. Our mother's heartbeat is the first drum we hear. When we hear that heartbeat, we feel a sense of belonging. And when a mother hears another heartbeat within her, she feels that sense of being needed."

Gearing up now for our TRC work in Quebec took me back to the province where my baby and I had spent our first intimate months together before her birth, as one body, two hearts. I was touched anew and further changed by the unfolding stories of other mothers, other daughters. This was, after all, the most universal of all residential school Survivor stories, recurring in almost every one of the nearly seven thousand we recorded. It was the story of premature rupture from home, from mother.

This day, a young woman was talking as much to the middle-aged woman sitting beside her as to me, the presiding Commissioner. She spoke first in Algonquin, introducing herself, faltering with the

Indigenous words. Then, with more confidence, she went on in French: "That's about all I know of my language. I don't hold it against my mom for not teaching me my language. I don't know what it was about residential school that made her think she couldn't speak it, or teach it to us, but I don't blame her. It wasn't her fault."

In another town, on another day, there was another daughter, with another message. But this time, it was for a mother who was not so close at hand and never had been.

> As we get older, we don't understand why our mother wasn't able to look after us. You're full of anger and hate. You end up detesting her, becoming prejudiced yourself and self-loathing of being Indian. Because Indians only drink, and you're raised in a white world that has nothing but bad things to say about Indians.
>
> And then at some point, you learn that your mother went to residential school and lived through many things. You stop blaming her. And you forgive. And today I am able to tell my mother that I love her, and I don't blame her for not taking care of us.

As Survivors shared their stories, young people were beginning to see their parents and grandparents in a new light, grasping better than ever before why things were the way they were in their families and communities. Their anger was shifting to understanding about so many things, including language loss, absentee-parenting, and lack of affection. As one Survivor revealed, "When my children were small they used to want to climb up on me and I wouldn't let them. I was afraid to. I didn't know what was right and wrong. When we were kids, we didn't know anything about those things they were doing to us." Childhood sexual abuse had crippled this man's ability to do the most natural of things—hug and hold his children.

Sexual abuse was not limited to male perpetrators; there were also female abusers. In Quebec we heard several Survivors give accounts of childhood sexual abuse by nuns.

On most TRC hearing days, a few clergy from various denominations would be present, usually representative of the church or churches that ran schools in the region where hearings were happening. Typically, their seminaries or theological schools had taught them nothing about their church's history running residential schools and the associated harms. Now, in showing up to listen to Survivors, they were learning stark truths and bearing heavy burdens for what individuals from their Christian traditions had done, or allowed to happen, to generations of children. At one such hearing in Quebec, after repeated accounts of sexual predation, a priest made a statement to the Commission but addressed the heart of it to Survivors. In a voice of quiet outrage and shame, he said: "If I were in your shoes, I don't think I'd like priests or nuns either. What happened to you is unspeakable, unacceptable, vulgar, indecent." I felt his words as a broken lament of betrayal from one who had devoted his life to Christian teachings of goodness, kindness, and love, the same lessons I had learned from many spiritual traditions over the years, including my own Christian upbringing.

In childhood, I always liked this particular Bible reading from Isaiah 11:6: "In that day the wolf and the lamb will live together; the leopard and the goat will be at peace. Calves and yearlings will be safe among lions, and a little child will lead them all." It resonated with me then. I liked this image of the child as the one leading, for a change.

My Commissioner colleague Chief Willie relates even more personally to this particular verse because of his last name—Littlechild. At one of our many lighthearted Commissioner dinners, he told Murray and me that his name had even helped him get elected as a Member of Parliament. In campaign debates, he would get the last word—and the last laugh—by declaring that even the Bible was on his side and quoting, "a little child will lead them all"!

Like today's challenge of reconciliation, that passage describes a new state of being: the coming together of perceived adversaries, the opposing powers of predator and prey, perpetrator and victim, in harmonious coexistence. From the earliest days of the TRC, we talked about reconciliation as being about respect. I often added that reconciliation also means change. How else to upend the current state of inequity? And from there, reconciliation also means peace. Peace in the hearts of individuals, peace in families, communities, country. Peace not as the opposite of war but as the opposite of social dysfunction, cultural disintegration, and spiritual collapse. And, always, with children at the centre, showing the way, leading us all.

When does a child become an adult? Throughout the Commission, I met adults, even Elders, who recalled still-vivid memories of their unresolved childhoods. As one Survivor said, "My inner child did not grow up. I grew up physically but not emotionally and spiritually. My outside body grew up but not the rest of me." Yet here they were now, leading the way for Canada: fighting through the courts to get a Truth and Reconciliation Commission and forcing adversarial churches and government to sit together with them, to hear them. Little children leading them all …

And when does a child lose their childhood, prematurely forced into adulthood? Is it at the moment of separation from everyone known to them? Of brutal, humiliating punishment? Of lock-up? Of rape? As we heard multiple times, such moments leave the child feeling outside of themselves and outside of the circle of any adult protectors, physically and emotionally on their own, physical and sexual prey to adults. Or is it when the child is forced to take on the role of protector-provider-comforter for those who are even more vulnerable? We witnessed accounts of this happening both at residential school and at home, in families that fell apart after children were taken away. In all my TRC memories, these recollections of children being forced into ill-prepared adulthood are among the most haunting.

Like the time in a Quebec school when little girls were left holding a dying classmate through her final moments, in the absence of any attentive adult:

> She was only eight years old. Handicapped. We protected her. Treated her as our baby. Dressed her up. Brushed her teeth. Combed her hair. To us, she was beautiful. Our little doll. One night, she was sick. I sang to her a little lullaby that Grandma used to sing to us 'til she fell back asleep. She had a fever. I knew there was something wrong. We wrapped her with her teddy bear like a baby. One girl ran downstairs to get the nurse. I sat on a chair and sang to her. I felt underneath, she was wetting herself. I think she's dying ...
>
> How long we waited! By the time she came, she had her nurse uniform on! Took her shower, makeup, and everything! When they took her down and put her in the ambulance, that's the last I saw of her. When they brought the body back near the church, they wouldn't let us see. We thought it was just lies. Her own parents didn't know in time. Only five people were there when we buried her. I went to get the little purple sweater she liked and her teddy bear to put into the grave with her. Even to this day I think about her little plate sitting there with just a number on it.
>
> A few years back, when we tore down the school, I told her dad, "I was the last one to hold your baby." He started kissing my hand ...

I clearly remember the aftermath of that story. Commissioner Littlechild and I were taken to the grounds of La Tuque Indian

Residential School, along with our Quebec Survivors Committee member, Madeleine Basile. Standing in a tight circle, a Traditional Knowledge Keeper from the health support team led us in a prayer of remembrance for all the children we had heard about who had died in this and other residential schools. In that moment, I was overtaken by the overwhelming sensation of little children clambering up my legs. I grabbed Willie's arm to steady myself. I was on the verge of tears and quietly confided in him that I'd just had the strangest feeling of the presence of children.

The sensation was so real, but it also sounded so incredible that I was hesitant to talk about it. That night, on the lengthy drive back to Quebec City after the La Tuque hearings, I took Chief Littlechild up on his offer from nearly two years before, when he'd told me I could always ask him anything about his cultural teachings. I asked Willie whether he thought the feeling of invisible children climbing up my legs while we were in the prayer circle was a product of my imagination after a very emotional day. Did he know whether this kind of thing could actually happen? And if so, could it happen to me as a non-Indigenous person? And if it was real, what was I supposed to do with it?

In his usual way, Willie did not jump to answer, but when he did, he was clear, undoubting, and highly respectful. "Yes, that kind of thing does happen," he said. "It can happen to anyone—but it doesn't happen to just everyone. It happened to you for some reason. They might be asking you for something. Maybe you have to wait and keep listening for that."

Then I told him about something I called "deep remembering." "When I hear these Survivor stories, it's the strangest feeling," I told him. "With every single hearing, I'm learning something new, but also, it's like I'm remembering something old. Deep remembering."

Recognizing Willie both as my fellow Commissioner and as a

Survivor, I said this almost apologetically, because I had never been to residential school and had not experienced the particular traumas associated with that. But even so, that feeling of familiarity kept coming back.

Sometimes, it was an account of sexual abuse—and I began to remember the secrets of my own early childhood. Sometimes, it was an account of mean teachers who would deny a child permission to go to the bathroom—and I suddenly remembered the hot humiliation of wetting my eleven-year-old self in a bright turquoise dress during a so-called enrichment class for gifted students. Sometimes, it was an account of being locked in a room or a dark closet or a cage or a prison cell and tapping on the pipes to see if anyone would answer—and I remembered the loneliness and terror of being quarantined with whooping cough: chest-ripping coughs becoming soundless gasps for air; throwing myself onto the floor in the middle of long dark nights, hoping someone would hear the thud of my six-year-old body and come save me.

That day in Quebec, it had been this experience of sensing children at the edges of my reach, an acute awareness of the invisible—and I flashed back to other moments of precious mystery in early memories with my two daughters.

Little Kyla and I peeked over the edge of the canvas blanket-swing hanging above our bed, just within my reach to rock and reassure. The traditional Dene crib held her new baby sister, Daylyn, just days old and sound asleep. In navigating new territory as a mother of two—thinking I could shield the older child from jealousy at the arrival of their first sibling—to make plain I was still fully on her side, I joked, "What the heck is wrong with that new baby anyway? Doesn't she know we want her to wake up so we can see her and get to know her?"

But my first-born did not smile or laugh to show she was in on the joke. Instead, this precocious little speaker said, "Mommy, she's just brand new at being alive in this world. Maybe she's just keeping her eyes closed 'til she decides whether she likes it or not." That wise child of mine—not yet five years old! Did she still remember something I had forgotten, recognizing the baby as a new life not yet fully landed from another plane of awareness, that place my Celtic ancestors refer to as "the thin veil" between worlds, a meeting place of the Ancestors?

Almost a year later, the baby sister uttered what I still think of as her own recognition across that thin veil. Daylyn was just beginning to talk. One day, she was perched in my arms, her tiny familiar heart beating next to mine. She was staring intently at an enlarged photograph on our kitchen wall of Dene women Elders dressed in vibrant shades of blue and red. The style and variety of moccasins in the picture could have filled a museum case; the wrinkles told a combined storyline of at least five centuries. They were grandmothers and great-grandmothers, perhaps even some great-greats. Yet this baby girl of mine pointed her tiny finger at them and said, "Babies."

She looked back at me. Was it for reassurance? To make sure I was listening? To teach me? She repeated, "Babies."

I have so many times wondered what she saw in that photo that I could not. What did she still remember, being so much closer to the source of life from which she had only recently travelled? Did she already understand, or had she not yet forgotten, what some of the world's oldest wisdom traditions teach? That we are all spirit. That we are all timeless, ageless, interrelated souls. That our essence gets passed down and around and across the generations. That we are all part of a much grander creation. Was this earlier moment another example of a little child leading me to a different kind of deep remembering? The TRC would soon offer me more mystical moments for such pondering.

Women were often in the lead at TRC hearings. Generally, they formed the core of their community organizing committees. Women often led opening and closing prayers. They made up the majority of those providing healing and cultural supports. They did most of the translations. Women were often the first to speak at a hearing, inspiring others to speak also, including many who had not originally intended to. Perhaps, as mothers and grandmothers, they felt most profoundly the early separation of mother and child that was at the heart of so much of the damage caused by residential schools. The statements we received, especially from women, whether old or young, a Survivor or one of the many intergenerational Survivors, almost always involved the severing, abandonment, and anguish of the parent-child breakdown:

> "Why did I lose my kids? Because alcohol came first. When my kids were taken away was the saddest time of my life! I am what I am today. What I was yesterday is a different story."
>
> "I never felt good enough as a young girl. All I ever wanted was a hug from my dad. I used to buy food and alcohol so people would hang around me so I wouldn't be alone. I never understood why he left me alone all the time. I can't imagine what they did to him to make him think he couldn't love his own child. I always thought it was my fault."
>
> "This epidemic, or genocide, or whatever they call it, it affects all of us. Sometimes you don't realize you can live a better life, because you don't know how."

Survivors didn't need their children or anyone else to point out their failings. They already blamed themselves harshly for devastating harms to their children, including, for some, losses they could never reclaim: "I killed my daughter with suicide." In the category of Survivor regrets, this truly was the biggest one—the regret of not knowing how to be a good parent and not being there for children who needed them, with dire consequences.

I try not to cling to my own regrets. With the blessing of time, I can no longer remember many things I have felt sorry about from my past. But I suspect the ones that stick with you are those where you missed the point altogether. Missed the moment. Momentous regrets. I carry one of these from the earliest days of the TRC.

In those days, I was sidetracked by a pervasive worry that I, as the one non-Indigenous Commissioner, would be seen and treated as the unwelcome face of the perpetrators, the government and church people who designed and ran residential schools, who, like me, were almost all descendents of European settlers to North America. As the lone female, I was especially sensitive to being associated specifically with Survivor memories of bad treatment from nuns. This remained a major apprehension and blind spot on my part, until we actually got to the hearings, where Survivors consistently treated me with generosity, kindness, and appreciation. The shame I had taken on was my own doing, bred from the prevailing attitudes and realities of my upbringing, especially toward women.

I grew up as the feisty little sister to two big brothers in a male-dominated family and world, where every mother I knew did more than her fair share of the drudge work on the home front and daughters were groomed to do the same. When I began working as a young professional, women became the silent secretary at every formal or informal meeting, while men made all the decisions and got the bigger pay, perks, promotions, profile, and credit. Women were still losing jobs for being married or becoming pregnant. Maternity benefits did not exist in most workplaces (much less paternity or family benefits). I spent seven months on strike with other Radio-Canada journalists for that hard-fought benefit. We were successful in a historic win, but because of the lengthy strike, I'd been off work for too long to qualify! As things slowly began to shift, I spent much of my professional life as the first or only woman in my various roles.

As a result of such personal experiences, I resisted any whiff of being forced into the back seat. And that's what I thought I was hearing from my male TRC colleagues in the flush of our first days together as a three-person Commissioner team.

We were in Ottawa, sauntering back to the office, still in the getting-to-know-each-other phase on that sunny day. The conversation over lunch had been light, sharing details of our families and backgrounds, and setting the standard for what was to become a norm for most of our times together—easy laughter and teasing. I grew up with plenty of that from my dad and have often been told I inherited his sense of humour and fun, but I can also be deadly serious and hypersensitive. Sometimes, the wrong trait kicks in.

Walking down the street, the two men in front, me slightly behind, I had just reminded them about an afternoon commitment. Murray said lightheartedly over his shoulder, "You're just like our mother. You look after us!"

"Yeah, that's right," Willie added with a smile.

Without a second's hesitation I said, "Oh no I'm not! You're big boys. You can look after yourselves. I'm not your mother. I can be your sister, but I'm not going to be your mother."

It was a significant misread on my part that led to one huge trip-up and, even worse, a missed blessing, which I still regret to this day, perhaps my only TRC regret.

Murray filled the awkward pause that followed with generosity. "In our ways, to call you our mother is giving you the greatest compliment. It's an honour."

In the years that followed, I have had so many reasons to reconsider the meaning of motherhood. I have been fortunate to have that honour bestowed on me again, and even to have it conveyed in ceremony.

In March 2013, I was presiding at community statement-gathering in Chisasibi—meaning "great river" in Cree—the largest community in the Eeyou Istchee homeland of northern Quebec. In 1981, the community relocated, redesigned, and renamed itself after the massive James Bay hydroelectric project threatened the old community of Fort George with flooding. The move was controversial, partly because of those who were left behind.

This day demonstrated that the memory of beloved children lingers long after their passing. Survivor statements included accounts and remembrances related to sixteen or more children who had died at the Catholic and Anglican residences associated with old Fort George schools. Survivors were concerned for the children buried in cemeteries at the old site. What if erosion continued? What about flood risk? Would the spirits of those children ever be free?

As always, we had set out two empty chairs to symbolize, honour, and remember the thousands of children who never returned from residential school. The final speaker told us that this day's hearings had helped her make sense of a recent dream where she was trying to bring little figures forward out of a grey zone and into the light. "I knew I wouldn't be able to because I was alone," she said. "I bought this rattle a while back, and when I saw the two chairs, I was drawn to them. We need to claim these children. We need to bring them home. They need to hear the chichigun. I need the mothers to come forward to help me, because they want to come home, and they need that rattle. I know they are coming."

I'll never forget what happened next. I was taken by the hand from the Commissioners' table and surrounded by the women of this community. In an instant, by some invisible cue, long withheld tears from the depths of grief overflowed from every direction against a backdrop of relentless rattling, shaking the entire room alert. Shaking me, as I received and held the most precious gift—that special rattle. The chichigun. That's the Cree word for it.

There is a similar Dene rattle called a bebí gogwa. I cherish the ones my three children held as babies, their tight little grasp on comfort and entertainment. Traditionally, rattles are made from dried and stretched animal skin, sewn tightly into a miniature, drum-like pouch to contain dried seeds. The pouch is attached to a whittled, wooden handle that's sometimes straight, sometimes rounded at the bottom for easier holding. The one gifted to me in Chisasibi is more beautifully decorated than any other I have ever seen. Both sides of the rattle head show a painted, black wild goose in flight, encircled in red. Babiche leather strings intertwine down and around the handle through pierced holes, weaving a design of seven diamonds, also painted red. They remind me of the seven sacred teachings the TRC followed as our themes for National Events, making this gift all the more meaningful.

Traditional rattles are not just used for babies but also in sacred ceremonies. This chichigun was for both. I'd experienced various gestures of gratitude at other gatherings, but this ceremony went well beyond thanking and honouring me as a Commissioner. I was acknowledged as a woman and a mother and a grandmother—just as I had been with that white eagle feather three years earlier in northern Manitoba. I felt like I was being recommissioned by this communal embrace of women—of mothers. It was a ceremony that immersed the entire room in decades of pent-up loss and immersed me fully into my own womanhood. The rattle wasn't really being *given* to me so much as I was being entrusted with it—with an instruction to keep it with me throughout my work, so that the missing children would know they were not forgotten, and so that their spirits could be released to find their way home.

From that day forward, I took the chichigun with me to every community and national gathering I attended through to the official end of my role as a Commissioner. It still travels with me. As I have been instructed by Elders, it will one day be conveyed to my first-born daughter—the baby who first heard my heartbeat in Quebec. She understands the rattle will one day be hers to carry forward. My chichigun—the children's chichigun—is still doing its work to help call out and bring home the ones who are still missing.

CHAPTER 13

Be Here Now

DECADES OF MY personal history reside in Quebec. As a teen, my first solo adventure away from my southern Ontario home was an exchange trip to Montreal to practise my newly learned French. At twenty, my younger brother and I ventured out hitchhiking and hostelling eastward to the Gaspé Peninsula. In my mid-twenties, I spent several weeks of a field placement there during my masters in journalism program. By my early thirties, I was covering the historic Quebec referendum on sovereignty-association—and then was immediately on a journalists' strike in the longest labour disruption in the history of Canada's national public broadcaster. I got through that strike with a magazine job in Premier René Lévesque's Aboriginal Affairs Secretariat, which took me to Indigenous communities throughout the province. Most significant of all, far away from both our family homes, Stephen and I got married in Quebec, formalizing a union that would forever redefine, challenge, and enrich everything that has followed.

All those experiences were possible because of undergraduate studies in French language and literature, which equipped me with French fluency and basic knowledge of Quebec society. As an anglophone student, raised Protestant, studying Quebec had seemed like learning about another country. You really couldn't talk about Quebec without talking about the *French* language and the *Catholic* Church. The unique, intertwined, and interdependent relationship between language and church has shaped the place. Historically, the Church's firm grasp was also bound up with government, as it was in charge of most provincial schools and many hospitals. In large Catholic families it was common for a son to be promised into the priesthood and a daughter committed to become a nun, a practice that constantly renewed the bench strength of the dominant religious institution. The Quiet Revolution of the 1960s finally dislodged the official grip of the Roman Catholic Church, clearing the way for state-run services and a more secular society. Things were still evolving when I moved to Quebec two decades later. Now, thirty years later still, I made new memories of this province in the months leading up to the fifth National Event of the Truth and Reconciliation Commission.

If any part of Canada has repeatedly claimed it has been put down by others, treated as inferior, and historically misunderstood, it is surely Quebec. But now, with the previously hidden horrors of residential schools emerging, the theme of our next TRC National Event would be a hard pill for Quebec and all Canadians to swallow: Humility.

Quebec has always seen itself as distinct from the rest of the country by the overwhelming fact of its unique history, language, culture, and majority francophone population. Quebec political voices have continually advocated for distinct recognition internationally and at home, where parts of this country have not easily valued or acknowledged a unique status for Quebec within the federation. Such beliefs have twice led to a formal referendum vote on a kind of internal separation from Canada.

But our TRC work would not be shedding any new light on Quebec as some kind of national, cultural underdog. Hidden within the provincial shadows was a very different story of cultural aggressor. Quebec's most powerful religious institution, the Roman Catholic Church, through its prominent role in the residential school system, attacked the language and culture of thousands of Indigenous children, both within this province and in all other parts of Canada. This would come as a painful surprise to many Quebeckers. Canadians, generally, had been unaware of residential school history before the TRC. But based on surveys conducted before we got going, Quebec citizens, in particular, had the lowest level of public awareness of any jurisdiction in the country. I recall conversations with otherwise well-informed people that began with "But we didn't have any residential schools here, did we?"—expressing that universal longing to see oneself on the right side of history. This was further evidence of how much Canadian history had never been taught, and the remedial education that would be needed in schools throughout the land.

The majority of residential schools in Canada—about 65 percent—were run by various entities of the Roman Catholic Church, most of them headquartered in Quebec. French was the dominant language of those Catholic institutions, and language became a weapon of church clergy and staff who ran the schools. Killing Indigenous languages was an intentional strategy for killing the transfer of cultural teachings and ties to family. Depending on the school, the times, and the teachers, both carrot and stick strategies were used for the kill.

From Survivors, we heard multiple examples of the stick: hot peppers on tongues, soap in mouths, pins through tongues, wooden blocks in mouths, strappings, severe beatings, and lock-ups. The carrot approach was something else: children were rewarded for *not* speaking their Indigenous languages. Each child got a certain number of chits or tokens to start, and the goal was to get more by calling out any classmate using Indigenous words and then confiscating their chits. The prize went to the winner with the most chits. Indigenous children were the innocent pawns in this game, set up to turn on each other, and, in the process, become unknowing accomplices in the destruction of their own mother tongues.

In most parts of Canada outside Quebec, the language imposed by residential schools was English. But in Catholic-run schools, the teachers were often francophones, speaking English only as a second language with varying degrees of proficiency. In many remote communities today, the language impact of residential schools is still obvious. The dramatic decline of Indigenous language fluency is well documented, but less often noted is the linguistic legacy of broken English. Anyone fluent in both languages might easily detect, as I can, that French-language phrasing is often superimposed awkwardly onto English.

As we teach our children to talk, we think of language as a tool of communication and education. But many residential school children experienced language as both an excuse for, and the voice of, punishment and abuse. Several Survivors told us that even the sound of French is a trigger for negative memories and emotions. They associate French with secrets, severe discipline, and a range of insults: "petit sauvage," "maudit sauvage," "sale petite," "petit vaurien." All over the country, we heard Survivor accounts of language abuse within the wider range of school abuses:

> "If you got caught talking Cree, you got whipped on the head and back. I still have headaches and deafness on the left side."
>
> "I can still hear my language in my mind, but if I try to speak it, my throat seizes up, just waiting for that hit across the back of the head."

"It damaged our thinking about our language. My husband and I worked hard to make sure our children did not speak Cree."

Within Quebec, the predominant language imposed in residential schools was French, and it was at least taught by French-language speakers. But that has left a different kind of harmful legacy: linguistic isolation. French has had the same devastating impact on Indigenous languages within Quebec as English has had in other parts of the country. But those Survivors now fluent *only* in French have also been cut off from easy communication with Indigenous neighbours, family, and colleagues who speak English in northern regions of this province, throughout Canada, and beyond. Over the years, I've witnessed how French-speaking Indigenous voices have been diminished, or even lost, in national conversations. In the nearly seven decades that national Indigenous organizations have existed in Canada, only once has a francophone leader from Quebec been elected to lead one of them for a brief interim period. I sometimes wonder if there is any group of Indigenous people in North America as lonely as those now left with French as their only language.

One Survivor's story I witnessed at TRC hearings in Val-d'Or was a worst-case language scenario: "Our family is Cree. As little children, we learned Cree. Residential school changed all that. My brother was sent to school in Amos, Quebec. He learned French. I was sent to Brantford, Ontario, to the Mohawk Institute. I learned English. When we came home after school, we had both forgotten Cree. I couldn't talk to my brother in French. He couldn't talk to me in English. We couldn't understand our grandparents, and we couldn't talk to each other." The phrase *two solitudes* took on a whole new meaning as I imagined the tragic divide between those two brothers.

In 1945, Hugh MacLennan wrote the novel *Two Solitudes* about the perceived lack of communication between English- and French-speaking Canadians, but the work of our TRC made it increasingly clear that residential schools had also forced divisions and ruptures at the most basic level of the family and across society. In a 2012 honorary lecture named for Madame Jeanne Sauvé, an inspirational journalist, parliamentarian, and Canada's first woman Governor General, I addressed that unspoken divide: "We must be honest about the real two solitudes in this country—between Indigenous and non-Indigenous citizens—and commit to doing tangible things to close the divide in awareness, understanding, opportunity, and relationship."

Here in Quebec, the National Event theme and ancient teaching of Humility helped illuminate the enormous challenge still before us in this country: reconciliation between the real two solitudes in Canada.

~

One of the oldest Survivors we heard from in the lead-up to the fifth National Event was ninety-eight years old. Well aware of her advanced age, she said she wanted to talk to the TRC before she left this earthly life. Fragile yet coherent, Suzanne Brazeau of Val-d'Or described, through a translator, her residential school regrets—not for herself but for her grandchildren. She said, "I look at my grandchildren. I don't understand them and they don't understand me. It makes me so sad that they don't know our language and our legends."

A younger woman sitting beside her, propping her up, punctuated the Elder's powerful words with her own: "My mother is my library."

How far is the library of a beloved Elder's teachings from a Canadian school library of errors and omissions? How far do residential school lived experiences of racism, humiliation, brutality, and loss stray from public school lessons about the history of race relations?

Our TRC Mandate included educating the people of Canada to fill in wide gaps in knowledge and understanding. With the fixed five-year term of our TRC, we had no time to lose in pointing out the past role and current responsibilities of schools and other educational institutions. I saw no point in sugar-coating the situation and preferred to hit the nail on the head with plain language I repeated early and often: "Education got us into this mess, and education is what's going to get us out of it."

We'd first met with the federal Council of Ministers of Education two years before to hammer this point home, challenging them to do better. We were advocating for the history and legacy of residential schools to become mandatory learning for every student, Indigenous and non-Indigenous. School policies and practices are distinct in each of the ten provinces and three territories, and their facilities, standards, and curricula are inconsistent. We met with the Council several more times over the life of the Commission, and each time more than half the ministers present were new to their education portfolios. We saw how a change in government, or a shuffle of ministers and departments, could stall and sometimes even derail momentum toward our new curriculum target. This underscored the need for consistent and determined political leadership for the work ahead. But beyond those in charge of the school systems, we also kept reaching out directly to the students.

Education Days were a big part of TRC National Events. With curriculum changes not yet in place in most schools, we brought students together to learn from our events. We had invaluable help from international practitioners in designing age-appropriate activities for young people. When we started in 2009 as the world's newest Truth Commission, one of the first offers of help we received was from the International Center for Transitional Justice, a kind of centralized brain trust based in New York for truth and memory initiatives globally.

They already had particular experience and expertise working with young people in post-conflict settings. I was the Commissioner tagged to work with them, along with a representative from our Survivors Committee, as they led two pilot workshops on our East and West Coasts, refining what would become our program for youth at our National Events. Charlene Bearhead, an educator from Alberta with far-reaching networks, later took on our TRC educational outreach with schools throughout the country. We knew that hearing directly from a wide range of students would be important for drawing our TRC conclusions in the area of education.

Always, TRC Education Day events brought together Indigenous and non-Indigenous students. For many, this was their first opportunity to gather and learn together about things that neither group had been taught in school. Most, including many Indigenous kids, had never learned them at home either. Always, these students and their teachers had prepared for the day with background materials we provided. Always, they had an opportunity to meet and hear first-hand from residential school Survivors and to experience cultural activities. Always, as the selected delegates from their schools, they came with a pledge to return and share with their classmates what they had learned. And always, before heading home, they had a chance to raise their questions, concerns, and expectations with what we called a panel of "adult listeners."

Different people made up the Education Day panel at each National Event, but each panel shared the same range of perspectives: an elected official or executive from a Ministry of Education, college, university, or educational foundation; someone with an operational leadership role in education, such as a superintendent or school principal; and an advocate for youth, education, and learning. The Right Honourable Michaëlle Jean—our very first TRC Honorary Witness—was that person at the Montreal Education Day panel. After serving as Governor General of Canada, she established a foundation in her name to use the arts for the ongoing education and well-being of youth. The final member and chair of the Education Day panel was always a TRC Commissioner. I did several, including the one in Montreal. The purpose of the panel was to listen, not to give speeches, and then to respond to what we heard with our commitments. Mine, on behalf of the TRC, was always the same—we would use what the youth told us in our conclusions and eventual Calls to Action related to education.

On this Education Day, close to a thousand teenagers packed the large, crowded hall at the Queen Elizabeth hotel in Montreal for the wrap-up panel session. That's where I witnessed the clearest challenge I'd ever heard to schools and educators. An articulate, outraged student declared, "You have taught us about the American civil rights movement. You have taught us about apartheid in South Africa. You have taught us about the Middle East, and the conflicts between Arabs and Jews. And in Northern Ireland, about the conflicts between Catholics and Protestants. You have taught us about the Holocaust and the wars in Europe and other parts of the world. But you have not taught us the truth about our own country!"

This challenge to do more, to do differently, to do better would have to reach beyond educators to politicians more widely. Schools are bound by laws, policies, and directives, and politically imposed budgets. We began to reach out more to federal leadership to drive home the point that reconciliation must be understood as a non-partisan issue. If ever there was a change in government, we needed confirmation that each party would honour ongoing reconciliation. That was the commitment the government and all national leaders had made in the House of Commons on June 11, 2008, when they publicly apologized to residential school Survivors and their families on behalf of each of their political parties. But as with territorial and provincial ministers of education, federal party leadership changes, too, and all parties had installed new leaders since those 2008 apologies were made. We needed them to honour those earlier vows.

The Commissioners met with Liberal and New Democrat Members of Parliament. We wanted to meet with Prime Minister Stephen Harper and his Conservative team too. He had given the 2008 official apology on behalf of the government and all the people of Canada, but it was widely understood that he had been legally bound to give that apology. Was it sincere? Our request to meet was never granted—neither with him as PM nor with his party caucus. A few Conservatives from the Senate of Canada did meet with us, but it was thanks to our personal connections as much as to their party. With recent federal funding cuts to long-term healing supports, including the Aboriginal Healing Foundation (AHF), our TRC, halfway through our Mandate, was now operating against a backdrop of growing cynicism about the sincerity of political goodwill. This was an early indicator that our eventual TRC conclusions would have to target and rely on more than just government support to ensure meaningful changes for the long term. Beyond educators, beyond politicians, we needed to keep reaching out to all sectors of society.

Ironically, the wider challenge to all Canadians did come from a former politician—Montreal's Paul Martin, former prime minister of Canada. The Right Honourable Mr. Martin was also highly regarded in the business world, and through his family-named initiative to support education and well-being in Indigenous communities, with its particular focus on growing financial and economic capacity. He was at this National Event to become a TRC Honorary Witness.

Mr. Martin said something that day that still stands out for me, and I've heard him say variations of it since: that for far too many years we have acted as if Canada is a European country imported from across the ocean and just a few hundred years old, rather than a place where other societies had already been living continually, in ancient civilizations, for tens of thousands of years before Europeans ever set foot on this continent. Such a powerful statement of humility from a man who once led the people of Canada—the people he was now challenging to see the country in a humbler light.

The variety of Honorary Witnesses introduced in Montreal exemplified the increasingly wide range of people pledging solidarity with the TRC and the ongoing work of reconciliation. Their ranks included NHL star Joé Juneau, former auditor-general of Canada Sheila Fraser, and Alanis Obomsawin, one of the most prolific, revered, and honoured filmmakers in Canadian history. This Abenaki superstar began her rich career as a storyteller and performance artist, model, and singer. Alanis knew about residential schools from her own family and community, and from her life's work of documenting such stories. She bore witness not in words but in song from her own traditions. She sang the Survivors a lullaby, rocking them with her voice, embracing the whole room. It was a song for all the years of lullabies never heard, to soothe childhood memories of tormented nights and to restore years of withheld nurturing.

On the road to healing and reconciliation, Alanis's song was also a challenge to Survivors. She challenged them to look back and take care of the wounds of childhood, to move past the shame and limitations of its secrets, but not to be lulled forever into the familiarity of its saddest songs. To wake up, restored and re-energized into the present, gathering strength, knowing that new songs are being written every day. And to look forward to the hopeful songs of the future.

The challenge of not getting stuck in the past is no small thing for residential school Survivors. Even those celebrating how far they have come in their healing often told us how fragile that is—how quickly they can be triggered by a food, a language, a smell; the sound of a shoe, a shower, a shout; the sight of a church, a long hallway, an EXIT sign.

Even commemoration projects, however well intentioned, can come with triggers. The commemoration project at the National Event in Montreal was a travelling exhibit about the residential school experience in Quebec, developed by a team at the stunning Indigenous museum and hotel complex in Wendake. It filled an entire conference room with interactive elements and multiple displays, including residential school hockey memorabilia. That was enough to grab the interest of Commissioner Littlechild. We had time to check it out during a break in the hearings, but once we got past the hockey display, another showcase tripped Willie up. It was a miniature replica of a residential school dormitory.

He stopped, he stared, he froze. And then, pointing, he said: "That's where my bed was, right along that wall, just by the window. And that was my friend's. That's his bedroll, all rolled up, just how it looked after he left. He was gone—we didn't know where. He never came back. We never saw him again."

I reached over, took his hand, and said, "Willie, look at me. You are not there anymore. You are right here, and so am I. I am right here beside you. You are not alone. Be here now."

Nothing more was said. Nothing more was needed. Willie the Survivor resumed his public role as Commissioner. But at the National Event closing, Commissioner Littlechild came back to that moment. I heard him talking about me in Cree—I recognized my spirit name. Afterwards, he told me it was a prayer of special thanks to me for help when he needed it.

Survivors throughout Quebec had offered countless examples of being there for each other, to help, to inspire:

> "We cannot change or touch what's in the past, but we have to understand it, to know why we are this way, and where we're going. Today we are going forward."
>
> "Vivez pas votre vie en arrière. Prends qu'est-ce qu'il y a de bon et fais ton chemin." [Don't live your life in the past. Take the good from it and make your way forward—move on.]
>
> "We were children. Now let's be heroes. Let's not let the government put us down anymore. Let's stand up for our rights and our freedom. We are not free until we let go of all the hurt and suffering that we went through in those schools."

The theme of Humility loomed large over the landscape of Quebec and all the regions before. A national picture was slowly coming into focus: That we create deep and lasting problems for ourselves when we act as if one group of people knows what's best for another group of people and their children. That both English and French have been used as weapons to destroy Indigenous languages and cultures. That high rates of addiction, mental illness, suicide, and missing people, especially women, are outcomes of residential school experiences and continuing traumas of separating children from parents. That there is great potential to worsen relations between Indigenous and non-Indigenous peoples by doing nothing or little in response to real harms and needs that Survivors have described. That Indigenous people want to believe that Canada hears them and cares enough to want to do something about it. That most Canadians who learn about the schools, including children, share a sense of outrage at what happened, are upset at not being told about it sooner, and genuinely want to help set things right. That schools, and all institutions of learning, have a huge role to play to redress the situation. That the human capacity for resiliency is enormous, given opportunity and circumstances. That

Indigenous pride and return to spiritual practices continues to grow. That individual acts of kindness, caring, and respect can and do make a positive difference. That Indigenous capacity for forgiveness is almost beyond belief. That reconciliation will take time. That there is emerging hope that things can get better.

I heard that resiliency and hope in the words of so many Survivors in Quebec:

> "Before residential school I was happily riding around on my dad's shoulders. I see where the schools have left us today. Still, we are strong. We are an extremely strong people."
>
> "I started not living in the past. I'm doing okay. I'm helping people too. We have to show more love to each other, respect each other. To tell each other we are proud. I am proud of you for what you are doing."
>
> "We are all on the path to healing."

The many highlights of the Quebec hearings and National Event had sharpened my insights into distinct challenges to educators, politicians, Canadians, Survivors—and to me. With heightened awareness of the importance of my role as a mother and a friend, and as ever more details of our national travesty unfolded, that was the other challenge that came from Quebec—to keep looking. I needed to face up squarely to the facts of what has happened in this country. We all do. The flame of Humility compels us.

As the TRC prepared to move on from Quebec, a society and landscape so historically dominated by church steeples and cathedral spires, I wondered how this place will want to be recognized in the coming years. How our work here might reshape the look and feel of things. I had heard both churchgoers and church leaders lament their own history. Their buildings still dot the landscape and dominate the skyline of most communities, but here and elsewhere, many sit increasingly empty. I have seen former churches converted to bingo halls and condominiums. Things are inevitably changing at the level of bricks and mortar. But I also remembered a moment from the opening sacred fire of this National Event. At one point, I had looked up and noticed eagles flying high above the tallest turrets. I left Montreal wondering what different kind of markers could be imagined by humble, hopeful, healing communities. Perhaps something more spirit-filled and enduring for the new horizons ahead.

The Bentwood Box: carved to honour Survivors; designed to inspire Expressions of Reconciliation. Carver: Luke Marston; Photo: Fred Cattroll

PART VII

HONESTY

BRITISH COLUMBIA

As you work to live a good life, always be honest with yourself and others. To be honest is to speak from your heart. Be honest with who you are and whatever you speak, but make sure your words show kindness.

—Elder Dr. David Courchene,
A Story of the Seven Sacred Laws

New moccasins, with colour and light to guide a Commissioner's steps, a special gift for the TRC journey from artist, friend, and Survivor Denise McDonald. Photo: Tessa Macintosh

Marie and Stephen, finding our way as a young couple. Family Album

Three children, the little blessings of our marriage: Daylyn, Keenan, and Kyla. Photo: Marie Wilson

Northern grandmothers, the heart of families and communities across time. Photo: Bob Landy

Four grandchildren to feed all our hopes: Maslyn, Ry'den, "Mimi," Tydzeh, and Sadeya. Photo: Kyla Kakfwi Scott

My fortune in family: Marie and Stephen with three adult children, two sons-in-law, and four grandchildren. Photo: Tessa Macintosh

CBC host Marie Wilson preps northern Canada's first live TV election with producer John Ridge and co-host Whit Fraser, 1983. Family Album

A lifting-up ceremony to humble and strengthen Commissioners Wilson, Sinclair, and Littlechild. AFN National Chief Phil Fontaine has our backs. July 3, 2009. Family Album

First gathering of the TRC Survivors Committee at the opening event, *Witnessing the Future*. Back row: John Banksland, John Morrisseau, Doris Young, Lottie May Johnson, Rebekah Uki Williams, Gordon Williams, Eugene "Big Bird" Arcand. Front row: Barney Williams, Commissioner Wilson, Chair Sinclair, the Right Honourable Michaëlle Jean, Commissioner Littlechild, Terri Brown. Photo: Fred Cattroll

TRC Commissioners induct the first TRC Honorary Witness, the Right Honourable Michaëlle Jean, Rideau Hall, October 15, 2009. Photo: Fred Cattroll

TRC Honorary Witnesses at the Alberta National Event, 2014. Robbie Waisman (Holocaust survivor), David Langtry (human rights commissioner), Joe Clark (former prime minister), TRC Commissioners Littlechild and Wilson, Jane Middelton-Moz (therapist, author), David Tuccaro (business leader), Bill Elliot (mayor), Jim Gladstone (lawyer, rodeo champion), Mary Simon (Inuit leader), Evan Adams (medical doctor, actor). Credit: NCTR

Commissioners Wilson, Littlechild, and Sinclair at Expression of Reconciliation ceremony with a guitar painted by Métis visual artist and author Christi Belcourt, 2015. Photo: Fred Cattroll

Northwest Territories offers adult moccasins as an Expression of Reconciliation to mark the completion of the first accredited Indian residential schools curriculum in Canada, mandatory for all students for high school graduation, 2015. Commissioner Wilson, NWT Education Minister Jackson Lafferty, Commissioner Littlechild, Survivor Committee members John Banksland and Madeleine Basile. Photo: Fred Cattroll

Elder and Survivor Committee member Barney Williams carrying the TRC eagle staff in a ceremonial grand entry processional. Credit: NCTR

Elder and Survivor Lavinia Brown lighting a traditional Inuit qulliq (stone lamp) as part of a TRC opening ceremony. Credit: NCTR

Mohawk Elder John Cri with Commissioner-Survivor Littlechild at a TRC Birthday Party, Montreal, 2012. Credit: NCTR

Ceremonial arrival of traditional canoe flotilla for the BC National Event, September 2013. Credit: NCTR

Commissioner Littlechild, seated, with Commissioner Marie Wilson wearing a moose-hair tufted hide and lynx cape by Dene artist D'Arcy Moses for final ceremonial day of the Alberta National Event, 2014. Credit: NCTR

TRC Commissioners, ITK President, and AFN National Chief lead the Reconciliation Walk before the release of the TRC conclusions, Ottawa, May 31, 2015. Photo: Fred Cattroll

Final Commissioner huddle before the release of the TRC summary report, 10 Principles of Reconciliation, and 94 Calls to Action, June 2, 2015. Photo: Fred Cattroll

"Truth and Reconciliation's Urgent Call for Political Action": a headline that speaks for itself, as fellow Survivors lift up and drum out welcome news. Photo: Fred Cattroll

Standing together: church and government defendants and Inuit and First Nations proponents of the Indian Residential Schools lawsuit and settlement. June 3, 2015. Photo: Fred Cattroll

Commissioner Marie Wilson in the heart garden outside Rideau Hall with granddaughters and Governor General David Johnston, a TRC Honorary Witness, June 2015. Photo: Fred Cattroll

The finale of Marie's 750-kilometre pilgrimage of healing and self-care along the centuries-old Camino de Santiago, Spain. Family Album

CHAPTER 14

The Longest Day

CONTENT CAUTION

It has been a challenge to recount my story of the Commission and stay true to one of the guiding principles in our Mandate: Do No Harm. This particular chapter might be one for Survivors to skip, or look away from, to take care of themselves. The Indian Residential School Survivors Society crisis line provides twenty-four-hour support at 1-800-721-0066. But for all others who are still learning, read on. Do not flinch. Do not hide. I cannot make it softer for you. This is what I witnessed. This history belongs to all of us.

IT WAS A beautiful sunny day. I noticed that, happily, because rain comes so often to the towering, ancient cedar gallery near this place on Vancouver Island. I was apprehensive. This was my first and only time at a TRC hearing at the site of a residential school run by the Protestant church I knew best: the United Church of Canada. The Alberni Indian Residential School started as Presbyterian in 1890 and ran for nearly thirty years until it burned down. In 1920, it reopened under the United

Church and ran until the early 1970s. An eighty-year stint covers many generations of schoolchildren, and that's just this school. There were several others in central and southern Vancouver Island. Local organizers at this hearing expected a big turnout of Survivors from all those schools, both Protestant and Catholic, over the next two days.

We were there under British Columbia's TRC theme of Honesty. As sickening school secrets continued to come out, I was increasingly asked how I could bear it, to hear so much terrible honesty from so many. How did I bear it? I only had to witness it; I didn't have to live it. I was an adult and knew how to reach out to those who love me for care and support. The kids in residential schools were children. They were alone. For most of their lives, they have remained alone, haunted by their experiences. Thinking they were the only one. Trying to make sense of it. Trying to forget it. And now, trying to tell their families, and trying to teach the rest of us. We *must* bear it. We must not look away. Surely that is the least we can do.

Hurt people hurt people. I learned this from years in healing fellowships, a lesson similar to that other one: we learn what we live with, practise what we learn, and then pass what we have become on to our children. That devastating transmission and inheritance of residential school traumas would be glaring under the burning flame of Honesty.

Port Alberni stands out among my memories, a beautiful and touching two-day event that included the longest day of TRC hearings. Close to a thousand people crowded into the bleachers of the gymnasium to bear witness. Young students in traditional regalia sang and offered gifts. Health and cultural workers accompanied every person about to give a statement, proceeding with them to the sharing table, surrounding them in cedar, strengthening their spirit. Everything unfolded with care and ceremony.

We started early. I was the only Commissioner there, glad to have other supports. Vina Robinson and Stan Matthew of the health support team met my practical and emotional needs. Two others prepared me spiritually for what was to come. The Honourable David MacDonald, known for his social justice activism both as a minister in government and a minister in clergy, was now a United Church consultant on the residential schools file. Privately, he and I prayed together in the tradition of the same church that was about to come under the microscope of many memories. I got further strength from Barney Williams, my beloved naniiqsu, the TRC Elder and Survivors Committee member who had adopted me into his family. This was Barney's home territory. Throughout these Vancouver Island hearings, he and his wife, Trina, were a constant support. Barney also entrusted me to his friend Ray Seitcher, a revered Tla-o-qui-aht Hereditary Chief and part of the Nuu-chah-nulth healing team. I shuddered as Ray brushed and crowned me with cedar, a headband of protection and a shield of prayer for every moment of these hearings.

The scene was set with the first Survivor's words: "They had former military, RCMP, football players, martial arts and judo experts in charge of us. How were these people screened? Was there a screening process? I don't think so. We view this place as an open wound. The after-effects continue today."

Interwoven veils of denial, shame, and silence were falling away. Survivors talked about physical and spiritual brutalization. They learned to keep their heads down and their mouths shut:

> "We were never encouraged to be proud of who we are, to be proud of our family. We were taught not to look at each other, not to appreciate each other."
>
> "We were taught only to watch out for ourselves and to take whatever was handed out to us."

"My best friend suffered abuse and I had no idea. He left us long before his time because of what he suffered here. I am here to give voice to my Ancestors."

"I don't want to feel this anymore. I went from being an A student to a D and E student. I failed a grade twice."

"Adult supervision? What a laugh! Our supervisor is in jail right now for numerous counts of sexual abuse. 'Mr. Jail Person' wasn't there for me."

"To the person who told me, 'It's all a lie,' I want them to hear what I say today. We are not liars!"

Children were so hungry they learned to steal, to scrounge, and to prostitute for food:.

"We used to trade food with one another when we were six or seven years old. We were starving."

"We used to sneak down to the bathroom and suck water from the tank in the toilet."

"We went on kitchen or garbage detail just so we could eat enough food from their scraps. Our faces would be just black from eating garbage. Look what *they're* eating. What do *we* get? Nothing."

"We got beaten for stealing food. Our own food. 'Cause they were hiding it. They didn't give it to us except when the inspectors came. Sometimes they took it back as soon as they left."

"If you give me a blow job, you'll get some nourishment."

They learned to fear and loathe the people and powers that did all this to them:

"I dare any non-Native person to give up their four-year-old child to an abusive institution to be raped, humiliated, to be denied their language, to be beaten and shamed. I dare you!"

"Do you know what it's like to get whipped across the face with a yardstick? To have the wrong tooth pulled?"

"Coming here as kids we were treated like cattle. I was assaulted by my supervisor. One night he caught me in the stairwell talking with my brother. He backhanded me while I was talking to my brother. I want to go home."

"I was brought into the gymnasium and whipped in front of everyone with a fire hose. I asked him how it feels to beat on a young, defenceless person. He said it feels good and hit me across the mouth with that fire hose."

"They would beat their way into us with sticks, straps, and whips. We were not allowed to be Indian. Not allowed to talk to our brothers and sisters. If we did, we were beaten severely. I shut down. I tried to become invisible."

"How this depraved man tormented us! He told me I had to make a choice between physical abuse or sexual abuse. Made me strip down and walk down the aisle that they use for church in front of the whole school."

"He said, 'You tell no one.' I didn't have to. My brothers already knew. They witnessed it. He left his hand marks around my neck. Left his fist marks on my face."

Some Survivors gave graphic details of the brutal, criminal lessons they received in sex education through pedophilia and sexual assault:

"I had no words for the parts of the body. I had no words for the things that were performed on me."

"It started off as tickling. It eventually turned into rape. He started introducing instruments into my hole, increasing the size of my body so he could penetrate me."

"When I was nine, the priest and Father comforted me—with erections. He laid me down to rest—arms held down, pants taken down—raped. He asked me to kneel down—not to pray but to give a blow job. I told the principal. He called me a liar and took me to the infirmary. The nun said it was an infection caused by piles. There was sperm coming out of my ass."

"I can still smell blood, feces, and semen all mixed together. I washed myself with toilet water."

"I started to wet the bed. Blood was coming out of my butt for over two years. I was stealing other underwear to hide it. So ashamed. Dirty."

"The Brother put a pair of girl's panties in my mouth every time he raped me. I became a loner. Never told anyone. Wanted to take my own life. Never saw my graduation day."

The personal cost of such deep, graphic sharing was visceral: retching, vomiting, gasping for air. I could see it before anyone else: a Survivor falling apart before me. How was I to know whether it was a heart attack or something else? For the first and only time, I asked whether there was a doctor in the house. It turned out to be a panic attack brought on by acute fear of a perpetrator still alive, still threatening: "This man is going to be out walking free in a few days. He got just a slap on the wrist, a couple of years, for these horrible crimes."

There was a long pause before we continued. This Survivor had more to say, followed by others, all recounting a relentless run of ravages:

"I hated white people. Every time I saw a white person I wanted to fight. That shadow would be standing beside my bed at night. If not me, another boy, going into that little cubby hole he had. I tried to tell my parents. They didn't believe me. They said, 'No, they are religious people. They don't do those things.' It wasn't the humiliation that hurt. It was what it did to me that hurt the most—thinking it was my fault."

"The nun used to go through the dorm and whip off our blankets and open the door so he could help himself to the girls."

"She used to take some of the girls and send them to the boys' side."

"She used to send us downstairs and call us 'dirty little girls' … I already knew I was."

"The nuns took off their pants and made me go between their legs. Said if I didn't, they were going to charge me with rape."

"I used to watch that nun and that priest in bed having sex. I wish they were here today so they could face me without having to get hit, strapped, or hit on the ass with a steel bar. It's like they were trying to disable me."

Finally, a fleeting moment of respite as another Survivor spoke: "I became dysfunctional, but not disabled. I love red roses. I always think of my mom when I think of roses. I wrapped myself in red roses. That's how I protected myself when I was being sexually abused. I would picture myself covered in red roses."

This description of a personal survival technique pushed me over the edge. My own mother loved red roses. Her death had been barely a year before. My eyes smarted and teared up as I felt her presence acutely, even as I tried to picture this former child before me, fortifying her small self with imaginary red roses amid the horror.

I called for the lunch break. To savour the moment. To escape the moment.

~

Lunch brought no relief. Survivors corroborated stories from other hearings in this region. If more Canadians had been in this room in 2013 to hear all the references to death and dying at residential schools, the 2021 discoveries of unmarked graves at Kamloops and other school sites might not have come as such a surprise. For some little children, it started on their first day of school.

> "The first day we witnessed a little boy, four or five years old, hanging in the basement, hung by a towel. We were all little boys."
>
> "They cut my hair. We all looked the same. I hid behind a door crying. Another girl was crying, too. We both thought somebody died in our family because they cut our hair. That is what it means in our culture."
>
> "We played in a playroom downstairs. I crawled into a crawl space. There was something hard in there. At first, I thought it was a rock—it was a skull! My supervisor saw that I saw it. That's when my sexual abuse started. I was nine."
>
> "I miss him so dear. My brother took his pain to the grave. I too was abused. I know he travelled with me to come here, to watch over me, as I do what I have to do for me, my family, our families."

Some of what happened at residential school prevented the very existence of a next generation:

> "This was a sterilization centre with a chief sterilization practitioner until the 1960s. And not just in the schools. It was much bigger than that."
>
> "Do I have any kids? No, I don't. The doctor told me you can't have children. They did something to you at residential school."

"Who the hell made themselves God to do this to me? Angry? You're damned right. Nobody wants to hear that story."

"What they did to me, I was never the same when I came out of it. I never had no kids. Now they know."

Here, as in other parts of the country, we heard more examples of lateral violence, and more graphic ones.

"This is the hardest time to share, with my own people. For politics, we hurt each other."

"Because of being gang-raped in residential school, I was sentenced and branded as a 'whore.' There are people I know who still consider I am not stable. I had to go away from this whole community for people to realize I have gifts. There is no greater pain than rejection by spouse and by community."

"All my abusers know who they are. Some of my abusers were in residential school. I was attacked by older boys. I was sexually humiliated by them."

"What triggers me today is what I had to do there. I was the enforcer. I was one of the monitors who had to do the staff's job. I was one of the chosen ones."

"The principal told us to do these things. I forced the little ones. I made eight bucks a month."

"I formed a gang in there. I'm not proud of it, but I wanted to survive."

"When I was carrying my son, I cried a lot. It was really emotional. My doctor said his ADD was because of what I went through when I carried him."

"If you don't listen, you're going to go to hell. I was already in hell—Alberni Residential School."

In the early evening of this seemingly endless day, I received an alarmed message from our vigilant executive director, Kimberly Murray. *What on earth are you doing?* she texted. *You were supposed to wrap up at four. You're going to make yourself sick.*

I can't stop, I told her. *There's close to a thousand people here. Some are still waiting to speak. I can't just turn them away.*

To me it was simple: If Survivors were still there, how could I not be? I was aware that my determination also had an impact on the health support and TRC teams, but no one was complaining. We were all taking our cues from each other. The room was overflowing with courageous, loving care, and we could all feel the transformation unfolding before us and within us. But we did take one important pause.

A group of a dozen or more senior high school students had been there all day to witness, intending to be part of a closing ceremony. They had to get home, so we held the ceremony early. They advanced toward me as a group, their regalia adorned with mini wooden canoe paddles. In their midst, their Elder was carrying something large and rectangular—a gift for me. It was a stunning black-and-white watercolour of an eagle taking flight, surrounded by green fern foliage, a picture of soaring hope and new life. To my eyes, it was a picture of them, and of this day.

But it wasn't over yet. We pushed on. With growing trust in the process, some familiar issues came into sharper focus, such as addictions. Some started at school, not after.

> "This is the place where I started my alcoholism."
>
> "I used to hate those people who hurt me. I learned to hate myself. I learned to hate others. The best hatred I ever had was diving into that alcohol. That's where I hid out for a long time."

Other issues surfaced here for the first time, including incest and its link to the child welfare system. Some of those affected were finally speaking up:

> "I expressed my anger inward. I was angry at myself because I was sexually abused so horribly—it happened at home! I was four years old."
>
> "I was sexually abused at an early age, before going to residential school. Two generations had gone before me."
>
> "I was mom to two younger siblings. Once, we got abandoned in a house. I don't know how long we were there. We witnessed a lot of incest. Sometimes adults would be looking for a younger girl or boy so they could molest them. I would hide under the bunk bed. When they couldn't find children, cousins would sleep with each other for their own sexual pleasure."
>
> "[It was always] my own brother that was going to look for me. I was abused by my older sibling."
>
> "My spouse was tied up and raped by their brother and their father."
>
> "I saw my uncle on top of his daughter. Will this pain ever stop?"
>
> "I was so abused sexually, incested by family members and extended family members. I used to sleep with rats because it was better than being raped and molested where I was."
>
> "Fear has been, by far, the strongest emotion of my childhood, from our parents' fits of rage to the toxic environment of other family members, always walking on eggshells for fear of being a trigger. Another dominating emotion was disappointment. Broken promises. Hope and joy turning to fear, disappointment, and anguish, waiting for a parent who was self-medicating and would never show up."
>
> "My parents were hard-core alcoholics. I became a parent to my siblings at age nine."

"I was seven the year both my parents died of alcoholism. I was in twenty-two different foster homes in seven different communities."

"If there is enough money to remove children, why is there not enough money to keep families intact?"

"Children get removed for overcrowding. Are we at fault for poverty? Are we at fault for lack of housing? And then moms can't get their own housing because of racism."

"We were apprehended at a young age. We were put into kinship care. We were sexually molested by family members. Then we went into the foster system."

"By the age of eleven we had been abandoned by our mother, taken from our father, sexually abused by other family members, put through a criminal prosecution process, placed in mostly white foster homes. Then the persecution and alienation of rejection by our own paternal family."

"Indigenous language was the language used by other family members talking about us. It was a tool that was off-limits to us, or a tool used against us."

"We eventually found ourselves in a loving home. We were made to feel like a traitor for our relationship with our white family who tried to foster connections to our culture, but who found themselves rejected by Aboriginal communities."

"The vast majority of kids in care are Aboriginal kids, and three out of four end up in non-Aboriginal homes. We need to be aware of what these kids are going through. They are living with this shame and guilt."

"This is not a past concern. Survivor parents and caregivers have to support children in care. Give them support to accept love in the homes where they land and the tools to live in both worlds."

What if I had shut the hearing down early? What if we had missed all of this tragic lived experience from such courageous young adults? And what if we had missed the wise advice they left us with, as ones who had lived through "the system" and knew what changes they wanted us to fight for?

> "We need to model healthy intimacy, healthy communication, and the ability to manage and control emotions."
>
> "I hope there will be an understanding of the intergenerational bondage that exists. So that our children and our children's children can grow up in a place of trust and love, not fear and pain."
>
> "If we continue to keep our eyes closed, we will continue as we are."
>
> "Protecting children is the key, and guiding them through. That is the most powerful way to mitigate all of this."

As several speakers pointed out here and in other jurisdictions, Indigenous children are the vast majority within the child welfare system—a repackaged version of residential schools that would lead the Commission to devote its first seven Calls to Action to this priority, with suggestions to urgently change the system. But for now, I wasn't the only one in this room wishing that elected leaders had also heard these statements, especially from so many younger intergenerational Survivors:

> "I wish the government was here, listening. To know what the hell they did to us. They have no idea."
>
> "I hope the politicians are listening as well, because they have to make a change in their lifetime too. To support the community where their support comes from."

"Ever since it started, I haven't seen the prime minister once, or the premier."

"I just pray that one day people will open their eyes and see what residential school did to us, without judging us."

"I had to go to treatment to become a better parent and grandparent. I don't know what it's like to be white. I have no clue. But I think maybe we should send the counsellors to Ottawa, so the government can go to treatment too."

"The TRC is about being given a voice to share our stories and teach others about the intergenerational impacts of those horrible schools. This process is about overcoming silence and invisibility."

We carried on with statement-gathering for sixteen hours, some of the richest hours of my life. The emotional outpouring toward the end was an uplifting rush of forgiveness, redemption, healing, and prayer—reclaiming of the circle of humanity.

"God, rebuild my brokenness. Touch my heart with kindness and compassion."

"I am starting my healing journey today. And I am scared shitless right now. This is the first time I have ever talked about it. I was only four years old when I was kidnapped from my community of love and care."

"I wanted to retaliate. As Grandpa taught me, it's much easier to hurt them, but it's much better to help them. It's not in our culture to take revenge on people who hurt you."

"I've learned through our own culture and traditions. I've learned to talk, not with my head down but with my head held high. My trials and tribulations are my teacher. Today I don't need to walk with shame and guilt."

"Those guys have passed on, and I've learned how to forgive."

"When I saw that person, I didn't run away. I forgave. Because I know what had happened to *them* in residential school."

"I am a father, grandfather, great-grandfather. How many times I thought I was not worthy. We need to break that cycle. I want to learn to love myself."

"It took me a long time to practise looking into that mirror. To say, 'I love you. I forgive you.' I'm gonna stop blaming God."

"An addict is told your addiction can be stopped. Let's do the same with residential school. We need to be more accountable for ourselves. Let's break the cycle."

"I'm fifty years old now and it took me this long to be proud of who I am. They didn't get the best of me 'cause the best of me is yet to come. This is not the evil place it used to be. Elders speak with honesty, truth, and respect, and that's the way I want to feel. Let me be a strong Elder."

"I am not here to talk about what happened to me in residential school. I am here to thank people for helping me. It made a big difference."

"I was an angry man. I was never a role model to my kids. But I am a good role model to my grandkids. For the rest of my life I'm going to work on it."

"The parenting skills I'm learning are from my children today. My grandson teaches me from school in our language. He'll correct me, and he'll laugh like an Elder does."

"I am here to reclaim my voice. I cannot be a little boy anymore. My daughter is teaching me how to hug and what it is like to feel. To feel again. I love it!"

"I live my apology today with my children, to break the cycle."

"My hope is that my grandchildren are happy in this world. I was picking blackberries with my little granddaughter. She bent down and kissed my arm. And I knew right then—there's going to be a change."

"We need to move from Survivors to Thrivers! We need to celebrate our victories. We are all connected. We come from smart, intelligent people."

"My life didn't start off very good, but it's sure going to end up a lot better. I even have a chance of going to heaven!"

"All people weren't bad. All preachers weren't bad. Too bad that these individuals could tarnish the names of the sacred places and the sacred beliefs of their own peoples."

"Indigenous people shouldn't be so hard on white people who are loving and kind. I'm happy today. I don't need to carry this story with me. And I pray to my Creator that you non-Native people don't carry that blame either. Support us; don't carry the blame."

"I ask that you pray to support other residential school students, who today are learning to cry. My heart goes to the life-givers. They are the ones who are teaching me to cry."

"Don't be afraid, because in the end, we are all one. And the guests here all need to stand behind us. Because it will not end until we all say it will end. I want to be part of your healing, and I need you to be part of mine."

"My wish is that everyone heals their wounded spirits so they can be whole, so they can be free. I just want all of you to understand I love you all so very much."

"What I carry inside is who I really am. I am proud of who I am today. To show love, kindness, to break down and show humbleness—that's where I am today."

"I realize I am not walking alone. I am walking with many. Let it go. Walk proud. All My Relations."

Around half past midnight, I heard the next Survivor's words as a hallelujah moment: "From where I started and where I am going is two different places, because I took my experiences and said, 'It's not going to happen again in my family.' I decided it was not going to bring me down. And it hasn't. And it won't."

Then, an intergenerational Survivor offered a kind of blessing for the whole gathering: "You guys are such a powerful, powerful bunch. My mom attended school here. Now I understand."

After such a long, unflinchingly honest day: the precious gift of understanding. I was both exhausted and revitalized by all I had witnessed, as kindness, determination, and wisdom outshone all the devastation.

As I write these words many years later, I have been wearing the cherished cedar headband first placed on me by Elder Ray Seitcher that early morning back in Port Alberni. He had offered me cedar and protective prayers. They carried me throughout those hearings, including that longest day. Today, I am thankful once again; as his cedar gift sits across my forehead, I can still feel its purpose and its power.

CHAPTER 15

Standing Up

VANCOUVER WAS A stand-out in so many ways. The British Columbia TRC National Event was our sixth—and the only one in September. We had moved around our TRC symbolic circle of flames to the theme of Honesty. Survivors elsewhere had often described June as "Freedom Day," when many (but not all) residential school children were able to go home for the summer. September, however, was the saddest month, when children went to school. It was a month of collective physical and emotional rupture in Indigenous communities throughout the country, and no Survivor gathered here would have forgotten that.

We started off-shore. Thousands of people showed up to witness our formal arrival—the re-enactment of an ancient welcoming ceremony. First, Murray and I joined a symbolic five-kilometre paddle in a flotilla of massive, elaborately decorated dugout canoes. Upon arrival, we all raised our paddles to indicate non-aggression. Chair Sinclair stood up to shout across the waters the peaceful intentions of the Commission. Only then were we welcomed ashore to do our work.

The next day, the public also showed up in record numbers for the opening land-based activity. Despite the pouring rain, a huge crowd under a colourful canopy of umbrellas gathered for a massive Reconciliation Walk through the streets and over the bridges of downtown Vancouver. That Reconciliation Walk drew an estimated and unprecedented seventy thousand people!

For months in advance we had nurtured positive relations with the city. As lead Commissioner for Honorary Witnesses, I proposed Mayor Gregor Robertson, who championed reconciliation efforts at the city, and Kwagiulth Hereditary Chief Bobby Joseph. Chief Joseph had led the BC Indian Residential School Survivors Society and was involved in negotiating the IRS Settlement Agreement. With fellow Survivor the late Alvin Dixon and others at the BC society, Chief Joseph had engaged widely with diverse faith communities, developing a rich network of cultural and civil collaborators in Vancouver and beyond. Later, Chief Joseph, several of his grown children, and other supporters formed Reconciliation Canada, an organization committed to public education and outreach to broad society. They were essential to the reach and impact of the TRC's colourful cultural kickoff in Vancouver.

But the BC setting also brought its particular realities and challenges. The greatest number of distinct Indigenous nations in Canada are in this province. This is the farthest reach from the eastern power centres of the government and churches that defined and shaped the Canadian residential school system, yet at some point, the four major denominations that ran schools all operated in this province—one Catholic and three Protestant.

Some of the most remote residential schools were located here, tucked away on one of the province's many isolated islands. Out of sight for much supervision. Out of mind for much accountability. Arguably the most high-profile of the many residential school lawsuits grew out of this province, too. The Willie Blackwater case made it all the way to the Supreme Court of Canada and played a key role in turning the page on government and church denial of massive and long-lasting school harms and criminality.

Other national news stories more indirectly related to residential schools have also unfolded from this BC region. They fall into the broad category of "residential school Legacy," also part of our TRC Mandate. The Pickton serial killings happened here. Painfully slow revelations from DNA samples on that farm indicated that a majority of the thirty-three confirmed victims were Indigenous women. Farther north in the province, recurring disappearances and deaths over many years of mostly Indigenous women has given a remote route a sad new name. Running between inland Prince George and coastal Prince Rupert, Highway 16 is also known as the Highway of Tears. Vancouver itself, Canada's third-largest city, includes an entrenched inner village with its own name and tragic reputation. The Downtown Eastside (DTES) is a gathering place of dashed hopes, heartache, and addiction. It draws its heavily Indigenous population from all parts of BC and many other regions of the country, all seeking a community of understanding, and, for many, a warmer version of homelessness in this wealthy winter country.

The DTES, the Highway of Tears, the Pickton farm—these are all residential school legacy stories. Survivors told the TRC of their connections to these places, of the experiences of family members or friends, those they knew who lived their lives in harm's way. Not all survived.

Vancouver was a place of contradictions. Even with the multigenerational residential school legacy unfolding in plain sight, at our TRC National Event this also became the first place in the country to announce a year of reconciliation. Later it declared itself a City of Reconciliation. The province was home to the first government to create a formal department for reconciliation (Ministry of Indigenous Relations and Reconciliation), and later, in 2019, became the first jurisdiction in North America to adopt the United Nations Declaration—the Declaration on the Rights of Indigenous Peoples Act was passed unanimously by the BC legislative assembly. The province has a designated First Nations Health Authority and a unique model of Indigenous leadership. More than two hundred distinct First Nations representing some thirty different languages come together to fortify their continuing claims and influence as a First Nations Summit. Despite the many documented losses, this is a place clinging firmly to deep cultural roots that long predate its British namesake.

In Vancouver, some real-time Expressions of Reconciliation played out at the gathering on the grassy, sprawling grounds and multiple buildings of the Pacific National Exhibition site. A provincial utility company had declared a professional development day so that all its managers could attend the TRC National Event as a major learning opportunity. The University of British Columbia did the same for its faculty. But willing governments, government agencies, and educational and corporate collaborators were no guarantee against angry flare-ups.

British Columbia was the first place we experienced semi-organized, though short-lived, protests. Although we tackled our work independently from any government, the TRC was bound by government rules, which meant we couldn't fundraise. We could accept indirect contributions, though, for travel and meals. With our limited budget, we were always seeking ways to bring as many Survivors as possible to TRC events. One willing corporate contributor to this event was also associated with a controversial industrial project within the province. The perception of dirty money from sponsors sparked the protests. It was a marvel to witness how patient listening and quiet intervention by one or two Survivors and health support workers eventually calmed things down, refocusing the issue on the presence and well-being of Survivors. Protests aside, anger sometimes just seemed to get stuck in the hearing room. It was rare, but it happened.

There were big crowds in Vancouver, so we had more than one auditorium at the exhibition grounds designated for sharing panels. The Commissioners split up sometimes, operating out of three different spaces at once. The Survivor I'm remembering now was signed up for my room, and I was alone to face him. He was alone, too. I could see by his walk that he was upset before he ever dropped into the designated chair at the table angled across from me. He was mad at life. At everything that had happened at school. At everything that had fallen apart since. He wasn't the first or only Survivor to be confused about the nature of our TRC. He thought we were a government Commission, and that I represented the government. He saw me as the face of all his troubles. The more he talked, the louder and angrier his voice became. He began moving around in his seat, visibly agitated. And then he stood up.

I immediately stood up, too. Didn't think about it. Just did it. I could smell danger. And I wasn't the only one. We were on a stage about three feet above the crowd. Out of the corner of my eye, I saw a quiet movement from the middle of the auditorium. Someone was heading toward an empty seat near the steps up to me. It was my spiritual advisor, Peter Short. He was almost always within my line of vision at National Events. Now, he repositioned himself, in case I needed a different kind of help. Then, from my other side, came a health support to be with the man.

I don't recall how many breaths it took, how many sips of water, how many quiet words to help the Survivor settle down, recompose. The stand was over. The room reclaimed its calm. I think the man was finally able to hear me as I explained, once again, that I was not working for the government. That his words were important for all of us to hear. That we honoured the courage it took for him to speak to us, that none of it was easy, and that he was not alone.

Immediately after this speaker, we wrapped the session and headed out for fresh air. A small crowd outside the door was gasping. There, in the lowest crux of the auditorium roof, was an eagle, its white head glowing in the sunlight, eyes piercing. It sat directly overtop of the stage area where the Survivor and I had taken our stands. I had never before seen an eagle perched so low—and never so close to those who needed to feel its presence and the sacred teaching of love it symbolizes.

~

I had experienced anger on the job before. Bullying too. I began my journalism career in my late twenties but looked younger. That didn't help my inexperience. I must have looked like a pushover to an elected official I interviewed back then. He appeared to be in conflict of interest, selling his own private property to the government while serving in public office. He was clearly unhappy with my line of questioning. There was an oversized desk between us, and this was an oversized person, his beet-red face fuming. He stood up and leaned forward onto his forearms, braced halfway across that desk. I was still earning my reputation as a junior reporter; I wouldn't get far if I started caving in to political bullies. I stood up, too, and leaned right back across that desk. We were practically nose to nose. I did not blink. He eventually sat back down. I did too. I got a good story, he survived the public reaction, and I internalized two lessons from that experience, both invaluable to my profession and to my life: 1) Get comfortable with being uncomfortable; and 2) Never fear standing up for truth.

Somewhere along the way I started standing up for Survivors. I was already standing up by speaking out for all of them in my role as a TRC Commissioner, and have been ever since. But in BC, in response to every Survivor who shared their experiences with me as the presiding Commissioner, I started to physically stand up.

From the beginning, the Commissioners had agreed that we would not be "interrogating" Survivors, neither cross-examining nor interrupting them. The only time I jumped in was to ask follow-up questions if they said something about a missing child, or a known death at the schools. We were developing the first-ever national registry for residential school deaths, and we needed as much information as possible, scarce and scattered as it was. Beyond that, we were there to listen to what *they* thought *we* needed to hear. We would explain the process, how much time they had, and how we would keep and signal their time. Many Survivors struggled with where to begin or end, so I started adding four guiding questions to my opening comments, intended to help them focus:

What was life like before residential school?

What do you want us to know about your school experiences?

What has life been like for you since school?

What would reconciliation look like to you?

I also explained that I would be taking notes while they talked because it helped me listen more carefully.

That's exactly what I was doing on another day in one of the other auditoriums—writing with a fury, scrambling to keep up with a different style of Survivor now speaking. Everything he said was in the present tense, but sometimes in the third person to distance himself from harsh reality, talking about himself as if he were someone else. He was beating the hell out of himself, revealing all his failings and flaws, beginning with a birth defect, as if that too were his fault. And he was reliving the worst of his memories. He began by describing day one of residential school:

> I cried all the first night. All the boys heard me and laughed at me. My spirit went into the cracks of the residential school, like being so ashamed. I'm so ashamed of being Indian, and how they taught me to be afraid. They brought a movie, and there was this beautiful white girl, crying and screaming. They were shooting Indians. When the Army came, we all stood up. We were clapping against our own people, 'cause we wanted them all to be shot.
>
> They brought us to bed. It really hurts me when they hurt us. I became like a sex addict with my life. I was so afraid of being gay. I have no boundaries. No parental skills. Went home. Met my wife. Had children. I look at myself in the mirror. I try to say, "I love you." I get so ashamed. I look down. How could I love me? How could I love my wife?

Then, as if suddenly returning to the present moment, he said, "Commissioner, I want to show you my pain." He gestured to a young man sitting at the table beside him who appeared to be in his late teens or early twenties—a son. I watched him bow his head and wince as his father resumed his rant, detailing the way he'd abused his son as a baby and his mother. The Survivor turned again to his son to say, "I love my scar so much. I love him. I want him to know I need him and I love him. My son is important."

By then I was wincing inwardly as much as the son. He was right there. But this father, so far removed in his mind from the present moment, was talking about his child as if he were invisible, labelling him "my pain, my scar, my pain, my scar …" The mother in me couldn't bear to watch the young man disintegrate.

"Excuse me, sir. Sorry to interrupt," I said gently, knowing I was breaking my own rules for how Survivors should be left to speak for themselves, trying to pull him back from somewhere else. "You've been talking about your son, but you haven't told us his name. He's sitting right there beside you now. Won't you please introduce him to us? I'm sure we'd all like to hear his name."

The father rallied to the present moment, told us his son's name, and then turned directly to the young man, and said:

> I love you, son. I love you, my wife. I'm a happy person, but I'm lost.
>
> I want to say thank you to all the non-Native people here today. We still have residential schools today but they are called foster care. There's no love, respect. We are condemned, controlled. We are a big business, we Indians. We are a big business.
>
> We have so much deep pain. We have so much deep shame. We have so much deep fear. We are confused. We want to be Indian, but we are white. I don't want to be ashamed of me anymore. I want to be normal and I don't know how.
>
> Can you respect who we are? Please remember who we are. Can you honour us in our way?

There could not have been a more fulsome expression of Honesty. He finished speaking, and that's when I stood up.

It was a spontaneous, solo standing ovation. After that, it became my regular practice—my personal tribute to the tremendous efforts a Survivor had just made toward personal and family healing, and toward the great reckoning of our country.

~

British Columbia was also a homecoming for our TRC Bentwood Box. At all our major events across the country since our launch years before, the healing energy of this cedar box had been available for Survivor contributions and to receive Expressions of Reconciliation from wide-ranging groups and organizations. In repeated public ceremony, TRC Commissioners and Survivors Committee members received their tokens, each one a commitment to tangible action—or a renewed commitment to do much better than in the past. It was their chance to step up, to step forward, and to hold themselves publicly accountable.

A broken chalice, a drum, baby moccasins—each now found their way into the Bentwood Box as an Expression of Reconciliation. The chalice was from a national Protestant church to symbolize its broken sacred promises of the past, and a renewed commitment to walk forward together on a path of truth and reconciliation. The drum was from a newly formed group of Indigenous and non-Indigenous youth—their pledge to continue learning together to the beat of the same drum. The baby moccasins were to symbolize first steps toward developing a new school curriculum about residential schools and other treaty matters—and a commitment to return with full-sized moccasins once completed within two years. Education minister Jackson Lafferty, himself a residential school Survivor, did return, making the Northwest Territories the first jurisdiction in the country to introduce a course on residential schools, co-developed with Survivors, and mandatory for *all* high school student graduation.

Then there was the one exceptional gift to the Bentwood Box, a rare collection of school records created by former students themselves, decades earlier, in the form of artwork. In the 1950s and early '60s, the late Robert Allard had been a volunteer art teacher at some schools in western Canada. Years after his death, his family gifted his personal collection to the University of Victoria. Dr. Andrea Walsh, an art anthropologist, uncovered about forty well-preserved paintings, realized they had come from the residential school context, and asked the TRC Commissioners for advice. Dr. Walsh showed us several large, vibrant paintings and a small pile of companion photographs. They were pictures of child-artists hard at work on the creations emerging before them. Now those completed paintings from the residential school in Port Alberni were displayed before us, long preserved on high-quality paper by a caring art teacher. Many paintings reflected childhood memories of life before residential school: village life, familiar birds, fish, and whales. They spoke a silent language of remembering and deep longing. Others depicted the new realities of school days, including buildings above ground, burial sites beneath. I don't think any of us anticipated their emotional impact. I noticed how quiet we were. Almost whispering. Sombre. Reverent. As if we were at a wake. In such an unexpected format, these paintings spoke new evidence of what Survivors had been telling us all across the country: that children died and were buried at Canadian residential schools. Art documenting life.

As diverse as they were, the paintings shared a common power. Throughout the TRC, we heard from adult Survivors, often elderly. It was easy to lose sight of the fact that our Commission was looking into harms and atrocities done to *children*. These paintings, clearly the work of young artists, also preserved a picture of Survivors as children, and what Canada had allowed to happen to them.

The paintings inspired an unprecedented kind of class reunion. Some had signatures, and with the benefit of Allard's photos, Dr. Walsh identified and located many of the artists, then arranged for Nuu-chah-nulth repatriation ceremonies to reunite them with their childhood masterworks, back where they had created them, in Port Alberni.

Some artists were harder to track down. After school, many had scattered—some lost to the streets. But more were found during a TRC event in Victoria when the paintings were displayed publicly for the first time. Some of the artists told me it was as if their lost childhood painting had found *them*, to help them find their lost self. As the paintings were ceremonially drummed into the main hall, each artist carried their painting for all to see, as if cradling a piece of their own reclaimed childhood.

By the time of the National Event in Vancouver, Dr. Walsh had produced replicas of the paintings. This time they would be drummed in to be placed into the Bentwood Box as an Expression of Reconciliation. The very first school accounts from the hands of children were about to become part of the TRC permanent record. But as it unfolded I experienced much more than a drumming-in of paintings. On the main stage with my fellow Commissioners, I wondered if anyone else could see what I was feeling. I could barely breathe. Similar to what had happened to me back in Quebec, I was suddenly consumed by a rush of air and a sensation of little children clambering onstage and all over my lap and chest. I felt the weight of their presence. For me, this was no longer about paintings. It was a drumming-in of the spirits of children captured *within* those paintings, an electric sense of living art, longing to be seen and remembered.

Dr. Walsh, upon becoming a TRC Honorary Witness, spoke of the power of the marks we leave. How artwork is a form of leaving a mark. Marking a time, a place, a life, or an experience lived. And of how artwork then marks those who encounter that art. I know how the experience of those residential school paintings marked me. I am told they have also since marked the lives of some of the very children who created them, lifting some out of defeat, returning some to school, raising some to new success. The children's paintings left marks that could reach through time to the adults they had become, inviting them home to their own healing.

Never would I question or doubt the power of the arts, of commemoration, of ceremony to breathe new life and transformation into the human realm. Nor would I lose hope. Just as loss and injury can leave visible and invisible scars, in the rebalancing of forces, I could see more clearly now how art and beauty can also leave enduring marks of light, to stand out beyond darkness.

Standing out, standing up, stepping forward. Slowly, with Honesty, we were inching our way toward Wisdom.

A prayer-filled tipi. Photo: Tessa Macintosh

PART VIII

WISDOM

ALBERTA

Wisdom is knowing your gifts and using these gifts to serve your fellow human beings. Living your gifts will define your identity and purpose in life. Your gifts are to help … bring peace and balance … To know wisdom is to know yourself.

—Elder Dr. David Courchene,
A Story of the Seven Sacred Laws

CHAPTER 16

Falling Apart

IN THEIR WISDOM, Survivors who brokered the Indian Residential Schools Settlement Agreement took the issue of healing seriously from the beginning. They insisted, as part of the deal, that Canada would provide cultural, emotional, and mental health supports to help implement it safely. One province stepped forward to figure out what that would look like—Alberta. The region's director general of First Nations and Inuit health for Health Canada, the late Herman Wierenga, called on Saulteaux social worker and therapist Brenda Reynolds to design and lead the pilot plan. She was doubly equipped, with her Western training and experience, and the teachings and healing values of traditional ceremonies from her culture. Personally, she had her own complex ties to the residential school story. Professionally, she brought particular insights from supporting young girls with the first abuse disclosures from Gordon's Indian Residential School in Saskatchewan, one of the last schools to close, in 1996.

Dynamic teams were developed, integrating Western-trained counsellors, therapists, and social workers with Indigenous healers and Traditional Knowledge Keepers. Some former residential school students were also trained to be part of the team, adding credibility for Survivors. The Alberta design became the model for health supports throughout the country. We observed throughout our proceedings that the Indigenous supports were called upon most often by anyone in need. It was an unprecedented, effective approach, not just for supporting Survivors but for uplifting everyone involved in this heavy work. I often thought this approach might work in other Canadian contexts and beyond, not limited to Indigenous realities. Trauma cuts across all cultures, as does the need for capable, innovative solutions to address the gap in available resources.

In January 2012, almost halfway through our TRC, we issued an Interim Report and about twenty early recommendations. These are often overshadowed by the ninety-four Calls that came at the end of our work, though several of them were interrelated or restated. By the time of the Interim Report, we'd already had the benefit of three National Events—in Winnipeg, Inuvik, and Halifax—and dozens of community hearings in those regions. The particular lessons from the North had left a deep mark, so the Commissioners made a specific and urgent call for healing centres in northern Canada, specifically the Northwest Territories and Nunavut, the two most isolated and underserved regions. We also called for the professional certification of Traditional Knowledge support workers. They had already proven to be a key part of the integrated health teams, supporting fellow Survivors and the Commission throughout our hearings. We reasoned that their work on the front lines of trauma was no less worthy of recognition than similar years of on-the-job apprenticeship in any other field of work that leads to a professional designation or accreditation. Many of those who supported TRC events are still working in the healing field today.

Some of them got their start thanks to the critically important work of the Aboriginal Healing Foundation. The AHF had been sponsoring community-based activities throughout the country for several years before the TRC got underway. One of the earliest invitations the Commissioners received was to one of their events in Calgary. Our core focus was Survivors, but younger speakers at this event sharpened our attention on intergenerational Survivors and what they had inherited. One speaker told us he was raised with extreme physical violence. He said he started off raising his kids the same way. When he learned about what happened at the schools, his anger changed to compassion. He began training to become a helper and started raising his kids differently.

The Aboriginal Healing Foundation was chaired by Georges Erasmus, a Dene Nation president in the 1980s and, later, National Chief of the AFN. He went on to co-chair Canada's Royal Commission on Aboriginal Peoples (RCAP) in the 1990s. In 1996, RCAP issued a monumental report with a significant section on residential schools that helped pave the way for our Truth and Reconciliation Commission, and for the Healing Foundation itself. Under the executive leadership of Mike DeGagné—who later became one of the first Indigenous presidents and vice-chancellors of a Canadian university (Nipissing University)—the AHF proved vital to our Commission. Many Survivors told us that without the benefit of Healing Foundation projects, they would never have been able to talk to the TRC.

I never forgot that point, and I sometimes wondered whether we were hearing only from the healthiest Survivors. Although a very high percentage of Survivors did give statements to the TRC—close to 10 percent of those alive at the time, a very high sampling by any survey standard—most who spoke said they had already faced addictions, and now were focused on healing. But what about those still suffering—those who didn't get the benefit of an Aboriginal Healing Foundation project, who never made it to the Commission, and perhaps never even knew we existed? I knew there were and still are countless ones who continue to struggle with school-related demons on the streets of Canadian cities, including those I know in Yellowknife. One of them became an important part of our family story on the historic day of the prime minister's apology to residential school Survivors in 2008.

After the televised event and community gathering, Stephen and I were too wound up with emotional exhaustion and exhilaration to go home. It was a sunny, warm June day, perfect for our first hard ice cream of the season. We were sitting with kids, grandkids, and cones on the benches outside the convenience store, a magnet for uninvited company. I'm usually friendly and generous with people living on the streets. Many of them are not originally from Yellowknife. Some, I know and recognize from their home communities, or they recognize me from my many years on television. But on this day I didn't want to be recognized by anybody, or at least not interrupted. I was feeling such a profound need to be with my family, to feel their presence fully in the aftermath of an apology acknowledging so many thousands of families ripped asunder by residential schools, knowing that our own family has been one of them. I wanted to lift up this day for us through the simple joy of eating ice cream together, a kind of celebration of the spirit, and a reassurance for grandchildren who had earlier seen their "Mimi" crying.

But what *I* wanted didn't matter. Down she sat, right beside me on the bench, reeking of her addiction and smiling the friendly, semi-familiar smile of the beautiful woman I know she once was. I think she was truly happy to see me. I offered to buy her an ice cream, but she said she didn't want one. I explained that I was trying to have a private moment with my family, after all the emotions of the apology to residential school Survivors. I thought she would pick up on that, knowing a bit of her story, but that's not where she went.

"Oh, you're with your kids? How nice," she said, not moving an inch. "Yeah, I've got a kid, too. I jus' love him so much," she said, slurring her words now.

"I didn't know you had a son," I said. "Does he live here with you?"

"No, he took off a long time ago, went way to the other side of the country."

And then she wandered off in her mind, muttering something under her breath:

"S ... F ... S ..."

Did I hear her right?

"Oh, I jus' miss him so much! I jus' wish he would come back to me."

"Why doesn't he come back?" I asked.

"Oh, why did he have to go and join that army anyways? Oh, my boy, I jus' love you so much—stupid fucking shit!"

It was too tragic to laugh, and too funny to forget, this distorted message of love and regret from a struggling residential school Survivor mother, all wrapped up in a drunken outburst.

That SFS moment was a real-time reminder of the lasting, intergenerational impacts of residential schools, and of the humanity of Survivors still suffering on our streets, often judged, often rendered invisible. That's why healing is such an essential part of truth and reconciliation, just as it said in the first paragraph of our TRC Mandate. We heard this so many times that the Commissioners began to think we should have been called the Truth, Healing, and Reconciliation Commission. Jokingly, we imagined three T-shirts made just for us, each bearing a single word but forming a powerful image when we stood side by side. But who wanted the Truth T-shirt? All three of us wanted to wear Healing! And we already knew that Reconciliation was far too wide a word for any one shirt—and far too big a concept for any one person. But we did cling to such laughter as a way to keep our spirits up, even as we took our work as Commissioners very seriously.

Murray teased Willie relentlessly that he was still "on probation." As Chair, Murray, the judge, joked that *he* got to decide whether Willie was really a Commissioner, and the jury was still out! Other times, at evening talent shows, Willie and I drew laughs with our silent duet, puckering lips, pretending to be singing fish.

And sometimes I was the sitting duck, when the joke was on me and the two of them were in on it. Once, we had a very early start for a lengthy drive to a post-Christmas event in Alberta. I had rushed through early-morning efforts to fix my hair so that it would last all day. The procedure involved rollers and a generous amount of hair-spray. I was in the van only a few minutes before one of them reached over and pulled out a curler I had missed from the back of my head. The teasing erupted—they were my saviours from public humiliation. We howled!

An hour or so later we stopped for breakfast, settling into a large round table in front of a pine-like indoor tree with a few remaining decorations from the holidays. Breakfast came and went, and we got back into the van. As I was adjusting my scarf, I felt something else attached to my hair. This time it was a tree ornament! That extra-strong hairspray must also have been extra sticky—unless, someone intentionally stuck it there?

The day unfolded with familiar heartache, and ended in reverent beauty. Tables and chairs were moved aside from the centre of the room. Family and friends carrying photographs of remembered loved ones from residential schools moved around an honouring circle to the reverence of slow drumming. Later, as we began a long, quiet drive back to Edmonton, I know we all carried the weight of that image in our hearts. But as we got closer to the city, tired and giddy, we also boosted ourselves back up, remembering my Christmas-ornamented head from that morning! I never did know for sure whether I'd been decorated by that tree, or by one of my fellow Commissioners. Either way, it gave us the laughter medicine we needed to wrap up a heavy day.

~

At community hearings in advance of the Alberta National Event, having health supports close at hand proved invaluable to many—including me. Alberta was the province with the most residential schools in the country, both urban and remote. I had already heard of one child seeing her own house burning down across town, helplessly watching from a school window. Until the end of the school year months later, that little girl had to live with the torture of not knowing whether her family was dead or alive. I had also heard of newborn babies buried in the foundations of schools. I had heard of boys forced to put on dresses and parade around to the taunts of schoolmates. Several victims of pedophilia had described how such abuse at the hands of priests, nuns, supervisors, other school workers, or older students had left them confused about gender identity and sexual orientation. There were countless descriptions of heartless, criminal places:

> "Indian residential school was like a concentration camp."
>
> "We did everything as a group. If we had been animals, we would have been a herd."
>
> "The food made me sick. I had to lick my vomit off the floor like a dog."
>
> "They treated us like cattle."
>
> "My school was a crime scene."

But these words were far from the heaviest part of a TRC day that is seared into my memory. For the first time, I heard of siblings punishing siblings outside of the school context: "My mom went to residential school. If we did anything wrong, she used to scare us and say, 'I'm going to throw you into the Mission.' She was very militant. If we peeled potatoes too thick, she would whip us with a willow. She would make our older brother do the whipping." This was the latest heartbreaking example of what Survivors brought home with them from the schools—an inheritance of cruelty.

In our multi-year process there were times when I would think, *Surely we have heard it all by now. Surely there are no new examples of atrocities against children.* But no. At every event, in every part of the country, there was always something else. Often something worse. I heard some of the worst at this hearing in Alberta. Was there no end to human depravity?

This Survivor's story had it all, starting before he ever set foot in residential school. First, physical violence, not against him but against his mother. She, holding one arm, crying out that her son was too young to go. A man in a black robe pulling on the child's other arm, stretching him apart, until the man's punch to the mother forced her to let go, and the child was dragged off and into the building.

Then, emotional abuse. The familiar story of nighttime bedwetting was followed by the additional mockery of name-calling. He got a derogatory nickname from a priest and beatings from classmates if he refused to answer to it. Then, the daytime incontinence that came with living in constant fear and the further humiliation that resulted. One day, he soiled himself while playing outside after supper in the winter. A Sister forced him to stay outside, cold, wet, and dirty.

> She came out and had a string with her. She tied one end of the string to my wrist and the other end to the pillar. Then she left me there to stand. I was really cold. Later, the night watchman came along. He was my uncle. He untied me and took me to the horse barn and the hay loft. I slept there in my dirty, wet pants. The next day a guy came along with a pitchfork. He didn't know I was there. He almost pitched me in with the hay to feed the horses! He took me back to the Mission and told them what happened. Sister told me to go upstairs and have a bath. She gave me a grey woollen women's nightgown instead of clothes and made me stay in the dorm.

Eventually, he got another set of clothes, but the brutality didn't end because he couldn't stop wetting the bed. This time, he was taken for a hot bath. The water was scalding, steam rising. Sister pushed him in, screams and all. He had blisters all over his body: arms, back, legs, feet. One of the Brothers carried him to the local hospital for a stay of five weeks. The priest told his father his son was sent away because he was sick.

And don't ever lose anything in this school. Not if you are this child. Not with *that* Sister around:

> It was laundry day. I lost my handkerchief. She accused me of using it for toilet paper. We had big outhouses at that school with twelve stalls. She called the priest, told me to put on my coat, boots, and toque, and Brother came to meet me with a crowbar. He took me to the outhouse, pulled off the floorboards and told me to crawl in there and look for my lost handkerchief. I crawled into about thirty-six feet of human excrement. I tried to walk fast but Brother said I didn't look hard enough and made me crawl back across again. Sister told me to take my clothes off outside the dorm. I had a bath. She gave me clean clothes and sent me to the classroom. No apologies.

> I was also sexually abused by the priest and a Brother. I was an easy mark for those predators. These were people of God, supposedly. I don't know what kind of a God they represented.

If only things had let up after residential school. But name-calling and related abuses trailed him.

> Physical pain lasts a short while. Mental, spiritual, and emotional abuse, bullying, name-calling, those hurt more and last longer.

I braced myself, sensing that his story wasn't over, bound for worse to come. It did. The man went to prison for the drunken murder of a friend's father. The one kind person—the only one who called him by his real name—became an innocent victim of this relentless run of rupture, torture, rot, and rage.

> I thought my friend would hate me. Instead, he said, "I forgive you. It was not you. It was the whole community's abuse of you. I was your friend before; I am still your friend." I have learned to forgive the abuses. I can forgive, but I can't forget. I try, to the best of my ability, to pray to Creator to forgive me.

Creator must have heard him, because the living miracle sitting in front of me was somehow able to survive and recount such a cold chain of cruel and criminal conduct.

But I was falling apart.

Two things saved me that day. First, those treasured health supports. I wrapped up the session and ran to the designated wellness room for personal care. Water, smudge, brushings, prayers, hugs, and tears. Maggie Hodgson, Liz Oscroft, and Brenda Reynolds were waiting there to help me. They had been listening to the man—and watching out for me. Second, I called Murray and Willie. I told them bits of the worst. It was enough. I felt less alone. Perhaps, by now, my inner wisdom helped save me by guiding me quickly to the two places where I needed to turn.

Before bed, I searched my notebook for glimmers of hope from this day to equip me for tomorrow. I rested on these words from another Survivor: "It's not only about the life—it's about the living. We are Survivors. Our Ancestors gave us life. We are still here and we are going to be here. They tried to kill us off. Put us in residential school. Call us dumb Indians. Little did they know. I'm grateful today for what we have, even though I came through hell. I am here today to support you, and to continue to help myself because healing is a lifetime journey."

Like most community hearings, this was a two-day event. The second day brought more of the familiar and still more of the shockingly new. And as with all other TRC hearings, it brought out some details that Survivors had never before shared with another soul. It also coaxed forward some Survivors who had never shared their story. What this one shared was a resounding inspiration to the whole room:

> I am honoured to tell my story for the first time today. I do love the little girl in me. I love the young person that was me. And I love the woman that I am today. I witnessed all my dad's anger. I was tired of living what he taught me: about anger, about alcoholism, about how to hide my pain. I'm very fortunate I pulled out of my situation. A lot of people didn't. Today I feel fortunate I'm alive. I lived to talk about my story and how I have changed it. I quit drinking and things began to change. I don't live in my head because my head can take me all over the place. Today I talk from the heart. I'm not ashamed anymore. I'm not that dumb Indian anymore. When I see my little grandchildren singing and dancing, it makes me proud. The government didn't win.

> We're getting stronger. We're going to get stronger still. And it begins with me, to continue changing myself, to make this world better.

That hopeful statement inspired another one from a much less common place—a non-Indigenous, non-Survivor from a local church. Often, especially for National Events, church representatives in the regions of our hearings helped behind the scenes with food, travel, and other practicalities. But once the hearings began, they usually stayed quiet, listening, bearing witness, often with bowed heads, wincing or weeping at truths that so often pointed a damning finger at their own institutions and at those who brutalized children while working in the schools they ran. But this church minister spoke up: "In the last two days, I have seen more positive modelling of forgiveness among Survivors than I have ever seen in all my years of ministry among Christians. Your stories have given me strength and resilience these last few days. To carry on and be that much stronger. You lifted me."

This was a day of fresh glimpses into the complexities of that F-word—forgiveness. We had often heard that forgiving government, churches, and parents seemed impossible. Today we heard that forgiveness was liberating, uplifting, even essential for healing and moving forward—and that forgiving oneself was the hardest. As an old Yellowknife friend had once told me, "Forgiveness is 'for giving forward' a load that is no longer yours to bear." This day was a demonstration of self-forgiveness and healing nurtured by the inspiration and support of others.

I left this Alberta community event with the words of yet another Survivor resonating in my head: "I came in here alone today. I'm not leaving alone."

I, the TRC Commissioner, had also been alone there. But I, too, no longer felt that way.

CHAPTER 17

No Wrong Way to Pray

IN 1974, I WAS on my way back to my teaching job in Ouagadougou in Burkina Faso, taking that unlikely, gruelling route across the Sahara Desert. This was that trip where the elderly pilgrim in the magnificent blue robe frantically chased his money in the wind. Also, the trip where, without a shred of outside communication, I received a clear premonition of my grandmother's death, later confirmed by telegram. And the trip that left me clinging to two inches of shade beside a random rock in the midst of the vast desert, praying for my life.

It happened when that truck we were hitching a ride on got stuck. Once the old man was back on, one of the two Canadians I was travelling with needed help, too. We pushed her up, but not fast enough. Three young women watched in disbelief as the truck moved on without us. We had nothing—no water, food, or means of communication. Most critically, no protection from the sun. I nestled beside a three-foot-high rock, starving for shade. Facing down my fear. Listening. Noticing. Marvelling at the spider suddenly appearing out of god knows where. Stretching my memory for the story of Anansi the spider, the West African trickster and shape-shifter. Praying for the truth of such myths. Praying for a miracle ...

The miracle appeared in a long black robe. I kept blinking dry eyes, thinking, *This must be how mirages play on you.* Closer and closer. It was lean and towering, a dark turban and robe offset by a red jerry can announcing the slosh of water. Closer, I could see a man with dark skin turned bluish from the indigo garments of his Tuareg people. No words were understood or needed as he guided us, following our own growing shadows across the sands, pausing for occasional swallows. He did not take one sip of that precious water. This was a Muslim holy season, a time for fasting. Desert or not, no food or drink had crossed his lips since sunrise. Yet in the worst heat of the day, he had come for us. By nightfall we made it to the makeshift camp several kilometres away—just in time for our new saviour to break his fast. If anyone had proposed conversion to Islam that evening, I might have been the first in line—I had just witnessed and experienced pure Islamic devotion in action.

Forty years later, I was a long way from the fear and loneliness of that desert. In March 2014, I was sitting inside a tipi on the grounds behind the convention centre in downtown Edmonton, overlooking the North Saskatchewan River. I was with my Commissioner brothers, Murray and Willie, taking in the warmth and light of the morning sun through the white tipi walls on the last day of the final TRC National Event. We had offered tobacco to a sacred fire before entering, and then I was seated to the right of the pipe carrier leading this spiritual ceremony. He began with this: "We welcome all of you to this ceremony. We know you come from many traditions, with your own ways of praying. You are also welcome here to join us in our ways. There is no wrong way to pray."

At other TRC stops, words of spiritual welcome, respect, and inclusion came with the same message: "All nations have been given a way to communicate with the Creator. No one way is better than the other because they are all communication with the one God. In our prayers we begin by saying thank you, then ask for direction in how to be, to speak, to listen. We need to come together in a good way. We come here to fix a life. To repair and prepare our spirituality, which is a way of life."

I was acutely aware of how privileged I was to be there, knowing what an act of defiance and reclamation it is for Indigenous people to pray in traditional ways. Many sacred ceremonies, songs, and drums had been outlawed in this country, within the living memory of Elders, including many Survivors who shared examples with the TRC of what they called "spiritual abuse":

> "My parents practised sweat ceremonies and all that. At residential school, they put this bracelet on me. It said, 'Pagan.' I had to wear that bracelet for everybody to see. I was five years old. I used to eat all those Communion hosts, trying to get that pagan-ness out of me."
>
> "There was all that name-calling. 'Pagan.' We didn't know what that was. So they showed us that picture at the end of the hallway. That is still stuck in my mind. There were these stairs, and at the bottom of the stairs were all the Indian people and the fire. At the top of the stairs was Jesus and all the angels. The only favoured ones were if your parents went to church on Sunday. We were the condemned. I really feared that God, and I always looked on him as a punishing God. Everything was a sin. When I left at seventeen, I thought, *Okay, I'm bad, so I'm going to be bad.*"

Before I began my role as a Commissioner, I knew about the spiritual brokenness of individuals, families, and communities. And I knew that a journey of truth and reconciliation would have to be a journey of spiritual awakening for our country and the spiritual strengthening of each and every one of us within it. But the TRC had also rattled my faith in organized religion. It was a horror and a humiliation to learn about what so-called servants of God, including those working under the banner of the church I had been raised in, had done to children. Truthfully, I had been feeling conflicted about institutionalized religion before I became a Commissioner. I have known countless good people throughout my Christian upbringing and adult life, but I have also witnessed and experienced the self-righteous blindness of some—arms of the church clinging to the sacrament while missing the sacred.

My time in Fort Good Hope was especially challenging on that front. First, there was our marriage. For our civil ceremony in Quebec City, we'd had a tiny wedding with just four guests: my parents, our little niece Bonny, and our mutual friend Bob Overvold. When we moved to the North, we decided, out of respect for Stephen's aging mother and other elderly relatives—all devout Roman Catholics—to redo our vows in a Christian ceremony at the local church. Our Lady of Good Hope is no ordinary chapel. It is a hand-hewn, century-old masterpiece of intricate, vegetable-dyed paintings, now restored as a stunning National Heritage Site. The community pump-organ player, Uncle Jonas, was going to provide the music. But it was not to be. I quickly learned that in this and other small communities, the local priest makes the rules. The ultra-conservative Father wouldn't let our wedding happen unless I converted to Roman Catholicism. I was raised a Christian and felt no less worthy than those from any other denomination or spiritual tradition. I was not about to change, and Stephen did not expect me to. The church wedding never happened, and Stephen's mother was left with her doubts about whether her son was ever actually married.

Then there was the baby. Our friends awaited him lovingly. He was born with a name. He had parents and family who welcomed him, adored him. And then he died, suddenly and inexplicably. The whole town was in mourning, and then the whole town was enraged. The priest decided the baby could not be put to rest in the church cemetery—the only one in town—because the parents were not married. Nobody could let this one go. The chief overruled the Church, and the baby was placed to rest with all the reverence of any other beloved child of the community.

And then there was the other wedding. Different town, different priest, but the same blindness to the immediate needs of those supposedly being served. The tiny community known in English as Colville Lake is about fifty kilometres north of the Arctic Circle, near the edge of the tundra. The place got electricity only in the early 1990s. Just a few hundred people live there. My sister-in-law is one of them, and this was her wedding.

The tiny log church was built by community members in the 1960s, designed by an American priest who decided to leave the pulpit, marry an Inuk dog-musher, and focus on painting, writing, and log-building. Limited capacity didn't stop the whole town from showing up. Stephen and I were among the lucky ones, squeezed into a short pew, kids on laps. Many others stood at the back, along the sides, and within earshot on the steps outside. This far north, it can get surprisingly warm, with midnight sun, little evening cool-down, and hot days lingering into September. We were sweltering before the ceremony even began.

This was a catch-up wedding. With no resident clergy, the bishop had flown in to marry four couples in what felt like a four-wedding assembly line. First, the grooms walked in single file to wait at the front. Then, here came the brides, one after the other, a parade of white glamour in sharp contrast to the rustic setting. The repetitive vows went on and on, four times the usual lengthy wedding service.

Then the bishop went on to instruct the couples on marriage, using visual aids for emphasis. "Man and woman are like this," he said, holding up a package of Kool-Aid and a clear glass pitcher. "One adds flavour to the other," he said, pouring some crystals into the water. Stirring it up to turn it red, he added, "When they get together and combine as one, that's like marriage." But that alone was no recipe for matrimonial sweetness. After a dramatic pause, with great flourish and emphasis, the bishop streamed in the sugar before concluding, "This is the love! The magic ingredient that makes all the difference in marriage!"

I wanted to laugh—and to cry. This was quite a stretch from the miracle of Jesus turning water into wine, and tone-deaf to the present needs of all those praying only for it to be over. Our little Daylyn had long ago lost interest. She was hot and thirsty, sweat dripping down her flushed cheeks. Her bright eyes were no longer glued to the fancy brides but to that tempting red pitcher. While everyone else scrambled to the back to get out, she clambered forward over the pews, beelining to the bishop.

"Can I please have a drink of that?" she asked politely.

Surprised and flustered by Daylyn's little plea, the bishop poured out a small glass with an awkward laugh. While he had been drinking his ceremonial wine, it had taken a small child to point out the practical need to quench the thirst of others.

This story came to symbolize for me what was always at the heart of our TRC. Children, now adult Survivors, had to point out the need for a Truth and Reconciliation Commission, and then plead before the courts to get it. For five years, these same children challenged the entire country to consider the practical needs of all our children on a much more far-reaching scale: Now that we know the truth, what can we do to help make things right? How can we quench that enormous thirst for respect and change and peace?

Fortunately, hope sprang from our TRC gatherings. Just as I had lived through those northern examples of a church withholding service, during our hearings I witnessed living examples of devoted service—church members listening acutely and responding immediately.

I was on my own at a hearing in northern Alberta when a former residential school staff member sat down at the hearing table normally occupied by former students. It was riveting and uncanny—what he had to say came out in the common order of a church service: adoration, confession, contrition, the ask of forgiveness, thanksgiving, commitment, and benediction:

> I learned from Native people. Elders are held in high respect. Not my experience growing up. I appreciated receiving that gift. After university I heard about a job at an Indian residential school. I like kids and I like Indian people so I went. We told stories in circles and I asked them how to say certain things.
>
> I took the kids for hikes. We came back late. The kids didn't get supper and I got a talking-to about following the rules. I was a supervisor with the boys. One twelve-year-old was very disturbed and kept running away. I didn't know why. Police brought him back. I tried to make him toe the line. One time he got violent. I manhandled him. I used violence to respond to violence. Both of us were covered in blood.
>
> Another time, the kid got away from me. Every time he didn't do what he was supposed to, I got into trouble. I lost my temper. I took my belt off and I whipped him. I don't know where that young man is. I have a feeling his life was tragic.

> There's a lot of things I didn't know then. This morning answers the question of why there was so much resistance. What I did is something I have never done since. I resolved even then that I would never do it again. I express my deep regret over what happened there. It wasn't right to do that.
>
> Thanks for this opportunity. I have felt welcome here today. I really appreciate that. It has been a way of cleansing myself. I hurt that boy. I hurt myself at the same time. I have always felt drawn to Native people. I have a deep respect for your culture and your spirituality.

Few former school staff spoke to the TRC. Few were willing, and many were no longer alive. Most of the statements we had were gathered at retirement facilities for clergy. So, this tearful outpouring from a former staffer at a public event was exceptional and long-awaited.

At a community event in Saskatchewan, a Survivor told the tragedy of losing his leg at residential school because of faulty farm equipment and delayed medical care. His artificial limb was now worn out, he couldn't afford to replace it, and the government wasn't helping. Within a couple of hours, a clergy member sat before me. "We have scraped together more than four hundred dollars to get Hugh's leg," he said. "The church took it. The church can at least help to get it back."

I was surprised and touched by this man's vulnerability and the humility of his words. It was far from the only example. Across the country, many Survivor statements highlighted the importance of spiritual healing:

> "There is only one great spirit. God. He created a beautiful child. Me. And he didn't create me like I was told: a savage, a dirty Indian. Man has tried to change and destroy us. Man has tried to play God."

"I went to residential school and I still say prayers. There is a religion there. The people were dysfunctional, not our Creator. I pray every day for everything and everyone."

"There's nothing wrong with the Catholic or any other faith. We know there were some people hiding behind that faith. Just stick to the teachings and learn how to forgive."

"I thank my grandfather for teaching me about our language and culture, and about being kind. I know from his teachings to forgive people for what they have done to hurt us."

"I had to forgive myself to Nass [Creator]. To say sorry to my children for my cruelty toward them. It's all I had ever known. My prayer is for healing for the next seven generations. Today I can do all things through Nass who strengthens me."

"I honour my dad. He was the one that taught me to honour the little flower in the ditch. He taught me to read the wind and the waters. My mom taught me songs and ceremonies."

"Grandpa used to say, 'Respect other people's way of praying, and they in turn will respect yours. If you do not, it will lead to wars.'"

"Today I don't believe in a punishing God. Prayer does work. You can't live in hate. I am my own worst enemy. If you start clearing that garbage out, your life will change."

"We don't have to earn a place beside God, to earn Creator's love. It sits within our hearts. We just have to let it be."

"I hope everybody heals. Our healing comes with our choice—talking to God every day."

"We're not dealing with individuals. We're dealing with the spirits of people. That spirit is holy. Each one of us has that. I look around and I see God's creation—beautiful people, love, respect. I look around and I see the wisdom of one person—Creator."

"Let our drums ring out. Let our songs of hope be heard. Let our children know there is a language within them. Don't let it lie dormant anymore. Let it be awakened."

"This TRC event has opened my eyes and my ears that we are not alone. There is hope. There is beauty. As long as we keep loving one another, we're going to make it."

"May great Creator—kind, compassionate, full of love—walk with you. We are all related."

Carrying within me the spirit of those sentiments from across the land, and now sitting in that prayer-filled tipi, I took in this Elder's welcoming words, knowing they would carry me through our final National Event, and knowing that this message would resonate within me for years to come: "Lucky for us, God speaks many languages. Lucky for us, there is no wrong way to pray."

~

Everybody showed up for the final National Event. Our TRC had continued to draw bigger and bigger crowds and much wider recognition. Of the thousands present for this event in Alberta, some 60 percent were non-Indigenous members of the wider community, compared to just 10 percent at our first major gathering four years earlier.

The draw to Edmonton was bolstered by the mayor, Don Iveson. With determined support from Calgary mayor Naheed Nenshi and Mayor Bill Elliot of Wetaskiwin, Mayor Iveson rallied municipalities throughout the province to commit to tangible reconciliation. Together with Mayor Gregor Robertson of Vancouver, Mayor Iveson also challenged all big-city mayors across Canada to learn and act. Edmonton stood out as Canada's first city to co-create a comprehensive Indigenous strategy. Over the years, several municipal leaders were acknowledged as TRC Honorary Witnesses, but only Mayor Don Iveson got an extra title for his heartfelt efforts. Indigenous friends and collaborators dubbed him *Chief* Don Iveson.

This was the last of the seven National Events prescribed by our TRC Mandate, though we still had much work and another year and a half ahead of us. For Chief Littlechild, this was also home turf. It was his Treaty Six territory. It was also a kind of second home to me and others from the Northwest Territories. I've driven countless hours on Alberta's northern highways and spent even more time in its airports. Road and air travel out of the North routes through Alberta on the way to almost anywhere else in the country. Northerners also end up here for specialized medical care and post-secondary education. Edmonton is a familiar hub and meeting place for north and south, with the fastest-growing urban Indigenous population in the country. The Alberta National Event was the perfect place for the meeting of hearts and minds, completing the flaming circle of the TRC logo with our last theme: Wisdom.

Alberta marked the completion of a circle in other ways, too. Five years earlier, in July 2009, we had done our first substantive presentation in this province. We were farther south, in Calgary. The Assembly of First Nations was holding its annual meeting with First Nations chiefs from every part of Canada. TRC Chair Sinclair's address to the AFN was an invaluable opportunity to introduce the new Commissioner team and our intentions, and to begin building a relationship with the newly elected national chief, Shawn A-in-chut Atleo. His predecessor, Chief Phil Fontaine, had brought the voice and perspective of a residential school Survivor to his role. Now, Chief Atleo would bring the equally important perspective of an intergenerational Survivor. He went on to support the TRC throughout his term and a half in office, regularly allowing us to update all chiefs on our progress. No other national Indigenous organization, nor any public or Indigenous government, gave the TRC as much opportunity to brief its leadership as the AFN did, first through National Chief Atleo, and then, just as consistently, through his successor, National Chief Perry Bellegarde.

Recalling how far we had come since those earliest days in Calgary, I felt optimistic heading into this marker event in Edmonton with its powerful theme. After thousands of kilometres criss-crossing the country, and hearing from thousands of Survivors, we hoped Wisdom would emerge for both the Commission and the country.

Our Grand Entry into the giant ballroom of the Edmonton convention centre was to the sound of Dene drum songs. I was wearing moccasins made at the start of the TRC by a special friend and Survivor. Denise McDonald is an accomplished Gwich'in educator, researcher, leader, and artist. In gifting me the smoked moose-hide moccasins to carry me through my TRC journey, she had said she intentionally created the intricate bead design to look like stained glass because it lets in so much light and colour. How right she had been. Five years later, I was especially grateful for the familiar comfort of these unique moccasins and drums. Both added to the beauty and emotion of my final day of receiving public statements as a TRC Commissioner.

Once again, the three Commissioners were in three different rooms, maximizing our availability to receive as many statements as possible. This was my fourth day to hear Survivors embrace the theme of Wisdom, even as several of them struggled to express their own understanding of reconciliation:

> "Reconciliation is not a program, or a process that has a beginning or an end. It requires difficult conversations and a commitment to move away from the status quo."
>
> "Healing is not a short process. It's how much you want to invest

in yourself. My reconciliation started inside myself, in reclaiming who I am."

"Reconciliation lies deep within our hearts. Wisdom starts with gratitude."

Gratitude. Of all the millions of words I heard throughout my time as a Truth and Reconciliation Commissioner, I think the ones I heard most often were "thank you." More often than not, I begin my public speaking with words I first heard from my spiritual advisor, Peter Short: "We give thanks for the gift of this day, and the grace that has brought us all safely to it." I turn to that invocation to bring my attention fully into the present, with a sense of gratitude that this day, and all of us in it, have been called to it, each of us a small part of a much bigger whole.

Many of the world's wisdom traditions make the connection between gratitude and grace, that peaceful calm that can settle wherever there is an opening for it. I witnessed its presence at every single one of our TRC gatherings. In multiple languages, from every corner of the country, person after person expressed thanks. Some were thankful for a few things about the school experience, some good things they got out of it: a res school family, a circle of lifelong friendships; fluency in English; the ability to play a musical instrument; the love of sports, especially hockey. But far more often, others simply said thank you for coming. For being present to pains, regrets, and hopes. For caring.

"Thank you for listening to me."

"Thank you for believing me."

"Thank you for helping me set down this great load I have been carrying around for all these years. I feel lighter now."

"I feel like I can finally breathe."

"I feel like today is my new birthday."

Over and over, I witnessed the grace of breath, of lightness, of new life, in a multilingual flow of gratitude: Thank you. Mahsi cho. Qujannamiik. Gunalchéesh. Klecko klecko. Hych'ka. Hiy hiy. Kinanaskomitin. Ekosani. Niá:wen. Miigwech. Nakurmiik. Wela'lioq. Merci beaucoup. Gratitude, in its many voices, in its universal meaning.

I knew that the main program schedule of the Alberta National Event did not include time for me to share my own thanks and closing remarks with the entire assembly. So, I wrapped up my final statement-gathering session a little differently than usual. When I was a presiding Commissioner, I took fast-and-furious notes, embellishing them with sticky tabs and coloured markers. My chaotic coding helped me keep track of themes, hopes, and quotes. As the TRC moved throughout Canada, I became known and valued for my closing comments. My synopsis of the day's statements was always as specific and detailed as possible. My fellow CBC broadcaster and friend Shelagh Rogers, one of our first and most active TRC Honorary Witnesses, called me "the great synthesizer." My crazy colour-coding was the key to that.

I never gave a lot of air to repeating the horrific childhood experiences shared at every hearing. Everyone in the room had already heard the worst of it, or lived their own version. True to our TRC Mandate principle of Do No Harm, I did what I could to make the close of each heart-wrenching day as uplifting as possible. So, in my summaries and closing remarks, I always zeroed in on the positive, inspirational things we had heard, something hopeful to cling to as a final memory of the day. Something to hold on to for the next steps forward in an unfolding healing journey. Something to reassure everyone in the room that I had been listening and, especially, that they had been heard.

But this last time in Edmonton, I wanted to do more than reflect Survivors back to themselves. I wanted to offer something from my heart, aiming at not just those in this particular room but also the thousands we knew to be watching online, including Survivors who had already spoken to us in other such rooms, at other such events throughout the country, over the last five years.

This was not a day for holding back. I allowed myself to feel and express full emotions as I spoke. I began by repeating something a Survivor had said earlier in the day: "When we share our stories and listen to each other, our humanity can begin to speak to each other."

In that same spirit of sharing, though less composed than usual, I continued:

> It has been the honour of my life to bear witness to your stories. And to be given more eagle feathers than I could ever have imagined, and certainly far more than I ever deserved. But mostly, to be given your trust and the honour of carrying your stories.
>
> I come from the North, from the Northwest Territories, and some of you may know that one of its more recent claims to fame is that of being the diamond capital of North America.
>
> Well, here is the wisdom of Mother Earth—that diamonds are born under great, great, great, and long-lasting, pressure. And they are stronger than any man-made metal or steel.
>
> So, as I see you, and as I have heard you all, I see you as sparkling diamonds. I see your incomparable strength. And I see your timeless and immeasurable value.

Even such words seemed so little. That is why I included another personal gesture. The last Survivor on my list had spoken, likely one who had waited to the very last minute to find the courage to sign up. When he finished, I did more than stand up for him. To mark the moment, I took off the TRC pin that I had worn every day of our hearings. I asked the Survivor to stand with me, and I gifted him my personal pin.

That pin was far more precious than he could have known. Its fastener was more secure than all other TRC pins. I had exchanged the original backing for a better one that I took from a Canadian Army veteran's pin—my late father's. It had long served me as a way of keeping my dad close to my heart, and keeping myself strong enough to soldier on throughout the emotional warfare of this work.

~

The closing ceremonies for the Alberta National Event were especially poignant. The Commissioners were on the main stage with our latest Honorary Witness inductees. Clinical psychologist Jane Middelton-Moz was one of the first Indigenous professionals in the field of Native American Adult Children of Alcoholics, multigenerational grief, and childhood trauma. Her community interventions and multiple books on trauma and healing have helped countless residential and boarding school Survivors across Canada and the United States. In her new role as a TRC Honorary Witness, she referenced her own hopeful message to individuals, families, and communities: "Connection is the correction."

Another new Honorary Witness was the Right Honourable Joe Clark, a former prime minister of Canada and homegrown Alberta boy. He used his unassuming local voice to appeal to the whole country when he said, "We as citizens have to help the larger Canadian population both see and act. Reconciliation in this context means coming together as a whole, with one purpose being to hear and to heal, and then a critical common purpose, which is to move forward together. If we fail to go beyond apology and regret—if we admit the truth and ignore the reconciliation—that would be to repeat the profound offences of the residential schools themselves."

Another TRC Honorary Witness from that day would also later become known as the Right Honourable. In 2021, Mary May Simon became the first Indigenous Governor General of Canada, and named reconciliation her top priority. In 2022, *Up Here* magazine featured a profile I wrote about her. She said her commitment to ongoing reconciliation, first expressed at our TRC event in Edmonton, was informed by her childhood experiences—not as a residential school Survivor but as one of the children left behind by them.

> Grade Six was one classroom, one teacher, and the policy of the day. The teacher made it quite clear we could not speak our language in school or on school grounds …
>
> At the end of Grade Six, kids were sent away to continue school … The administrator said we weren't eligible because our father was a white man. We were the only family in Kuujjuaq refused … Women would come and hug us and would be crying. They missed their children so much that they almost treated us like we were their children … My father home-schooled us. If he hadn't, we would never have been educated.
>
> Reconciliation seems like a broad term. But in my language, in Inuktitut, it is about relationships. It is a way of life. It is not something that ends. Reconciliation is going to be for life.

Mary Simon's motto as Governor General, the first ever in an Indigenous language, reflects her attitude to the ongoing challenges and potential of reconciliation: "Ajuinnata. It's a phrase of survival and determination, whether in the face of storms, starvation, or stalemates. On the land or in personal, community, or political circumstances:

when the going gets rough, you find a way to carry on ... Ajuinnata. Let's keep trying. Let's keep going. Never give up."

As the Commissioners stood on the stage with our new Honorary Witnesses and representatives of our Survivors Committee, we were acutely aware that this last National Event marked another milestone in the journey of our Truth and Reconciliation Commission. Although private statement-gathering would continue for years to come through the National Centre for Truth and Reconciliation (NCTR), the Commissioners had heard our final statements from Survivors.

Usually, after the birthday celebration and closing remarks, we would stand for an Honour Song, then more drum songs to accompany our procession out of the hall, with our eagle staffs, ceremonial flags, spiritual advisors, and podium dignitaries. Instead, Eugene Arcand, our Survivors Committee member known as Big Bird, took the microphone. He asked the three Commissioners to stand at the front of the stage. He recognized us in the name of all Survivors. He called us Warriors. He called for a Victory Song.

Exalted, exhilarated, exhausted, exposed, I stood there, holding raised hands with my co-Commissioners, afraid to look anywhere in particular in case I lost it. I spotted my daughter Kyla near the front of the crowd. The emotional impact of that instant was overwhelming. All our Commission work had been for her—and for all the next generations of children in Canada. I overflowed. She saw my need and rushed over. And there, in front of thousands, I wept uncontrollably into the arms of my eldest daughter, our roles profoundly reversed. It could not have been more public. It could not have felt more intimate. Mother and daughter, reclaiming and embracing the vital, essential space of the love-bond.

It was a lot to savour such an honour. Big Bird had called us Warriors for our work seeking justice, truth, and harmony. And we had called on Witnesses from across the country, asking them to do the same. Perhaps, on the final stage of this event, the shared Wisdom we were finally grasping was that Survivors alone could not do this work. Survivors alone could not make the country understand. Calling all Warriors. Calling all Witnesses. We were all in it together now. We needed to be. There was still a long way to go, as we guided Canada along its rough trail from ignorance to possibility.

The seven flames of the TRC logo and TRC journey by master beadwork artist and Survivor Lucy Ann Yakeleya. Photo: Tessa Macintosh

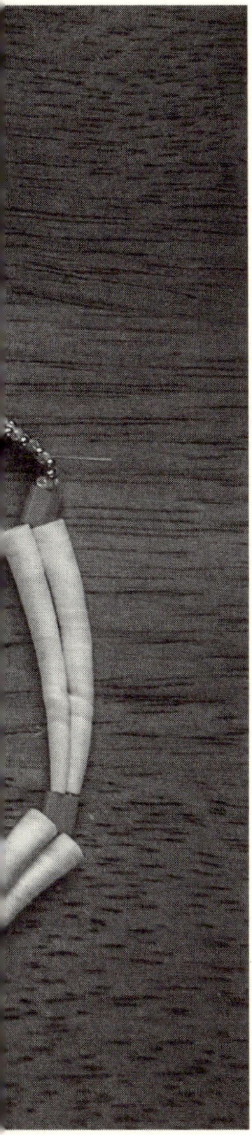

PART IX

THE ENDING IS JUST THE BEGINNING

Peace is not just the absence of conflict; peace is the creation of an environment where all can flourish, regardless of race, colour, creed, religion, gender, class, caste, or any other social markers of difference ... If you want to make peace with your enemy, you have to work with your enemy. Then he becomes your partner.

—Nelson Mandela, first democratically elected president of South Africa and Nobel Peace Prize Laureate

CHAPTER 18

Ethical Space

JUNE 2, 2015. There would be no turning back from this day. The curtain was about to rise on a national Truth and Reconciliation production, one that had been in development for the past six years. Our original Mandate of five years was extended, because of the time we lost going back to court to force the government and the Catholic Church to release records to us as the Settlement Agreement had ordered them to do. The TRC was back in Ottawa, the capital city, where we had been ceremonially lifted up as Commissioners. Now we, in turn, were unveiling our best efforts to lift up the whole country.

After all that the Truth and Reconciliation Commission of Canada had heard, Survivors, the media, and everybody else in the world who'd been paying attention was waiting to find out answers to two important questions: What do we do about it? Where do we go from here? Revealing our TRC 94 Calls to Action—a kind of master to-do list for the country—would be the centrepiece of this ceremonial closing. It was also a celebration.

I was the lead Commissioner for this Closing Event, and the liaison between the TRC and an external advisory committee that included representatives from all parties to the Settlement Agreement, reflecting the spirit of reconciliation we were advocating for the country. Designated staff from the Assembly of First Nations, Inuit Tapiriit Kanatami, federal government, and catholic and protestant churches all worked together. BC-based Reconciliation Canada participated as a community organization. From the Kitigan Zibi host Algonquin territory, Survivor Margaret Cote and Elder Peter Decontie guided us all.

Early talk was of a one- or two-day event, but we settled on four—the same scale as prior National Events. But unlike them, with their overall themes, the closing would have four distinct daily themes, each with key messages and related activities. After months of planning, my innards were churning as I headed into these four days, determined to savour every moment.

Day One's theme was a call-out to the whole country, proclaiming *We Are All In This Together*. We were called the Truth and Reconciliation Commission *of Canada*. This day's theme was to keep that focus on all of Canada, as we addressed Canadian history, Canadian harms, and a Canadian challenge. This was the sacred work of healing broken spirits, broken relationships, and a broken country.

We began the day quietly, semi-privately, with the ceremonial lighting of a sacred fire to burn for the next four days. I tear up again at the memory of blending ashes from the fires of all the earlier National Events into this new and final fire. Thousands of Survivors throughout the country had cried out their childhoods to the TRC, and their tissues full of tears were transmuted into these accumulated ashes.

The Day One call for sacred togetherness fell on a Sunday. Many of the churches that were involved in running residential schools were now involved in the work of healing and redemption. Special church services were held throughout the city before the first public rallying event.

The Walk for Reconciliation started on the Quebec side of the Ottawa River. Thousands showed up, including Premier Kathleen Wynne of Ontario, the first *provincial* leader to commit to including Indigenous and residential school history in their schools. As we set off, the crowd swelled on all sides. A massive reconciliation banner spanned the full width of the road in front of us. As I slipped farther back, I was happy to recognize many Survivors who had given statements to me. Drummers from various parts of the country found each other and edged toward the front, energizing us forward. I saw Wab Kinew among them, one of our youngest TRC Honorary Witnesses, a musician, broadcaster, author, and soon-to-be politician. Wab is also an intergenerational Survivor. He was walking in memory of his father, Peter, who had helped lead our Commissioners lifting-up ceremony back at the beginning; like so many other former residential school students, he had not survived to see this journey's end.

Shouts of good wishes showered us from the sidewalks and an overpass along the five-kilometre route to the downtown heart of the capital city. I felt sun on my face and lightness in my step as we reached the grounds of city hall for a celebration concert. It was also our first and only outdoor ceremony to induct a TRC Honorary Witness. First, I explained the significance to this new Ottawa audience, repeating words I had said countless times over the previous six years: "Witnessing is not a spectator sport. It is full contact. It requires a commitment to engage with others. It takes presence, participation, practice, and action." Then my fellow Commissioners joined me in pinning Buffy Sainte-Marie, in 2015 still acknowledged as an international musical pioneer in the call for Indigenous rights and justice. The instrument she played that day made the moment all the more memorable. It was a master-crafted guitar, a personal gesture of reconciliation commissioned by Bill Blakeney, a lawyer for the Catholic Jesuits and a generous participant throughout the TRC. Métis artist Christi Belcourt embellished that spirit through her own creative mastery. An intricate display of her hand-painted, interwoven flowers covered the body of that guitar as it offered up its first song of reconciliation.

Day Two awakened with its own theme—*We Still Have Lots to Learn*. We need to keep teaching our kids; we need to keep teaching our country. Education was a core part of our TRC Mandate, and the majority of our soon-to-be-released Calls to Action included an educational aspect.

This was another Education Day, bringing hundreds of Indigenous and non-Indigenous students together to witness and learn. So, this was the perfect day to induct another Honorary Witness: Sylvia Smith, educator and founder of Project of Heart, a program that started in Ottawa-area schools where students learned about residential school history and painted their understandings and hopes onto miniature wooden tiles. Over time, and with the collaboration of Alberta educator Charlene Bearhead, Project of Heart spread westward, reaching adults from colleges to corporations. It stands out as a humble reconciliation gesture that grew in its potential to help educate the country. We inducted several others who had made huge educational contributions as Honorary Witnesses. Clara Hughes, Canada's only summer and winter gold-medal Olympian, championed national campaigns for public awareness on mental health and wellness, which was so often directly compromised by residential school legacies. Former NWT premier Stephen Kakfwi brought together Canadians for a New Partnership, a collaboration of former national chiefs, Inuit and Métis leaders, and former prime ministers to advocate for national reconciliation, and to model it through the group's own diverse, non-partisan composition and collective voice.

Public art displays and performances also played a major educational role at this event. The National Arts Centre (NAC) hosted a tableau installation created by the Legacy of Hope called *100 Years of Loss*. The NAC also showcased excerpts of *Going Home Star*, the dance commissioned by the Royal Winnipeg Ballet and championed by TRC Honorary Witness Tina Keeper, a former Member of Parliament, actor, director, community activist, and intergenerational Survivor. The ballet was a visually stirring teaching tool for audiences and dancers alike, and the post-performance dialogue was riveting, connecting residential school Survivors and the dancers who had interpreted their stories. Down the road at the National Gallery, a different art form—a courageously raw documentary of the inherited impacts of residential schools. Director-actor Georgina Lightning's personal story of loss and healing called *Fantasies of Flying* was supported by the Survivors commemoration fund. The after-show dialogue was anchored by Dr. Evan Adams, another TRC Honorary Witness. His parents met at residential school. He understands better than most the health costs of carrying the relentless weight of trauma, experienced and inherited. "As a medical doctor, I know that it is completely normal and natural to heal," he said. "It is completely unnatural to not heal and to let wounds stay open and fester." For the room full of Survivors, the film was an inspiration. For members of the public, it was yet another eye-opening insight into the unfinished work of healing, and the continuing need for learning and teaching—whatever the platform.

~

The theme for Day Three was the heart of the matter: *Reconciliation Is about Respect and Change: The Truth and Reconciliation Commission's Calls to Action*. This was what everyone had been waiting for—our findings, conclusions, and recommendations to the federal government, as our Mandate stipulated. But we had decided long before on two important elaborations of our Mandate. First, we would not use the term *recommendations*. That label sounded optional, suggestive at best. Easy to avoid and put on the shelf to gather dust along with other reports. Ours would be Calls to Action. Tangible, specific, urgent. Second, we would not limit our Calls to the federal government. They would apply to all sectors and levels of government and society.

There had been a third matter on our minds in that final year, as we made our way toward the finish line: the elusive definition of reconciliation. The opening passage of our TRC Mandate talked about the overall purpose of Truth and Reconciliation as the freeing of spirits. How could our Calls to Action capture and protect that spiritual dimension when sacred promises and covenants from the past, including treaties, have been broken or have landed in court over technicalities? With the benefit of hundreds of community events and seven National Events behind us, we had gained wide-ranging insights to include in our findings and reports, but the concept of reconciliation persisted as both the most challenging and controversial—and the most hopeful. When Hereditary Chief Bobby Joseph became a TRC Honorary Witness in Vancouver, he spoke about older teachings: "Ancient concepts of reconciliation were embedded in all our traditions. We are here to rediscover our oneness. Canada will redefine itself and find its soul for the first time."

In June 2014, we convened a special dialogue with Traditional Knowledge Keepers to help us capture the full meaning of reconciliation, guided by their diverse cultural teachings and understandings. Representative Elders from diverse nations and regions throughout the country, and our spiritual advisors, joined us in Winnipeg for a two-day circle to explore these ancient concepts. Most were also residential school Survivors. Following early-morning ceremony, we moved into a large University of Manitoba space with natural light, access to outdoor greenery, and, most essentially, room enough for this large, rich circle of wisdom. This was not a public event and not live-streamed on the internet, unlike our usual statement-gathering sessions. It was a focused, intimate dialogue at tables arranged for a circular flow of sharing. The Commissioners were in the circle, too, eager to gain new insights.

Our TRC Elder Barney Williams set a hopeful, reverent tone with his first words, connecting what his Elders had taught him to what he and these other Elders would now be offering to us as Commissioners: "The Ancestors are excited today. They are feeling the joy of what we are trying to do here. These things that we have taught you that you must carry forward. These things that we have given to you that you must give to the world." Over the next two days, the dialogue fed on itself, circling and re-encircling the room in an elliptical flow as the weight of each Elder's words gave way to the weight of the next, building on each other, as if in an emerging gyre of enlightenment.

The Commissioners had agreed on three broad questions to shape the dialogue. We wanted guidance on past teachings, present realities, and future visions. First, to explore those traditional understandings, we asked: What does reconciliation mean to you and what are your teachings about reconciliation and forgiveness? We received a wealth of replies:

> "I have no idea what reconciliation means. I do understand ceremony. We need to do more ceremony."
>
> "Ceremony is our negotiation with Creation. Negotiating our survival. There are always Witnesses. The bureaucratic management system is with paper deeds. Our deeds to this land were in our songs. There was no paper."

"Ceremony reveals the answers—to receive that vision that can become a collective vision. We are challenged to walk in the footsteps of our Ancestors. To tread softly."

"Our stories of reconciliation and forgiveness tell of our belief that everything was equal—the land, animals, sun. Out of our beliefs we developed practices to survive. Songs came out of those practices, like evidence, agreements of our belief system. From stories to beliefs to practices to songs. That is our documentation."

"My great-grandmother was there at my birth. She touched my head to the Earth, to Mother Earth, to introduce me to her as one of her children."

"Our first responsibility is to our own people and this land. Our second responsibility is to other peoples in relationships on this land."

"Our relationship with birds, plants, animals, and fish for food, shelter, clothing, transportation, and teachings kept us in sacred balance with the lands and with ourselves. When you lose that, you get out of balance."

"Whatever we achieve in life is through the blessings of the Spirit. We have a responsibility to teach all those who come to our homelands how to act as proper human beings. We have a responsibility to speak on behalf of our Mother, the Earth."

"We need spiritual principles to answer what is reconciliation, what is kindness. You have to live a good life at all times with all people. That's what I understand to be reconciliation."

"We all have trickster transformation stories. I believe in transformation. All our stories talk about transformation and the ability to change things to get through."

"Am I speaking the language I should be speaking, singing the songs I should be singing? I could meet the challenges before me, if I remember who I am and don't try to be someone we are not."

> "There are parallels in the words that have been given to all the nations. Our Ancestors gave it to everybody. The voice that you hear is not mine, but the voice of our Ancestors. We say it differently, but we are all looking for that light again. Reconciliation is the destiny of Canada."

Our second question to the Knowledge Keepers was aimed at present-day realities—the continuing impacts of residential schools. We asked the Elders: What is needed to make reconciliation possible? They responded:

> "We have been invisible in our own lands for a very long time. We were good strong people. Now there are so many sick. What's going to happen to the land, to the children, to our people, if nothing is going to change? You see our land. Don't you see us? Don't you see the people?"
>
> "Canada is the perpetrator that continues to usurp our sovereignty. We cannot rely on the willingness of the perpetrator. It is always fighting over dirt and toys, resources and power. It has to stop. We have to be the catalysts of change. Let us start our healing. Encourage all to go back to their protocols and practices, stories and songs to find solutions, because we really need them. The past is not through with us."
>
> "The reality today for so many of our families and communities is abject poverty. How do I find value in this hardship to move away from blame, shame, and judgment?"
>
> "This country is founded on Indigenous nations. Why are we creating lateral violence against each other? You cannot bring ceremonies and land-based teachings into courtrooms. Men, get out there and teach those young men how to be men, protectors."

"We are Warriors, looking to bring peace to a dysfunctional family where there is abuse. In forgiving our worst enemy, we have to forgive ourselves. I am my brother's keeper. Some Christian teachings were very similar to Anishinaabe beliefs—in the morning, be in prayer. We need to keep lighting that fire every morning."

"At the end of residential school, I was civilized, Christianized—and lost. My first lesson in reconciliation was with my Elder. He told me I was not white, black, or brown. Not a Christian or a Catholic. Not an alcoholic or sober. I was a human being—Anishinaabe."

"I wasn't raised in the life I live today. We have to find our way back home to who we are. There's a lot of un-learning to do, while surrounded by things that control our thinking and way of being."

"If you seek solutions, go back to the beginning, recognizing the spirit that is within everything, the gift of life itself. We are in a state of crisis. Mother Earth has loved, protected, clothed, fed, and housed us. We do not own the land. We owe our existence to the land. We have to respect our life-givers. We are the people that can set a new direction, which is really the old ways."

"Our way of life is a spiritual way of life. In reconciliation, I am more interested in teaching my grandchildren how to love each other and how to love the land. We need kindness, that universal value. We need to embrace and take care of the human family. Be fearless and always stand up for the children."

"There is a large intergenerational gap in our societies. I am responsible for the long story, our oral history, traditions, knowledge systems, ceremonies, language. I'm not fluent, but I can pray in my language."

"Reconciliation is about working together. We are all on a journey and need to learn how to forgive. We cannot keep blaming nuns and priests and residential school. You can't undo it. You just have to be

> proud of who you are. Love yourself. Love your neighbours. Forgive one another. Start healing. Nobody can do that for you."
>
> "Forgiveness has a lot to do with how we understand reconciliation. Your responsibility is to free yourself. Allow yourself to be the person you are meant to be. That's what reconciling is. Putting things back together in a good way, in balance, back to the centre again."

Our third question was about how to move Canada forward on a new pathway: What should our Commission say about reconciliation? The Elders reinforced what our TRC Mandate had said from the beginning—that reconciliation involves everyone:

> "Reconciliation is to go back to our original understanding of relationships, and the teachings of honesty, sharing, strength, and kindness. Harmony with ourselves, harmony with each other and harmony with the Earth and Creation. That will take all of us."
>
> "Western management practices have completely displaced spirituality from any decision-making. We need true co-management and environmental stewardship."

Their message was clear: Reconciliation is not an Indigenous or a political issue. Reconciliation is a non-racial, non-partisan issue. And it includes reconciliation with the Earth. Countless Survivors had told us about the importance of their lands and waters—that their identity was connected to them. But these Knowledge Keepers took it further, making stewardship of the environment and kindness to the Earth everyone's responsibility. I had first heard this concept years before at the United Nations Permanent Forum on Indigenous Issues. Haudenosaunee Elder and scholar Chief Oren Lyons spoke of the urgency of standing together, beyond the divides of race and politics, to avoid the looming environmental destruction of our shared world. In turn, these Elders from vast, diverse homelands within Canada were telling us the same thing.

They also drew links between identity, spiritual values, and education. "We have failed as parents, as aunties and uncles. Getting a good education is not enough if you don't know who you are. We need to teach our young people our language, laws, religion, and culture. When our children go to school, they should graduate with love, respect, and kindness." The Knowledge Keepers advised Indigenous Peoples and Canadian institutions to come together, honourably, generously, in true recognition:

> "We have been so divided by outsiders. We have to strengthen what we are still holding. Those who forcibly took from us have to help restore some of what was taken. They spent billions trying to destroy us."
>
> "Our people are literally crying on the streets. Reconciliation is the furthest thing from their minds. They just want to get better. Healing needs to address hurts, including collective community hurts, [and] the three big indicators of wellness: housing, education, and employment."
>
> "I believe in adaptation, not assimilation. I truly believe Canadians want better. We want to move from managing welfare to managing wealth. What would it take to share? Maybe the government needs to hear this, to learn to share, instead of always being the number-one boss."
>
> "Reconciliation is all about me. I have to take the best of the white man's world. And I have to go to my land. How does the concept of reconciliation deal with this? We need to take our two ways apart to

dialogue in ethical space. To find parallel processes of truth, love, and honour in that ethical space."

Hearing the Knowledge Keepers use the term *ethical space* reminded me of the many times I had asked Indigenous-language speakers in various parts of the country how they would express reconciliation in their language. Their answers were often some variation of words meaning respect, good relations, kindness, peace. One version stayed with me, perhaps because it was in the dialect of the K'asho Got'ine of my Fort Good Hope family. Perhaps, also, because it came from a Survivor friend who perfected her language skills working with someone we both adored—the late Mary Wilson, a beloved auntie from Stephen's side of the family. Mary's protege, Lucy Ann Yakeleya, became an invaluable TRC colleague during our work in Northern Canada. Over many conversations, she explained her own Dene understanding of the spirit of reconciliation as rakeralets'edusi, meaning "to become two again"—not one in front of the other, on top of the other, or instead of the other.

A century ago, a great northern Dene leader, Tlicho Chief Jimmy Bruneau, described a similar vision, instructing his people to recognize the perspective of the white man while also hanging on to Dene teachings, traditions, and skills. His translated words have become a cultural slogan—Strong Like Two People. This guiding philosophy and way of life still resonates in the North today in community decision-making, school curricula, and on-the-land guardian programs.

From the Mi'kmaw traditions of eastern Canada, different wording for a similar idea has spread into the academic world. Etuaptmumk, a concept credited to Elders Albert and Murdena Marshall, is referred to in English as "Two-Eyed Seeing": one eye for seeing through the lens of Indigenous ways of knowing, one eye for so-called Western or

Eurocentric knowing, both world views acknowledged with neither one seen as better or enough on its own.

For the Traditional Knowledge Keepers at the 2014 dialogue, ethical space was not a right way or a wrong way, not an old way or a new way, and not a neutral kind of no man's land between Western ways and Indigenous ways but an active space where different perspectives come together in parallel respect and humility, a space for ethical exchange of expectations, experience, and expertise.

The Commissioners came away from that dialogue with a growing consensus around the meaning of reconciliation. Not an absolute definition—we already knew we could never nail it down to one simple thing—but an agreement on its ongoing nature, its spiritual dimension, and its basis in relationships: with self, with each other, and with the natural world. The Traditional Knowledge Keepers guided us toward what became the 10 TRC Principles of Reconciliation, which serve as the foundation of our 94 TRC Calls to Action.

And so, on June 2, 2015, we had all that we needed to share our conclusions. This third day of our Closing Event was when we released four defining documents: an Executive Summary called *Honouring the Truth, Reconciling for the Future*; a compilation of statements called *The Survivors Speak*; 10 TRC Principles of Reconciliation captured in *What We Have Learned*; and a proposed road map forward in ninety-four specific areas, the *Truth and Reconciliation Commission of Canada: Calls to Action*.

Three TRC Commissioners took turns at the podium delivering a lengthy message to Canada. First words? Our name and Commissioner title. Immediate response? Three spontaneous standing ovations before we could say another word.

Chair Murray Sinclair began with our overarching conclusion that residential schools amounted to cultural genocide. The room erupted!

I'm not sure anyone heard much of what he said after that first controversial mouthful.

After Chair Sinclair captured the big picture of our work and findings, Commissioner Littlechild, as a Survivor himself, focused on the voices of Survivors. He also spoke about the United Nations Declaration on the Rights of Indigenous Peoples as the first principle and framework for all reconciliation, and sports and athletics as one of the ways forward.

I focused on two main messages: education and missing children. Education is a ribbon running through the majority of the 94 Calls to Action. I stressed the need for relevant and honest curricula in *every* provincial and territorial educational system, mandatory for *all* our children, to fill in the glaring errors of omission from the past. We also need remedial learning across all sectors of our society, including many professional sectors, to help those who have outgrown classroom education to catch up as adult learners. And we need compelling efforts to inform newcomers, as part of their official welcome to Canada, and to engage them in the national project of reconciliation that now also belongs to them. It is one of their shared responsibilities in a new country.

As for the estimated thousands of residential school children still missing from their families, I stressed our calls to find them through combined efforts, resources, influence, and know-how. My voice quavered as I told the room the gruesome, shameful, haunting numbers. We had confirmed thirty-two hundred child deaths, and another thousand who died within a year of leaving the schools. I shared other cruel statistics: in half the cases there was no recorded cause of death, a quarter had no gender identification, and a third of these children died without even the most basic detail being recorded—their full names. This was only what we had tallied so far, the bare beginnings of a national student death register—something that no level of government had ever bothered to do. The TRC took up that effort unfunded, despite our requests for financial support to advance the work.

Following our speeches, the plan was to ceremonially transfer all our work to the safekeeping of the new National Centre for Truth and Reconciliation. Establishing a national research centre was part of the TRC Mandate. Tom McMahon championed the visioning and legal work needed to fulfill that obligation. Ry Moran led the TRC's Survivor statement-gathering, and then became the first director of the NCTR, hosted at the University of Manitoba in Winnipeg. During the hearings, Survivors had expressed anxious hopes and expectations for the centre. "The stewardship of that information—who will keep and maintain that? That is *our* property, our information. We have the right to control that information. No one else has that right."

The NCTR was established to archive and preserve everything gathered by the TRC, and to continue receiving, analyzing, and documenting residential school information, never again to be scattered, lost, or buried. Canada could never again deny this shameful part of our shared history. No future Canadian could claim this didn't happen. Most important, all of the previously non-existent Survivor statements, now recorded as oral history, would speak for posterity. That was the sacred trust we repeated to Survivors as we welcomed and encouraged them to share at hearings. The TRC collection included recorded public and private statements and sharing circles, as well as poems, songs, films, drawings—whatever voice and format worked for Survivors to express themselves—and hundreds of symbolic Expressions of Reconciliation from the wider population.

Crucially, the NCTR is also the keeper of the National Student Memorial Register, as it continues to update the identities and tally the thousands of children who died at residential schools, many buried in unmarked graves and unknown sites. So much effort is still needed to find and identify the missing children.

This was the perfect moment in the Closing Event for us to publicly hand off to the National Centre for Truth and Reconciliation to carry on our work. But there was a change of plans. After six years, the Commissioners were suddenly invited to meet for the first time with Prime Minister Stephen Harper. Considering we had written to him on specific matters before, with no response, we were conflicted. But the federal government would be key to addressing several of the Calls to Action we had just announced, so we went to his corner office in the Parliament Buildings. I was distracted, thinking about what we were missing—the program our committee had planned so carefully. The prime minister's comments were casual and non-substantive; he said little about our conclusions, though we assumed he had been watching the live-stream. His questions suggested he wasn't aware that our work was not yet officially complete. His government had agreed to a further six months for us to ensure French translations of all volumes of our final report.

Meanwhile, a panel of international experts across the street was applauding our report, with the Reconciliation Principles embedded in the United Nations Declaration on the Rights of Indigenous Peoples, and expectations for Canada to do better. They were also applauding a message conveyed from the secretary-general of the United Nations, supporting our work.

But at that moment, sitting with the prime minister of Canada, I was still savouring the enormous relief I had felt a half hour earlier when that room erupted. Survivors and intergenerational Survivors had told us loudly, with hands and feet, that we had gotten it right. We had heard them loud and clear. Still, I could not have imagined how far, wide, and long that nationwide call-out for reconciliation would continue to resonate in our national consciousness.

Day Four arrived like a breath of fresh air with its forward-leaning theme: *This Ending Is Just the Beginning*. The TRC Mandate had singled out reconciliation, describing it as both "ongoing" and "an individual and collective process." Our Commission's work was coming to an end, but the country's work was just beginning. As our Chair had said the day before, the TRC had described the mountain; others would now need to take up the climb.

Yesterday's event had been huge, public, and all business. This day's was more intimate, by invitation only, a mix of the sombre, ceremonial, and celebratory. The purpose was to acknowledge the people who had walked with us on this TRC journey, to leave sacred symbols of reaching our destination, and to honour children. The new generation was the point of all our efforts.

We returned to the place of our *Witnessing the Future* opening ceremony six years before, but with a different Governor General host. Their Excellencies Governor General David Johnston and his wife, Sharon, had recently joined the ranks of our TRC Honorary Witnesses and readily agreed to tailor their Rideau Hall residence to our needs. We took our places in the circular seating that again filled the grand ballroom. Each Commissioner was accompanied by a spouse, a child, and a grandchild—a gift after so many lonely TRC days.

My youngest grandchild was born after the Commission started and was now in school. I had missed many chapters of that little life. My kids and grandkids, and especially Stephen, had all paid the price of my relentless time away. Sometimes, what landed back home with them was an exhausted, emotional mess, plagued by noisy nights full of nightmares. Having family there that day honoured their cherished support to us—and embodied our hopes for them. Three unforgettable images of hope still stand out for me from what unfolded next.

First, many voices offered a shared opening prayer, in sequence: TRC Elder Barney Williams, residential school Survivor; Archbishop Gérard Pettipas, Roman Catholic Church entities; Archbishop Fred Hiltz, Anglican Church of Canada; Rev. Stephen Kendall, Presbyterian Church in Canada; Rev. James Scott, United Church of Canada; and Sarah Fontaine-Sinclair, granddaughter of the TRC Chair. Collectively, these voices represented Survivors, those brave children of the past; the churches who in so many ways failed them in their schools; and the children of the present, with all their youthful potential to guide Canada on a new way forward. "Hear our prayer of hope," Sarah concluded, "and guide this country of Canada on a new and different path."

As I sat with these prayerful words, I remembered the many we'd lost along the way, since our Opening Event—countless Survivors across the land, some of our own Survivors Committee members and TRC staff, friends and family members ... Mom. Many did not live to see this day, yet each in their own way contributed so much to it. In this final circle, we held them in our hearts and thanked them, along with many others.

Second was the image of all the most senior representatives of the parties to the Indian Residential Schools Settlement Agreement finally together for the very first time in our TRC. In addition to all the Survivors, Assembly of First Nations National Chief Perry Bellegarde and Inuit Tapiriit Kanatami president Terry Audla represented the two largest plaintiffs in the court case that resulted in the TRC. Their predecessors were also there. Former national chief Phil Fontaine and former ITK president Mary Simon had been on the front lines of this fight and received the 2008 official apology from Canada on behalf of their Peoples. Chief Fontaine was also a party to the Agreement in his own name as a former student. His Survivor voice had been loud enough to harness the concerted action of every court in the country and force two large, national, improbable defendants—Canada and the churches—to negotiate a settlement.

Prime Minister Stephen Harper and Opposition leader Justin Trudeau were there for Canada, two would-be opponents sitting together in the non-partisan spirit of reconciliation, demonstrating its possibility. Roman Catholic bishops and Sisters and their legal representatives as well as Anglican, United, and Presbyterian leaders represented the churches. Former Supreme Court Justice the Honourable Frank Iacobucci and lawyer Kathleen Mahoney each played central roles in bringing all these parties together and brokering the historic out-of-court Settlement Agreement that led all of us to this climax.

These parties did not all come easily or willingly to this reckoning in Canadian history. Some of them had to be dragged through court more than once to get here. But in seeing them all together, I thought that if Canada was now able to stand back from itself—to appreciate the value of what had happened since, and how it unfolded—we might begin to see beyond our national shame to a country with a courageous model to offer other nations seeking truth and redress. But that would be possible only if there was a sincere and timely response to our findings.

The Commissioners acknowledged and thanked them all: the Survivors who fought to have their residential school Truths brought to Canada's doorstep, through their representatives on the TRC Survivors Committee, and the parties who walked with us during the TRC, however hesitantly. We also acknowledged those who helped grow the circle of awareness and commitment to ongoing reconciliation: the TRC Honorary Witnesses who joined us along the way; a growing list of philanthropic, professional, corporate, and community organizations; colleges and universities; and an encouraging number of territorial, provincial, and municipal governments stepping forward to do their part, especially in education and curriculum changes.

Each Commissioner marked the occasion with a few words before placing something precious inside the sacred TRC Bentwood Box that had travelled with us from the beginning, and that had received so many diverse Expressions of Reconciliation from all parts of the country. Chair Murray Sinclair placed a copy of our reports—the history, hurts, and hopes of all that we had heard. Chief Wilton Littlechild placed the beaded basket holding the ashes of six years' worth of truth-telling tears—and secretly sneaked in a hockey puck, representing the sport that saved him and many others at residential school.

I shifted us toward reconciliation, repeating what I had said so often throughout our work: Reconciliation is not a short-term TRC project that ends with our Commission. Reconciliation is an ongoing, everyday process, a long-term commitment to a new way of living together in a shared country. Reconciliation is just beginning. It will take everyone, across all sectors of society, to move Reconciliation forward, to keep it alive.

Unforgettably, I asked all the mothers and grandmothers to stand as I placed my most sacred object in the Bentwood Box—my chichigun. I had carried it, as it had carried me, through every TRC hearing since the women of Chisasibi had entrusted it to me. It represented a constant, rattling reminder of the promise I had made to those women on behalf of the Commission, and so to Indigenous mothers throughout the land—that their children would never be forgotten. It was hard to set it down, remembering how long and far this baby rattle had accompanied me and the thousands of lost children it represented.

But soon enough, children's voices replaced that empty feeling. Just outside the door, fanfare, fountains, and five hundred kids were waiting for us, leading to the third image I would never forget. An uplifting finale was orchestrated by TRC Honorary Witness Cindy Blackstock, widely known as a relentless fighter for children's rights through her First Nations Child and Family Caring Society and before Canadian courts and tribunals. When we talk about children as our greatest hope for reconciliation, I have often heard Dr. Blackstock say it best: "We are working for a generation where Indigenous children don't have to grow up recovering from their childhoods and non-Indigenous children don't have to grow up saying they are sorry."

These young ones outside were bussed in from several urban and outlying schools. Children who didn't know each other before that day were now lined up facing each other, forming a human arbour for us to walk through as we left Rideau Hall. A couple of students near the door handed us the same thing that the others were holding—wooden stakes with construction-paper hearts on top. We were guided between two rows of smiling kids waving their hearts for all to see. Each heart was unique, decorated to reflect something their schools had taught them about residential schools. We all planted our stakes along either side of a winding pathway through Rideau Hall's park-like grounds, gardens, and fountains. Together, they gradually grew into a collective art installation—a heart garden. My throat seized at the messages on some of the hearts: *Truth* ... *Sorry* ... *Forgive*... *Remember* ... *Every Child Matters* ... *Love* ...

Standing alongside those firmly planted children's hearts, with my granddaughters on either side of me, I felt surrounded by love: expansive, all-inclusive love. I breathed it in—love as essential to this present moment, knowing this ending was just the beginning.

CHAPTER 19

Rock On

I KEEP THINKING about that rock. For years, a rock sat partially buried beside our house. It was smack in the middle of the only path connecting the front yard to the back, and right where an upstairs corner of the house jutted out. Don't trip on the rock; don't whack your head on the corner. Get the picture? In winter, out came the snowmobile. Helmeted heads became much bigger targets, while a frozen snowcap increased the height of the rock, forcing machine and driver ever closer to the immoveable overhang of the house. Getting around the protrusion in the pathway, your machine might hit a rock on one side, or your head might hit a wall on the other—literally, we were caught between a rock and a hard place. It was time to tackle that rock.

How hard could it be? I had harvested quite a few rocks over the years for garden borders and a stone sidewalk. This one looked slightly bigger than those. It stood about a foot or so above ground, maybe a couple of feet in diameter. I had a good trowel, crowbar, and rock trolley, a strong back, a beautiful sunny day, and a half hour to spare, so I decided to finally get at it. I expected to be digging for about ten minutes, down and around all sides to loosen the soil, and then pry out the rock to roll down toward my trolley. Fifteen minutes in, I was still digging sideways, still scraping away the crown of what was obviously a much bigger obstacle. It was a good three and a half feet wide! The rock we had been dodging and tripping over for years was only a top hat on the head of what was actually a very large boulder. Think iceberg!

I am a determined person. I don't give up easily on people, ideals, or projects. I did not want to give up on this rock. But it was clear this was no half-hour job. Nor a one-person job. Stephen and I have lived rich and compelling lives, professionally and personally. We have loved each other long and well, despite extreme differences in background, upbringing, and personality, and despite our own limitations and failings. It has always been interesting; it has rarely been easy. This particular period was not an easy time for us. So, of course, he was the perfect person to ask for help with the rock!

The space was too tight for any equipment, so we continued the excavation by hand, wrestling it out together. Stephen and I dug and scraped, pried and pushed. We wedged one side in place while scouring around and beneath the other. Family and friends witnessed the curious mission, offering encouragement and suggestions. We persevered, not for hours but for days.

This rock affair became intimate. There we were, flat on the ground, face to face, breathing in each other's air, both arms fully extended, jointly wrapped around this massive rock. One hand gripped the rock's crevices for stability, to keep from falling head-first into the hole; the other hand dug out sand, pebbles, and baby stones, removing them from the mother rock. At times, we overlapped as we balanced and dug, our hands touching on the crown, our trowels scraping against each other below as we plunged farther into the unknown depths. It was the most intense, purposeful, face-to-face time I'd spent with my too-busy husband in far too long.

About a week into these evening encounters, the rock finally began to round out. We were still only halfway there, but at last we were getting to the bottom of it. When we hit the curve at the bottom of the boulder, it was so far down we could barely reach it. Could we move it? We pushed and grunted together from the same side. The rock shifted, ever so slightly. *We can do this!* It would be like pushing a stuck car out of a snowbank, rocking it back and forth until it's freed up to move forward. We are experts on Canadian winters. The hard part was over!

What were we thinking? This rock was never going to roll forward; it was still trapped by earthen walls on all sides. Instead of pushing, we now had to figure out how to *lift* a two-ton rock up and out of a hole. We tried, to the best of our strength and ability, and the limits of our tools. We were running out of steam, strength, time, and patience.

Stephen, defiant, was newly inspired. If we can't lift it up, we should bury it—deeper!

We inched away at the supporting earth beneath the boulder, forcing it to drop. We went to extraordinary, obsessive efforts to rebury this massive rock, deeper than before. No longer to trip us up. No longer to be seen.

But the rock still won.

With the huge mound of earth and all the stones around our worksite, we had lost track of ground level. We refilled the hole, intending to level things out. But there, still smiling at us, was the top of the rock! It did sink significantly but not completely. It was no longer as threatening as before, but it was still visible. Unavoidable. Determined.

My experience of the Truth and Reconciliation Commission has been rich in teachings, many from Indigenous Elders, some about rocks. In many Indigenous cultures, rocks are referred to as grandfathers, ancient as they are. Certain kinds and sizes are used in sacred ceremonies to seek guidance from Ancestors. Rocks are considered to be alive, as with all of Creation, part of the interconnectedness of all living things. Elders have said we are all here to support, serve, and teach each other.

It is no longer difficult for me to think about that rock as my teacher. The memory of it frequently invaded my thoughts over the TRC years as I heard statements from residential school Survivors and others all over the country. And now, I have finally seen what the rock was trying to teach me.

Today, that rock reminds me of the truth, in truth and reconciliation.

I think first about the rock itself. How it was targeted, exposed, dislodged, destabilized, and then buried again, surrounded by finer-grained soil. How we tried to make it look like it never existed, like this never happened.

And I think about my husband, the one who'd said, "Let's bury this deeper." As if he understood the rock, understood that the rock could participate in diminishing itself. Stephen, a residential school Survivor, described the same solution I'd heard from thousands of other Survivors during the TRC. After years of traumas—stripped bare, displaced, redefined—what had they done as adults to survive the impact of those childhood experiences? Like that rock, they buried themselves under the weight of their own destabilization. They did it with denial, anger, self-loathing, and self-medication. Seeing themselves as the forgotten ones, they too tried to forget about what had happened—to bury themselves.

And I think about myself, from my perspective as the one standing over that rock. Lording over it. Deciding it had been in our way for too long. Trying to control it. Deciding it was time to get rid of it. Separating it from its groundings. Using force and strength in numbers to displace and relocate it. Now, with the benefits of age, experience, and many life lessons in humility, I recognize the stubborn presumption of expecting that something much bigger, older, and with far deeper roots could be transplanted and redefined by self-serving will, invasive tools, brute strength, and awkwardness.

But the rock did not completely cave in. It faltered. It resisted. It is altered and diminished on the surface, but by its very existence and inherent nature, the rock stands firm, refusing to be invisible. Because of the experience we shared, it compels me to see it with new awareness. Whenever I look down upon it, I see that the rock is looking skyward beyond my human shadow. I may keep stumbling as I get familiar with its new shape, its reassertion of itself, but there is no ignoring it. It isn't going anywhere. That rock will surely outlast me and our superimposed house. Meanwhile, we are sharing the pathway.

Today, that rock reminds me of spiritual healing and relationships. It reminds me of the reconciliation, in truth and reconciliation.

~

Six weeks into his new job, Prime Minister Justin Trudeau's words to a national Assembly of First Nations chiefs captured the heart of the TRC's 10 Principles of Reconciliation. "There is no relationship more important to me—and to Canada—than the one with First Nations, the Métis Nation, and Inuit," he said. "It is time for a renewed, nation-to-nation relationship with First Peoples: one that is based on the understanding that the constitutionally guaranteed rights ... are a sacred obligation that we carry forward ... based on respect, co-operation, and partnership."

When Trudeau's Liberal Party swept Stephen Harper's Conservatives out of office on October 19, 2015, my first thought was to recall Trudeau's unconditional commitment to accept all ninety-four of our Calls to Action back at our TRC Closing Event in June, while he was still leader of the Official Opposition. As Canada's new prime minister, he quickly endorsed and recommitted to implementing all the TRC Calls to Action. For the first time in history, he named an Indigenous person to a top job in Cabinet: Jody Wilson-Raybould, a lawyer and former BC regional chief, became Canada's minister of justice and attorney general. And he outlined specific TRC-related expectations in his mandate letters to all Cabinet ministers.

It was a hopeful, heady time. Murray, Willie, and I were still standing as TRC Commissioners, but not for long. We had six whirlwind months to take our TRC Calls to Action on the road and talk them up with as many of the sectors named within them as we could—the national Indigenous organizations, churches, schools, colleges and universities, professional and philanthropic sectors, corporations, and always, as much media as possible. We seized our last window of opportunity as TRC Commissioners to get the word out. That proved to be a critical advantage for our TRC.

And we started to see hopeful signs of people and organizations moving stones, rocks, and even old mountains of resistance to make new things happen. The heart garden of our Rideau Hall ceremonial closing grew into a wide initiative of heart gardens springing up in schoolyards all over the country. Headstones in Canada's national Beechwood Cemetery were enhanced with new commemorative plaques to expose the role of prominent individuals in Canada's residential school system. Duncan Campbell Scott's headstone was rewritten to paint a more truthful picture of him as an architect of the Canadian residential school system, which the TRC concluded was cultural genocide. Dr. Peter Bryce, whose grave had been without a plaque, now has one to acknowledge his heroic efforts and the professional price he paid for blowing the whistle on preventable, death-trap conditions at the schools, which Canada ignored. And a new commemorative rock there has been etched to honour all residential school children.

The inertia of familiar old ways of doing things might be one of the hardest mountains to move, especially within institutions. But there, too, visionary people were stepping forward. Rosemary Thompson had been an essential collaborator for our Closing Event activities and a strong influence in her senior role at the National Arts Centre. Her NAC president and CEO was renowned visionary leader the late Peter Herrndorf. He started rethinking the original mandate of the National Arts Centre, historically an institution for English and French only, through the eyes of reconciliation. Soon after our Closing Event, he announced the National Arts Centre's first-ever artistic director of Indigenous theatre. He appointed Kevin Loring, a playwright, actor, and Governor General's Award winner for his book *Where the Blood Mixes*, about the intergenerational effects of the residential school system.

Many honours came flooding in for me and my fellow Commissioners following the December 2015 official close of the TRC. In January 2016, Montreal's McGill University, through its Institute for the Study of International Development, invited me to design a senior-level seminar on the Truth and Reconciliation Commission of Canada for graduating and post-graduate students. The academic background of my class was wide-ranging, from political science and law to education, from medicine to anthropology, from social work to history.

During my first session as a professor of practice, I invited everyone to self-identify however they chose. A third of the class was Indigenous. They said this was the first time anyone had ever given them a chance to introduce themselves as they wished to be known. Another third were international students. They had a lot to say about the stereotypes they held of Canada before arriving here. They thought all those from northern Canada were "Eskimos." They had no idea that half of northern Indigenous people are not Inuit but from several distinct First Nations. They also thought all Indigenous people in southern Canada wore feather headdresses. Most poignantly, one young African woman said she was surprised by two things when she first arrived in Montreal. The first was that the Indigenous people of Canada were not all dead. The second was that, based on what she could see, they all lived on the street. She later said that what she learned about the TRC helped her see Canada and the First Peoples here in a whole new light.

One assignment I gave was a group project. The students had to select one or more of the TRC Calls to Action and design practical policies for putting them into effect. My twist on the assignment was that they would also be graded on how their group functioned, which they had to document, describing how they ensured that all members were valued, active participants. Without exception, the groups reported that this had been the hardest and most beneficial part of the assignment. It had forced them, and allowed them, to learn so much from and about each other, and *that* had improved their overall results.

In their personal essay reflections, many said it was the first time in four years of university that they had ever knowingly had Indigenous classmates; the first time they had been invited to experience subject matter on an emotional level; the first time they had realized the importance of assessing human impact in determining public policy, including involving those who will be directly affected by such policy. One student summed up the personal impact like this:

> I wish to embrace reconciliation by acknowledging in my daily life my participation in society as a treaty person. I will encourage others to learn more about Indigenous Peoples and Canada's colonial history whenever possible. I sincerely hope that the TRC is the beginning of a turn of the page in Canadian history. By calling clearly and succinctly for decisive changes throughout Canadian society, the Truth and Reconciliation Calls to Action also illustrate the current situation as a

> lack of all the things called for. I am still unsure of my place in all of this. Reconciliation for the moment means working on making myself the kind of citizen worthy of sharing this land with the First Nations, Métis, and Inuit peoples who share it with me, my family, my community, and my fellow settlers. This can mean holding back to listen to myself and others, and it can also mean stepping up and acting when the time is right. It is a lifelong process of learning that I am glad to have begun.

We ended the seminar with a fantastic feast. One of the Indigenous students opened the meal with hesitant words she was learning from her child's daycare, a language nest. The moment was painful—touching beyond words to imagine a preschooler teaching this young mom how to speak a language nearly lost—yet so hopeful. The entire class seemed rewired to pay closer attention to challenges and possibilities, sometimes right in front of us. One of those was the Hochelaga Rock.

The rock near the main McGill entrance was far off to the left, beyond all foot and vehicle traffic, out of sight, out of mind. It wasn't that it was in the way; it was that it was *out* of the way. Parks Canada placed it there in 1925 to commemorate the Iroquois village that once stood near McGill campus and the original name of this community. I first noticed the rock and its plaque in the early TRC years while wandering around the campus before a presentation. It bothered me that it was so hidden—displaced, just as the village and original name had been. I'd been mentioning it over the years since to anyone who would listen, now including my own students and several other faculties where I was a guest speaker during my time there.

The year after my seminar on the TRC, and following a 2017 Task Force on Indigenous Studies and Indigenous Education, the Hochelaga Rock was moved to a prominent spot on the walkway in front of the main gates of McGill University. I cannot claim that our class moved that rock, but I know we played some small part in moving the minds that moved that rock. It now sits for all to see, no longer a forgotten chunk of history.

~

On the advice of health supports, I developed a personal self-care plan for after the TRC. It included a 750-kilometre walk along the ancient Camino pilgrimage trail from southern France across northern Spain. It took well over a month, a kind of walking meditation. It also featured rocks . . .

At the highest peak along the Camino, there is an iconic iron cross. For centuries, pilgrims from around the world have placed stones from their "homes" (and homelands) at the foot of it, a symbolic setting-down of something they have been carrying. For many it was the loss of a loved one or some other emotional load—a turning point in their lives. My walk was to honour residential school Survivors, and to help set down the load of their stories shared with me, and through me.

As I walked, the iron cross suddenly appeared out of nowhere, simple, unadorned, sitting atop a tall, slender timber. Although I had travelled with a few small rocks from home, I didn't feel ready when I finally came upon it. Every day I had been looking for a better rock. I wanted a strong and beautiful heart-shaped rock. One that would feel just right to honour the Survivors as the children they had been. But I had not found one. I had nothing good enough to place for them.

Tired, cold, and vulnerable after two weeks of a gruelling hike, I felt wobbly and dejected as I hung my head, empty-handed before this summit of Creation. That is precisely when a beautiful rock appeared at my feet. A perfectly formed heart about the size of a baseball. Just the big, beautiful stone I needed for so many thousands of children. I didn't find *it* so much as it found *me*.

I climbed up to the base of this ancient pilgrimage cross to place the Survivors' heart, to leave a piece of my own heart there. Happy and emotional. The wind had been flying since the day before and now continued to whip my eyes and help me, finally, to cry. To cry and cry.

I took many beautiful shots of the Camino that day, as the high-altitude mountaintops transitioned from snow on hardy alpine flowers and shrubs to red-soiled pathways, to trails through the gorse and heather of Scotland-like landscapes, and finally back down to the first little villages, and the next humble hostel to wrap up a teary, blustery day. I had set down something heavy, and I slept in the welcome feeling of its release.

I wonder what release we might feel as we continue to set down the load of heavy truth about Canada. How might we reimagine Canada itself, this country so shaped by rocks, mountains, and the great Canadian Shield? With the Indigenous name we long ago gave ourselves—Kanata—I hope we might begin to see ourselves as a proud Indigenous country, homeland not only to the oldest rocks on Earth but also to some of the oldest nations on the planet, a place where, over the past few hundred years, countless newcomers from around the world have been made welcome. Do we remember this? Are we a land of sacred values or a place of economic ventures? Do we value the rocks, lands, and waters more than the people who are attached to them and defined by them? Are some identities in our midst considered worthier than others, more deserving of recognition, accolades, and celebration?

The TRC provided a rich opportunity to reconsider our ways of being as a country, as we acknowledge that Canadian laws created the residential school system, not Indigenous laws. The mess the schools created is Canadian history, not Indigenous history. As inheritors of that history, it belongs to all of us to do something about the fallout. Most of all, it belongs to all of us as the architects and drafters of the future of Canada. How shall we be remembered as the Ancestors of tomorrow?

And now I'm thinking again about that stone carver I met all those years ago on Baffin Island. I think about all the rough and jagged edges he started with. About him holding that previously impenetrable stone up to the light. About how much sweat and dirt and grinding he had to put up with as he felt his way forward, toward beauty. I think about the wisdom of the carver's words: "Keep lifting it up. Keep looking. Keep listening. Waiting for the animal to appear."

My TRC journey has been like that. How hard we worked to chip away at the rough and broken edges of our country's history, holding long-held secrets up to the light to expose hidden truths, to reveal inner strengths and beauty, waiting and listening to so many words of wisdom, from coast to coast to coast.

Even now, although I am no longer a Commissioner, I am still chipping away at truth and reconciliation in the ways that I can, still waiting to see what else can emerge. Waiting for the great transformation. Waiting for the most beautiful animal possible to appear. I think that animal has a name. I think it is Canada.

I'm also remembering the first sweat lodge we entered together as TRC Commissioners all those years ago. Rocks transformed that ceremony, too, when I was given a spirit name. A Cree Traditional Knowledge Keeper instructed me to go home and learn how to say that name in Dene, and to consider what its meaning would be for my life. With respect and humility, allow me now to reintroduce myself with that precious name, bestowed in sacred ceremony. In Cree, I am Kiwetin Nikamon. In Dene, I am Dánihts'i Beyéné. I am the Song of the Northwind. Perhaps the song I have been called to sing is in the words of these pages. I am right here with you. At the centre of a shared world. We are *all* north of nowhere.

EPILOGUE

New-Eyed Seeing

OVER THE YEARS since we signed off on our Commission's work, my vision has changed. I notice how my leading public role in this drama has reshaped how I see almost everything. The TRC experience gave me a new, persistent filter on my thoughts and a new baseline of measurement:

> How much did that cost compared to the cost of running an entire national Truth and Reconciliation Commission?
>
> How bad was that atrocity compared to residential schools?
>
> How long was that adult held captive compared to a residential school child, and how much attention did the media pay?
>
> How much money did that person get in compensation compared to what residential school Survivors got for the loss of entire childhoods?
>
> How much more precious was that lost child compared to the thousands of residential school children we've only started to look for?

It is relentless, this comparative way of seeing things.

I don't mean *two*-eyed seeing. Not in the way Elders have described it, where both Indigenous and so-called Western or Eurocentric ways of knowing are acknowledged and considered, neither one seen as better, and neither one—on its own—the complete picture.

More like *new*-eyed seeing. I now see everything through the lens of residential school history and its wide, gnawing impacts on this country. This filter is more honest and haunting, yet hopeful in its constant flashing back and forth. For me, it just won't let up. It cannot.

Our TRC launched an unstoppable reconciliation process intended to benefit individuals, families, and the country as a whole. Throughout, we witnessed extraordinary examples of individual and collective healing, confession, forgiveness, and acts and gestures of reconciliation. I was touched by every single statement I heard. Back then, as the Commission was still unfolding, my new way of seeing things was already kicking in, moving me with deeper perspective. I first started noticing it during a brief return home.

Picture two little boys cuddled up together at bedtime. The one named Ry'den was three; the bigger boy, Tydzeh, was seven. These little boys live within my heart. They are my grandsons. I was home for a few days to be nourished by family in the midst of the relentless TRC schedule. I asked the smaller one if he wanted to sleep with me. He said, "No, I want to snuggle with Tydzeh." For a split second, I felt a twang of rejection, and of guilt. He was so small, and I had been gone too much and too long.

And then I caught myself. For I realized he had not rejected me at all; he had made a choice. And I thought, *What a blessed choice he gets to make*. Shall I sleep beside my big brother, whom I adore? Or shall I sleep beside Mimi, who is also here to cherish me, help care for me, comfort, and teach me? This little one got to choose between two versions of feeling secure and loved. He had a voice, and he got to use it.

I was moved to tears of hope for how these little boys would grow up thinking about themselves. They have strong Dene names, know traditional prayer songs, and have an extended family of parents, grandparents, official and unofficial aunties, uncles, and cousins, all part of their daily lives, anchoring their sense of self-worth, belonging, relationship, responsibility, and identity.

This bedtime scene especially moved me in its stark contrast to the other images I was picturing, where countless little boys and girls were huddled alone in their rows of residential school beds, far from home, bedsheets sometimes tied down around themselves in desperate efforts at scanty protection as they pretended to be asleep. Children who grew up with numbers instead of names; without the comfort, kinship, or security of nearby brothers or sisters, parents or grandparents; alone, often hungry and cold, too often sick, and far too often afraid, abused, ashamed, abandoned, and angry. Such scenes superimpose themselves in my head, moving me, some days, almost beyond bearing.

From the depths of discouragement, disgust, and disillusionment to the heights of hope for happier homes, healthier lives, and more hallowed homelands, I am constantly moved by this perpetually jarring juxtaposition of all that has happened, all that still is, all that is being reclaimed, all that has been promised, and so very much more that has yet to be delivered.

On the most difficult days of the Commission, I felt knocked off my bearings as a Canadian, one raised on lauded notions of "the True North Strong and Free." In those dark TRC moments, I did not recognize our country as the one I had thought we were. And I did not feel proud to be part of the one that I now realize we have been. As the one non-Indigenous Commissioner, as someone who was raised in

Christian traditions, I at times felt the entire weight of the residential schools on my shoulders. I at times felt that I bore the face of the perpetrator, and I felt deep shame at the superior assumptions, transplanted government, and superimposed religion of my Ancestors.

As the one female Commissioner, as a mother and a grandmother, I ached at the raw and painful accounts of the forced removal of children, of the little ones feeling forsaken, abandoned, and unloved, and of the lost anguish of the parents left behind.

Yet on the most uplifting days, I was also moved by what I call "living miracles": residential school Survivors who publicly reclaimed their names and professed their right to be happy; those who lived years of self-inflicted abuse declared that they had finally learned to love themselves; those who grieved their failures as parents finally received, in the midst of a crowded room, the gift of cherished words from their child—"I love you, Dad," or "I love you, Mom," or "I don't blame you," and "I forgive you"; those who found, seemingly beyond all deserving, words of forgiveness for the churches who ran the places where they were harmed; and traditional spiritual leaders who invited all—Indigenous or not—into the ancient sacred ceremonies that Canada outlawed for decades. I can still hear their welcoming words of simple reverence: "In the eyes of Creator, there is no wrong way to pray."

At times, what has moved me is a hollow feeling of disappointment, sadness, and regret, especially for so many of our elected leaders who were not present to witness the truth-telling at TRC gatherings. Mostly, I have pitied them for all that they missed—all that rich public dialogue in unprecedented gatherings of residential school Survivors, sitting together with non-Indigenous Canadians from all walks of life: from young students to former prime ministers and governors general, judges and teachers, hockey heroes and Olympians, mayors and scientists, doctors and broadcasters, business and church leaders, international friends, newcomers to Canada, and so many others. All of their declarations as Honorary Witnesses moved and uplifted me, as each one pledged to continue bearing witness and influencing others about the impacts of residential schools, so that the country can shift to new understandings and new realities. New-eyed seeing.

It has been an endlessly moving transformation. Survivors have slowly come to realize that they are not alone, that what happened to them when they were little was not their fault, and that they deserve to see themselves as the very brave children they were. Many have come to believe that things *can* change for the better, and to realize that a growing number of Canadians from all walks of life are beginning to see what really happened, to care, and to stand with them.

Which brings to mind another memory of hope. This time, I see two little girls sprawled before the warmth of a fireplace on a cold spring day. The six-year-old, Sadeya, was taking turns playing with two things: a modern electronic game that made her laugh and the timeless homemade dolls that had previously entertained her mother and her auntie. The older one, Maslyn Setahlay, was keeping an eye on her cellphone while beading her first pair of traditional moccasin uppers. This eleven-year-old did not choose a conventional flower or geometric design; instead, she created her own stylized version of the Tree of Life in unexpected colours from her imagination.

I continue to see such potential in these precious granddaughters of mine. They were clinging to those things of infinite value from their roots, while simultaneously embracing and exploring all the new possibilities at their fingertips. Remembering the poignancy of that moment, I feel such gratitude for the children in my life—and complete reassurance and hope in the children of our country, past and present.

Children are the heroes of the residential school story. Determined, undefeated children have pushed and pulled Canada to new pathways of healing, redemption, and spiritual strengthening. They suffered for so many years before speaking up, many from their Elderhood—and some even from their graves—to bring about this moment of national reckoning. The country heard this most resoundingly on May 27, 2021, with a media announcement that rattled the world. Modern ground-penetrating radar had identified 215 anomalies suggestive of unmarked graves on the Kamloops Indian Residential School grounds in British Columbia.

I was devastated by this news but not surprised. Part of my dismay was that the rest of the country was so shocked. Survivors had repeatedly told us about friends and relatives who had disappeared or died at the schools and, sometimes, about being forced to help bury them. Those were the only moments when I interrupted a Survivor's statement, seeking as much information as possible about the deceased child's name, age, where they came from, and anything else about how, where, and when they died. Throughout the Commission, we continuously spoke about those children who never came home. We devoted the entire fourth volume of the *Final Report of the Truth and Reconciliation Commission of Canada* to missing children and unmarked burials. I related grim statistics about lost children in my closing remarks at the release of our findings. That was six full years before the Kamloops announcement. Still, both citizens and politicians were shocked, devastated, incredulous. Beyond personal heartache, I also felt deep discouragement. Had nobody been listening to us back then? Had everyone already moved on? Was it all just easier to forget than to accept? Now, it seemed the spirits of those little children wouldn't let that happen—as if they were speaking up from unmarked burial sites near schools throughout the country, forcing everyone to pay attention, beginning with Kamloops.

In some ways, Kamloops is where my TRC journey really began. There's something about the place. The powerful feel of it. I experienced it the first time I set foot there back in 2009 for my first solo outing as a TRC Commissioner. First, the school tour. The old residential school building is still standing. Those few schools that remain add to the important physical record of Canada's 150-year residential school history. Former students were tour guides, but there was little need; as I experienced it, the school spoke for itself. I wandered through the upper-level dorms, dining hall, rec hall, down the basement hall to the left, the shower room. The creaks and moans. The overwhelming sense of dread. I left the place rattled, almost gasping for sunlight. Those media reports ten years later were about new physical evidence of what my spirit had already felt on that first day at the Kamloops school.

Next, the gathering in the nearby powwow arbour. I spoke, I danced, I witnessed: like the time the entire dance circle froze when someone spotted the down of an eagle feather on the ground and the reverential care in picking it up and safeguarding it before the dance could continue; and that first massive birthday cake for Survivors; and the unforgettable Survivor who said the hardest transition he ever had to make was from residential school back to his home community, and the easiest one was from residential school to prison. He felt right at home there. Residential school had prepared him: incarceration, confiscation, aggression, humiliation, segregation, starvation, predation, degradation, violation, self-mutilation, suicide, and murder. His story drew a straight line between residential schools and the criminal justice system. How loss of family, language, and traditional skills led to loss of identity. How grief, rage, and violence led to despondency, addiction, and crime. How it all flowed toward being locked up, a relatively easy shift because of prison's sickening similarity to the schools that had started the whole cycle in the first place. Another Survivor once said, "I went from residential school straight to prison, and I felt right at home, for my prison is within me."

Kamloops was marked by brutal honesty mixed with hope, as seen in one Survivor's reaction to learning of a young teacher who got fired for defending the kids. "This is the first time I have ever sat like this with different people. I've been listening, and now you are all listening. In this circle—when we are all sitting together, looking at each other, eyeball to eyeball—in this kind of circle, there is no place for a lie." He forecast perfectly what would later become the TRC theme for the BC region: Honesty. Eyeball to eyeball, with no place for a lie.

These memories from 2009 travelled with me as I returned to Kamloops in 2022 with TRC Honorary Witness, now Her Excellency, Mary Simon, Governor General of Canada. The year before, the world had witnessed the calm, measured dignity of Kúkpi7 Rosanne Casimir, chief of Tk'emlúps te Secwépemc, the first to speak publicly of the revelation of unmarked school burial sites. What an anniversary. An apple orchard below the school had become sacred ground, dotted with fluorescent ribbons to mark the detected sites. At the base of the largest tree, I placed a token carefully selected from the treasured stones of my travels. It was solid granite, starkly black and white, both colours sparkling as if shot through by stars. For me, it symbolized little voices shouting out of the darkness into the light.

Inside the school, in the children's dorm, the down from an Elder's eagle feather floated across the floor toward me, calling me to pick it up. The Elder, watching, told me later I had done the right thing, I had understood.

Then a return to the powwow arbour, where I witnessed a new generation of hope, captured in a scene so beautiful, I choked up. A little girl dressed in pink regalia was beside her mother in this huge crowd, drumming, with her left hand. She had access to all the things that previous generations had been denied by federal laws and residential schools—a mother, natural left-handedness, traditional clothing, the drums and ceremonies of Indigenous spirituality, and a large gathering. Even the prime minister attended this one. Weeks later, his federal ministers announced an Independent Special Interlocutor for Missing Children and Unmarked Graves and Burial Sites, expertly led by the former executive director of our Truth and Reconciliation Commission, Mohawk lawyer Kimberly Murray. Despite a limited two-year mandate, her conclusions are bound to guide the work of finding and identifying the missing children for years to come.

Monitoring progress will remain critical in several areas. On December 15, 2020, the TRC Commissioners issued a joint statement to mark five years since the release of our final report, expressing urgency and frustration at areas of inaction. We noted that the National Inquiry on Missing and Murdered Indigenous Women and Girls—something we had advocated for in the TRC Calls to Action—had already completed its work to address horrendous levels of violence against First Nations, Inuit, and Métis women, girls, and Two-Spirit people, concluding with further calls for transformational change. We also noted Indigenous lives lost to systemic racism in health care and continuing high rates of poverty, incarceration, and child apprehension. Most critically in our fifth anniversary statement, we emphasized the unfulfilled TRC Call to Action that would be essential for monitoring progress in all these areas—an independent National Council for Reconciliation. In an ongoing way, it would track, assess, and report to Canadians annually on all aspects of national reconciliation, both challenges and progress. As of 2024, we are still waiting for that kind of annual accountability.

Some days, I have to work hard not to feel discouraged. I still see disproportionate Indigenous destitution and despair on our streets. I see evidence of the lateral violence within Indigenous families and communities that so many Survivors named. It remains a crippling force with a long reach and enduring impacts. I see the pain of controversies like the one surrounding the Indigenous identity of international icons such as Buffy Sainte-Marie. But as we Commissioners repeatedly said, reconciliation is hard and takes time. I know that voters will have the last word on whether individual politicians and governments have lived up to their promises. It is clear from national and local examples that political leadership is inconsistent, political will is fragile, and hopeful relationships can fall apart. But I also know that it falls to all citizens, as the democratic bosses of those leaders, to remain vigilant, paying attention to Indigenous rights as human rights, and insisting that governments live up to their national and international obligations on behalf of all Canadians.

For now, in circling around my memories of the seven flames of our TRC logo—the seven sacred teachings that held all our efforts together—I know in my heart that what we did has illuminated and changed this country forever. The TRC job was gruelling, painful work. But it was also an incomparable gift to witness regeneration of strength and hope, and to reimagine possibility and potential:

> "What happened to me, Canada? You killed my spirit. When I left school, I did not know who I was. I did not know my identity. I was lost. I didn't know who or where I was."
>
> "Today I believe in prayer. I also believe in Elders. I am thankful to them for helping me find my identity. I found my identity through my culture."
>
> "Disclosing our stories, we can never forget them, but we can use them as teaching tools. We can say, 'Let's put a stop to this. Let's work together. So that our grandchildren can stand together in a circle.'"
>
> "Canada. Beautiful, Canada. Enough. Please. Enough."

As a country officially committed to establishing respectful relationships between Indigenous Peoples and the people of Canada, surely some of what is required is for us to imagine what is still possible, far beyond anything we have yet seen. During the TRC, in the context of our Mandate to inspire ongoing reconciliation, I often shared a family story.

I was observing my youngest granddaughter's dance class. She was barely nine years old.

The regular teacher was sick. The replacement got to know this group of little dancers by asking two questions: What is your favourite colour? And what is your favourite animal?

"Pink, pink, pink, pink, pink ..." Around the circle they went. This was ballet, after all. As for the animals, the girls named dogs, cats, horses, bunnies, and birds—except for my granddaughter. She said *her* favourite animal was the unicorn! On the way home, our conversation in the car went like this:

"My girl, you *do* know that unicorns are not *real* animals, don't you?"

"Of *course* I do, Mimi! But I like to believe in my *own* imagination!"

That eternal possibility of the imagination. To speak up for it. To dance toward it, no matter the detractors, naysayers, or cynics. No matter those who say it is impossible, unrealistic, or cannot exist, simply because we have neither seen nor done it before. Are we too old to believe in our imagination of the country we can yet become? Or are we too blinded by prior assumptions and presumptions?

When Willie, Murray, and I were announced as Commissioners in 2009, Phil Fontaine was still AFN national chief. He called for our "expertise, insight, and sensitivity." It was a gentler version of what Willie Blackwater said, as head of the National Association of Residential School Survivors, and famous for his landmark lawsuit victory against residential school perpetrators: "The message I want to send to them is to remember who they represent—human beings who had been attempted to be dehumanized by the government system. We are traumatized people who are just crawling out of our horrors. We need a place to share stories that's safe."

I hope the enduring impact of the Truth and Reconciliation Commission of Canada will stand as evidence that we did both of those things: we brought forward the best of ourselves; and we convened safe spaces to keep Survivors at the heart of our work, so their voices could be widely heard and never forgotten, bringing this country closer together.

We were three. Littlechild, Sinclair, and Wilson. Truth, Healing, and Reconciliation.

We each brought forward what Chief Phil Fontaine had called for—our respective expertise, insight, and sensitivity. I believe we even strengthened the whole, by standing together. Behind the scenes, we frequently debated and occasionally struggled—frustrated, tearful even. But we also knew how to soothe ourselves, to reach out, often across great geographic and cultural distances, with talk and tobacco, to renew our vows to Survivors and to each other, and to grow our affection for each other. Unlike the Canadian TRC before us, and many others around the world, we kept standing.

At our very first meeting, Willie brought a braid of sweetgrass and shared one of its teachings. He demonstrated how the grasses, once braided, become too strong to break. We, as three Commissioners, would need the cleansing and strength of our three strands to get us through such hard work. Sometimes, I think we simply loved ourselves, and each other, to the finish line.

I learned another sweetgrass teaching from the Elder who first helped me see myself within a sacred circle of life-giving womanhood—the one who gave me a pure white eagle feather in northern Manitoba. It turns out, her name was Stella Blackbird. I never got to see her again before she passed, but I did finally get to put a name to her beautiful face and to recall the profound message she had given me with that feather: "This one, of course, is for you … It is white and pure and most sacred, because you are woman and we are the life-givers. Now you are the mother watching out for all our children."

Stella's name came to me as a surprise gift one quiet Saturday morning. I was screening the first version of *The Unforgotten*, a Canadian Medical Association film made by my old neighbour and friend Dr. Ewan Affleck. It's about adverse Indigenous experiences with the health care system. But it was Stella Blackbird's quiet voice that made the film most memorable for me: "I used to have long hair—braids my mother made. They are the antennas to the Spirit world, to the Creator. And they shaved us, and put kerosene on our heads, and then I developed this shame to be an Indian. Today I know I am not a savage. Our people were very spiritual."

In addition to residential school, Stella's people had been violently evicted from their traditional territory, displaced for a provincial park. In the fight to reclaim those lands, Stella devoted herself to reclaiming her relationship with the natural world, teaching others about traditional plants and medicines, and finding her way home. "These plants are our brothers and sisters. They have a purpose like we have a purpose. To survive. To heal one another. That's their gift to us, and for us to honour that. For the last thirty years I've been travelling here and there, to find me. Where I belong. Today I belong here."

Her on-screen words sounded to me like Stella's version of what my mother-in-law, Georgina, had said about belonging at the very centre of her own world: north of nowhere.

Stella's notion of belonging went beyond geography, though,

reminding me of something I'd learned decades earlier. The South African notion of Ubuntu also invokes the dignity and interdependency of all human beings. But Stella went beyond even that—to her Indigenous world view of All My Relations—belonging in relationship with *all* living things, not just human. "I do belong. I am part of everything. I am one of those trees. The grass. And you."

In that moment, I absolutely felt part of her. I laughed out loud when one scene showed a glimpse of her wearing a one-of-a-kind embroidered shawl—I'd long since given up looking for that shawl, lost in the early days of the TRC. How happy I was that it had ended up with her. How honoured I would have been to give it to her in person. Instead, I remember and honour her whenever I pick up my white eagle feather and say her name. Stella, meaning "star."

These days, I've been thinking a lot about Stella and the sweetgrass teaching she offered in that video. "Sweetgrass represents the hair of Mother Earth. When you look, after it's braided, it only has two. You never see the third one. It's the man and woman—and the child to come. Man. Woman. Child."

Maybe that is what we have done through the TRC. We have given birth to reconciliation, as that child to come. At the very least, we have assisted at its birth. And now what? I know there is still much truth to be known. I also know that both truth and reconciliation can happen at the same time. Not one first, and then the other. Each can continue to unfold in our midst, informing and inspiring the other. I know this because, as a TRC Commissioner, I saw and heard thousands of residential school Survivors demonstrate that to me, to themselves, to their families and communities, and to the world.

Now, for reconciliation to survive in our midst, we must *all* continue to breathe life into it, in our everyday lives as individuals, governments, and broad society. Encircle it, nurture it, help it grow.

All of us, being related. All of us, being right here, where we are. At the centre of our own lives. Belonging. All part of that circle of interconnected relationships.

I see myself in that circle. From all that I have lived, all I've been taught, and my new-eyed seeing through many rich perspectives, I know that progress will ebb and flow as it always has, that we will continue to live through disappointments and breakthroughs, and that determined hope and goodness will outshine all other forces.

I am hopeful that other countries may benefit from the examples of the Truth and Reconciliation Commission of Canada. Many parts of the world are facing their own truth, memory, and healing needs. During our TRC and since, I have been invited to speak in Finland, Norway, Denmark and Greenland, southern France, New Zealand, Peru, and various parts of Australia and the United States. The United States, in particular—Canada's next-door neighbour—has its own boarding school history. Invariably, groups and organizations want to know the background to our Commission, why we had one, and how it succeeded when so many others around the world have failed. But most of all, they want to know how our work relates to them. What can they do to contribute to the big work of reconciliation? I hope my first-hand Canadian perspective may offer insight, inspiration, and ideas helpful to such efforts in other national and international contexts.

My reflections have been both public and personal because I have been personally moved by the work we have done, as have countless others. But many still need to learn, and the big work of reconciliation is far from over. May my words contribute to ongoing education and a deeper understanding of why Canada needed a Truth and Reconciliation Commission in order to take an honest look at itself. It is still my hope that our TRC has indeed helped remove our national blinders, that voices that had been silenced have engaged us all in a national conversation that is ongoing, and that Canada can move forward in a new way that serves as an example to the rest of the world. We are inching forward, but we are still a long way from the greatest country we can yet become.

I hope that what an unprecedented seven thousand Survivors have said in recorded statements to the Truth and Reconciliation Commission of Canada will be widely heard, diligently taught in all our schools, and perpetually commemorated, lest we forget. My hope is that as a result of the Commission, we will listen to the longing in Survivors' voices, and find ways to walk each other home to a greatness not yet known. That we will bring patience, compassion, resources, and skilled care to supporting those who are still in the midst of gut-wrenching healing journeys. That we will support the reclamation work that is underway, as stolen languages and cultural practices are restored. And that we will begin to fill the glaring educational, economic, and socio-political gaps, so that Indigenous children can grow up feeling proud and certain of who they are, knowledgeable of their languages, histories, and heroes, and so that all of Canada may be enriched in national wisdom and international reputation by the rebalancing of a shared country.

My hopes come with promises. To the Survivors in every region of the country who have entrusted me with your stories, I will remember you. I will never stop talking about your bravery as children and your resilience and leadership as adults.

To the thousands of children who died in, or as a result of, residential schools—the lost and missing children—I promise to do whatever I can in the continuing push to keep looking for you. I carry you in my heart and will bear witness to your precious and unforgotten lives for the rest of my own.

Then there's the promise to myself—to keep doing what I can to breathe life into the TRC Calls to Action and contribute to a justly shared country through the infinite possibilities of ongoing reconciliation.

As the saga continues, may we keep our eyes and hearts open to each other. May we learn the lessons of injustice, hardship, and failure, and act with determined hope for what is still possible. May we respect the worth of each and every life with its potential to make a difference. And may we hold to belief in the universally sacred teaching of love, which lies at the heart of all possible reconciliation, with its power to transform everything—a life, a relationship, a country, a world.

Hį̨dú gogha kádi.

For now, that's enough.

Acknowledgements

To acknowledge is also to celebrate.

An extraordinary celebration unfolded during the evolution of this book—I reached a milestone birthday in the midst of the worldwide pandemic known as COVID. Even so, I wanted to celebrate, by acknowledging the many circles of community that have influenced my decades. It became the best birthday I could ever have imagined! A progressive party across ten time zones!

Food favourites and birthday cake prepared by my daughters arrived on our doorstep, uniting our three isolated households in a shared meal. A complex schedule of Zoom calls unfolded over twelve hours and three continents. I was told when to sign on, but not who else would be there. That was the great surprise, as beloved faces from past and present chapters of my life appeared on successive calls. It was the best gift—a virtual visit with so many who have enriched, marked, and blessed me, whether family of birth, family of marriage, professional families, or adopted families of the heart.

That birthday cracked open many rich memories that spilled over into the chapters of this book, giving it new shape as glimpses of my personal and previous lives became interwoven with scenes of my life as a TRC

Commissioner. I am forever grateful to my children for planning that love-infused celebration. And to my party guests from various parts of the world, I acknowledge all of you as treasured human milestones on my life's journey. In unpredictable ways, you each marked my own steps forward toward the Commission.

Many I have loved are now among the Ancestors. Their lessons also proved invaluable to understandings I would need in my Commissioner role. My parents, Neil and Ellen Wilson, taught me hard work and service, kindness and love. Grandfathers Aaron Wilson and Archie McLellan demonstrated hardship, sacrifice, courage, and determination never to give up. Great-Grandma Ellen Harnett, Grandma Ethel McLellan, and Grandma Mina Wilson gave me insights into the wounds of motherless children, and those forced into early adulthood. They also taught me the joys and generosity of singing, dancing, and laughter. Our little niece Yvonne taught me the incomparable devastation of losing a young child, and Auntie Mary Wilson (Barnaby) showed me the profound power of belonging as a pathway to healing.

Uniting the north and south of my life is a continuing enrichment. It equipped me for the TRC in unanticipated ways, and I thank my extended Wilson and Kakfwi families for that. My three brothers, Thom, Bob, and Tod Wilson, were my first playmates, friends, teachers, and heroes. Our childhood experiences together helped me, by contrast, to feel the acute loss in every residential school Survivor story of forced separation from siblings. Many beloved aunts, uncles, and cousins showed me the comforts of extended family, as identity, as community. My own three children blessed me with the deepest bonds of motherhood. Thanks to them—Kyla, Daylyn and Keenan—I registered the agony as Survivors described how the love-bond was severed when they were taken away, some never to be returned. I especially thank my Survivor husband, Stephen, for trusting me with the depths of his own experiences, and for cradling me through the recurring nightmares of the thousands of residential school stories I witnessed, and then revisited for this book.

My own story has new meaning because of the children of Canada's Indian residential schools system. I acknowledge and honour them all. They suffered through the schools and fought to have the Truth and Reconciliation Commission, which I was privileged to help lead. Before witnesses and the world, Survivors spoke up for themselves and on behalf of others who no longer could, awakening the consciousness and the conscience of a Commission and a country.

I specifically acknowledge, thank, and name the TRC Survivors Committee: Eugene Arcand, Ray Arcand, John Banksland, Madeleine Basile, Terri Brown, Lottie May Johnson, Wilton Littlechild, John Morrisseau, Barney Williams, Gordon Williams, Rebekah Uki Williams, and Doris Young. Your presence, honesty, and wisdom helped the Commissioners complete our big work together. I also make particular mention of the Inuit sub-Commission directed by Robbie Watt and Jennifer Hunt-Poitras, supported by Jeannie Maniapik, Frank Hope, and Lucy Ann Yakeleya, who ensured the TRC heard widely from Survivors in the remote top one-third of Canada, in many languages and dialects. To Lucy Ann, a further thank you for your expertise with Dene words that appear in this book. Mahsi cho! As for my fellow TRC Commissioners, I shall forever honour and cherish the Honourable Dr. Murray Sinclair and Chief Dr. Wilton Littlechild. We travelled far because we travelled together.

Deeper reflections on my TRC experiences were only possible once it was over. In 2016, McGill University invited me to develop and deliver a course on the Truth and Reconciliation Commission of Canada. The class response to it proved that education could change minds and attitudes. I am sincerely thankful to Dr. Phil Oxhorn for that opportunity, and to my former students for the rich lessons we exchanged. Among other things, you helped me decide to share my TRC experiences and perspective more widely.

Three stand-out individuals were essential to my earliest efforts to expand my reflections into a book. Dr. Debby McNaughton never let up on telling me I should write one. Joyce Busch listened to early, disconnected writings and always asked for more, reassuring me that it was important for everyone to hear. Whit Fraser, now His Excellency as viceregal consort to the thirtieth Governor General of Canada, was my first radio boss and journalism mentor, more recently becoming an award-winning author. He gave me a deadline for the first step of this book, and then cheered me on as each chapter took shape.

Still, it took many months of writing and sifting through countless notebooks to reveal the larger story I was actually trying to tell. I was so journalistically programmed toward objectivity and telling *other* people's stories that I couldn't see the obvious—that this was *my* story and *I* was the lead character. I owe specific and particular thanks to my longtime friend and journalistic colleague Dick Gordon. His incisive, challenging questions clarified that point.

Digging down, digging deep takes time and uninterrupted space. I was offered several safe havens for developing the original concept and various chapters of this book, some for days and others for weeks at a time. I gratefully acknowledge the international Rockefeller Foundation for its generous residency in Bellagio, Italy, at the beginning of my writing, with special thanks to Nancy MacPherson for introducing me to it. Deep thanks, also, to the Peace Village retreat centre in New York state, where Judy Rodgers and the Brahma Kumaris community provided calm and encouragement as my final draft emerged.

Various basements, attics, bedrooms, houses, cottages, cabins, and kitchen tables were generously offered by Brenda Reynolds, Sally McLean, Nora Sanders, Debby McNaughton, Pam Del Maestro, Jane Myles, Jeanne Carroll, Joyce Busch, Jamie Scott, Barbara Gordon, Laurie Sarkadi, Kyleigh Schieman, Eric LeReste, Melissa McCrackin, Cristine Bayly, Jennifer Moore-Rattray, and Cynthia Reyes. Whether you were there or not, your spaces helped me find the words. Some of you also read early drafts and gave much-appreciated feedback. I additionally and particularly thank therapist and author Jane Middelton-Moz for your writing feedback, occasional emotional guidance, healing support for my family, and the practical enticement to get me to the finish line—a beautiful pen for author signatures!

I am most indebted for rock-solid professional backing and cheerleading. Shirarose Wilensky, my cherished editor at House of Anansi Press, championed my story, guided me through unfamiliar waters, honoured my words, and respectfully finessed a way through the excess. My deepest thanks to you, Shirarose. I also acknowledge and thank your colleagues at Anansi, with special mention of Semareh Al-Hillal. Together, you honoured, trusted, and encouraged me. I would also like to thank Publisher Karen Brochu, as well as Lucia Kim for the compelling book design.

The book's cover is a glimpse of the magical beauty of the North, thanks to my talented photographer-friend Tessa Macintosh, who weathered biting cold to capture this image of me. I can still see you, lying in the snow, barehanded, persevering with every angle to capture a perfect light before diving into your mitts! Thanks also for your contributions to pictures within the book, as well as the National Centre for Truth and Reconciliation (NCTR) for providing several others from the TRC collection. Fred Cattroll of Big Guy Pictures in Ottawa has an unparalleled treasure trove of photos from major Indigenous gatherings over the decades. Chi-miigwetch, Fred, for your gifted eye, and for capturing and generously sharing precious scenes of historic TRC moments.

My most heartfelt thanks also go to several individuals whose revered names and thoughtful, generous words further enrich the cover and inside pages. I am extremely grateful to each one of you for the time and care you devoted to reviewing *North of Nowhere*, and associating your good reputations with my book. For the audiobook version I thank Matthew Montour and Blair Stainton for their sharp technical skill and careful listening, and David Stinson for overall support.

I have always said that the work of the Truth and Reconciliation Commission was spiritual work, to attend to the broken and mending spirits of individuals and of Canada itself. I owe tremendous thanks to many who have supported my own spiritual health as a woman, mother, Commissioner, and emerging author. Many are specifically named within the pages of this book. Several others have also supported and guided me. In addition to my spiritual advisor Peter Short, I particularly acknowledge and thank my "cell sisters": Sue Short, Nora Sanders, Elaine Stewart, and Donna Allen. I also name and honour Elders Rick Lightning, Maggie Hodgson, Barney Williams, Dave Courchene, Jane Meader, Maria Campbell, Stephen Augustine, Rebecca Martell, Moïse Rabesca, and MS Naidou, as well as Father Jean Pochat, the Very Reverend Dr. Bill Phipps, Caroline Poag, Penny Ballantyne, Reverend Russell Daye, and Reverend Susan Chisholm. Over the years, each one has offered me specific guidance and care. Mahsi cho to all of you.

I celebrated my completion of this manuscript with the gift of travel, circling back to South Africa to a spiritual and environmental retreat within the sacred heartlands of the White Lions of Timbavaati. With new insights from my time there, my final acknowledgement goes to the White Lions Protection Trust, with a deep bow of thanks and respect to Linda Tucker, Protector of the White Lions. In the spirit of "we are all related," your inspirational work in protecting an endangered species and restoring a threatened homeland has reinforced my profound belief in the possibility of reclamation, restoration, and rejuvenation. Reflecting in this light, I see more clearly the importance and value of my *own* contributions to the harmonious co-existence of all living beings. I recognize myself as a messenger of hope, peace, and Reconciliation. I offer this book in that spirit.

Marie Wilson
Yellowknife, Denendeh
January 15, 2024

Notes

"What We Have Learned: Principles of Truth and Reconciliation," ehprnh2mwo3.exactdn.com/wp-content/uploads/2021/01/Principles_English_Web.pdf.

"Truth and Reconciliation Commission of Canada: Calls to Action," ehprnh2mwo3.exactdn.com/wp-content/uploads/2021/01/Calls_to_Action_English2.pdf.

"affirm the right to a just and equitable measure of self-government . . .": John Paul II, "Apostolic Journey to the United States of America and Canada: Meeting with the Indigenous Peoples in Canada: Address of His Holiness John Paul II," transcription of a speech given at Fort Simpson, Canada, 20 September 1987, *The Holy See*, vatican.va/content/john-paul-ii/en/speeches/1987/september/documents/hf_jp-ii_spe_19870920_indigeni-fort-simpson.html.

"*There is an emerging and compelling desire* . . .": "Schedule 'N': Mandate for the Truth and Reconciliation Committee," *Residential Schools Settlement: Official Court Notice*, residentialschoolsettlement.ca.

"You represent the former residential school students …": Michaëlle Jean, speech at the Witnessing the Future Launch Event, Ottawa, Canada, 14–15 October 2009, video recording, posted by National Centre for Truth and Reconciliation on 11 February 2021, archives.nctr.ca/MDO109_E1.

"Today, we recognize that this policy of assimilation …": Stephen Harper, speech transcript, "The Day of the Apology," *Government of Canada*, modified 27 May 2015, rcaanc-cirnac.gc.ca/eng/1100100015657/1571589032314#.

"Indian children should be withdrawn …": John A. Macdonald, from "10 Quotes John A. Macdonald Made about First Nations," *Indigenous Corporate Training Inc.*, 28 June 2016, ictinc.ca/blog/10-quotes-john-a.-macdonald-made-about-first-nations#:~:text=It%20has%20been%20strongly%20impressed,of%20thought%20of%20white%20men.

"There is no relationship more important to me …": "Statement by the Prime Minister of Canada after Delivering a Speech to the Assembly of First Nations Special Chiefs Assembly," *Prime Minister of Canada Justin Trudeau*, 8 December 2015, pm.gc.ca/en/news/statements/2015/12/08/statement-prime-minister-canada-after-delivering-speech-assembly-first#:~:-text=The%20Prime%20Minister%2C%20Justin%20Trudeau,the%20Métis%20Nation%2C%20and%20Inuit.

"The message I want to send to them is to remember …": Willie Blackwater, quoted in The Canadian Press, "3 New Members Named to Truth and Reconciliation Commission," *CBC*, 10 June 2009, cbc.ca/news/canada/3-new-members-named-to-truth-and-reconciliation-commission-1.805250.

"I used to have long hair …": Stella Blackbird, in *The Unforgotten*, short film, directed by Dr. Ewan Affleck and Christopher Paetkau, theunforgotten.cma.ca.

Index

DR. MARIE WILSON (CM, ONWT, MSC) spent six years criss-crossing the country as a Commissioner of the Truth and Reconciliation Commission of Canada. She has spoken throughout North America, Europe, Australia, and New Zealand on the potential of reconciliation. Born in Ontario, she has lived, studied, and worked as a journalist, teacher, professor, trainer, and executive in Canada, France, Burkina Faso, South Africa, and parts of South America. She lives in Yellowknife, Northwest Territories.